Third Wave Feminism and the Politics of Gender in Late Modernity

Shelley Budgeon
University of Birmingham, UK

© Shelley Budgeon 2011

All rights reserved. No reproduction, copy or transmission of this publication may be made without written permission.

No portion of this publication may be reproduced, copied or transmitted save with written permission or in accordance with the provisions of the Copyright, Designs and Patents Act 1988, or under the terms of any licence permitting limited copying issued by the Copyright Licensing Agency, Saffron House, 6-10 Kirby Street, London EC1N 8TS.

Any person who does any unauthorized act in relation to this publication may be liable to criminal prosecution and civil claims for damages.

The author has asserted her right to be identified as the author of this work in accordance with the Copyright, Designs and Patents Act 1988.

First published 2011 by
PALGRAVE MACMILLAN

Palgrave Macmillan in the UK is an imprint of Macmillan Publishers Limited, registered in England, company number 785998, of Houndmills, Basingstoke, Hampshire RG21 6XS.

Palgrave Macmillan in the US is a division of St Martin's Press LLC, 175 Fifth Avenue, New York, NY 10010.

Palgrave Macmillan is the global academic imprint of the above companies and has companies and representatives throughout the world.

Palgrave® and Macmillan® are registered trademarks in the United States, the United Kingdom, Europe and other countries.

ISBN 978–0–230–58090–9

This book is printed on paper suitable for recycling and made from fully managed and sustained forest sources. Logging, pulping and manufacturing processes are expected to conform to the environmental regulations of the country of origin.

A catalogue record for this book is available from the British Library.

Library of Congress Cataloging-in-Publication Data
Budgeon, Shelley, 1967–
   Third-wave feminism and the politics of gender in late modernity / Shelley Budgeon.
     p. cm.
  Includes bibliographical references and index.
  ISBN 978–0–230–58090–9 (alk. paper)
  1. Third-wave feminism. 2. Feminism. I. Title.
  HQ1155.B83 2011
  305.4209′049—dc22
                                                  2011013738

10 9 8 7 6 5 4 3 2 1
20 19 18 17 16 15 14 13 12 11

Printed and bound in Great Britain by
CPI Antony Rowe, Chippenham and Eastbourne

For A.J.T.K.

Contents

Acknowledgements	viii
1 Introduction: Defining the Third Wave	1
2 A Post-Feminist Gender Order	22
3 New Femininities and Feminist Subjectivities	49
4 Experiencing Third Wave Feminism	77
5 A Politics of the Self	103
6 The Limits of Choice	130
7 Generational Dynamics and Feminist Futures	156
8 Closing Reflections	182
Notes	193
Bibliography	195
Index	207

Acknowledgements

I am grateful for the support and encouragement given to me throughout this project by friends, family, and colleagues. Some of the ideas contained in Chapter 5 were presented as part of a chapter published in R. Gill and C. Scharff (eds), *New Femininities* (2011, Palgrave MacMillan) and are reproduced with permission of Palgrave Macmillan. I would like to thank the editors at Palgrave for their patience and professionalism. The early stages of the project took shape while I was spending time at the Centre for Women's Studies and Gender Research in the School of Political and Social Inquiry at Monash University. The final stages of completion were undertaken with the assistance of POLSIS colleagues at the University of Birmingham and with the much appreciated backing of Colin Thain. Thanks to Will for being so resilient and for helping me fight the battle on two fronts. A special thank you to Soots, for your calming influence and consistency of character. Finally, my deepest thanks to Andrew for helping to create a home for me to return to at the end of the day.

1
Introduction: Defining the Third Wave

Since the early 1990s a set of literature which identifies a 'third wave' of feminism has been developing, often provoking lively debates about where feminism has been and where it is going. The concerns examined in this literature and the problems that are identified are linked to the second wave of Western feminism associated with the 1970s and 1980s. However, in this literature the case is often made that feminism has reached a key turning point in its development and that questions must be asked about its applicability to contemporary gender relations and transformed late modern social conditions. Third wave feminist assessments of the state of feminism therefore aim to offer a corrective to established tenets, so that feminism may have greater resonance with women's lives today. The contemporary context is one in which the structure and meaning of gender relations are undergoing substantial questioning, due in part to advancements achieved by women; societal changes brought about by the restructuring of economies; increased cultural diversity; the proliferation of technoculture and the expansion of information technologies; the dynamics of globalization and the rise of global capitalism; crises of environmental degradation; diversifying sexualities and intimate practices; changing demographics; and declining economic vitality (Dicker and Piepmeier, 2003: 4). It is now also accepted that feminism itself is characterized by diversity, fragmentation, and a series of internal contestations. One response to the uncertainty resulting from all of these developments is to declare that feminism and the study of gender has reached a state of crisis in which there is little agreement about *why* the study of gender is still relevant and

1

how best to proceed with the project of feminism. Meanwhile popular perceptions of gender relations now in circulation often suggest that feminism has achieved most of what it set out to do, and so it can now safely be relegated to the past (McRobbie, 2009).

Nevertheless, the role that feminism occupies within contemporary society continues to be subject to extensive and ongoing scrutiny. For a considerable length of time, debates have waged around which aims and objectives ought to be pursued within a context where greater levels of gender equality have been achieved and women's autonomy has been enhanced. In response to the question 'what is feminism' Delmar (1994: 5) writes that many would agree that feminism asserts that women suffer discrimination because of their sex; that women have specific needs, which are negated and as such are left unmet; and that solutions to these problems require substantial transformation of the social, economic, and political orders. Attempts to move beyond these baseline claims towards a more comprehensive definition are frequently confounded by disagreements over how gender relations are best theorized in late modernity and by disputes regarding what practical strategies those different theories call forth for addressing the problems that concern feminism.

Deliberations on fundamental questions such as these illustrate that, in practice, terms like 'feminism' or 'feminist' are challenging because they represent a diverse set of perspectives and constituencies. In these conditions, claims to knowing what makes a 'genuine' or 'proper' feminist are problematic; nevertheless, at times analyses of the contemporary state of feminism reveal a desire for a return to authenticity and coherence – ideals often projected onto a mythical feminist past, associated with the women's movement of the 1960s and 1970s. From other quarters the imagery of a unified feminism, founded upon a commonly held experience of womanhood, has been challenged and replaced with metaphors of fragmentation. It is claimed that difference, not commonality, has become the characteristic most associated with contemporary feminism, and attempts to define feminism ought to give way to the acceptance that contemporary feminist practice features by a substantial degree of ambiguity and disagreement. This indicates that it has become problematic to assume that a clear-cut connection can be made between women's lives and the assumptions underpinning the variety of feminisms that have emerged. Current debates signify that knowledge about feminism's object – women's lives and experiences – has become more uncertain, requiring a set of strategies that often invite debate rather than consensus.

> An analysis of the shifts and changes which have taken place in the meaning and content of 'womanhood' for feminists is intrinsic to any study of feminism as a specific body of thought or practice... what concept of woman is being mobilized, or indeed, as far as contemporary feminism is concerned, whether a concept of woman is being employed at all. (Delmar, 1994: 16–17)

Assertions that a third wave of feminism now exists raises questions about how this particular feminism fits with other versions. What conditions make another wave necessary? Whom does this wave speak to and/or for? What is this wave setting out to achieve? If third wave feminism exists, what is to be made of the declaration that feminism has 'died out' and lost relevance? Claims made on behalf of third wave feminism are far from uncontroversial, and indeed the significance of the phrase 'third wave feminism' is the subject of a debate yet to be resolved. However, the complications that now characterize feminism do not undermine, but rather constitute the conditions that allow the claim that third wave feminism has come into being to be made. Third wave feminism is born out of contradictions, complications, and a lack of predictability; and it carries these features into its self-definition.

A contested site

Third wave feminism is a contested concept, made even more so by a self-conscious evasion of any clear definition on the part of many feminists who advocate for a third wave perspective. While such a move is indicative of its post-structuralist affinities and a commitment to widening the parameters of a feminist agenda, to those engaged in feminist research this deferral or denial often appears to be unhelpful. It is not surprising, then, that a considerable amount of effort has been spent on developing a working definition of the third wave; and yet, despite these efforts, debates about what third wave feminism signifies continue. Dean (2009: 335) argues that the 'third wave' functions as an 'essentially contestable signifier that may be taken up and *used* by feminist academics and activists in a plurality of different ways'.[1] If this is the case, then one might question whether positing a third wave has any political or practical purchase for feminism. The amassing literature on third wave feminism, however, indicates that, despite conflicts over definitional issues and inconsistencies in usage, the phrase 'third wave' is meaningful insofar as several dimensions are repeatedly associated with it and these cohere to the extent that it is feasible to regard them as constituting a distinct form of feminism.

In a comprehensive analysis undertaken by Arneil (1999: 255), third wave feminism is defined as a 'new body of thought, distinct from second wave feminism, which is characterized by notions of identity, difference, contradictions and embodiment'. Third wave feminism signals a break with previous feminist theory by fundamentally challenging the dualisms associated with Western thought. Second wave feminism effectively critiqued and destabilized the foundations of dualisms such as nature/culture and private/public, in which women were positioned in relation to men as a devalued 'other'. These dualisms had served to construct and naturalize meanings attached to the categories of male and female, and by challenging them second wave feminism politicized the processes through which gender difference came into being – thereby revealing the artificiality of those differences which historically had been used to justify gender inequality. From the perspective of third wave feminism, this approach is ultimately limited, insofar as this strategy retains a dualistic structure that is mapped onto the categories of man and woman, albeit with a political aim to integrate women into mainstream structures and social institutions. Third wave feminism is defined, first and foremost, by a deconstructive impulse that seeks to challenge the construction of these categories and to insist on starting from the perspective of multiple differences rather than from a position that advocates equivalence. This is a position that begins by affirming difference in two senses. Firstly, difference is significant insofar as third wave feminism seeks to move the emphasis in feminism away from a strategy which focuses on equality or sameness to a perspective in which women's difference from men or 'otherness' is embraced. It is in this sense that the starting point for third wave feminist critique is the specificity of women's experience. The second dimension of difference emerges from the recognition that starting from women's experiences involves working with the multiplicity of differences that constitute these experiences, therefore third wave feminism 'embraces the diversity and differences in perspectives among "women", ultimately straddling both "one" and the "other"' (Arneil, 1999: 186).

This emphasis on difference translates into a set of key concerns, around which third wave perspectives unify. Firstly, this position is clearly demarcated from second wave feminism but explicitly sets out to expand upon the groundwork established by previous feminist activism and scholarship; therefore both continuity and discontinuity with those previous practices is evident. Secondly, third wave feminism involves a commitment 'to continue the feminist legacy of assessing foundational concepts', most notably the signifier 'woman'; and, thirdly, it attempts 'to embrace the challenge of moving feminism, as a political movement without the fixity of a single feminist agenda in view' into the future (Siegel, 1997a: 56). A commitment to affirm difference complicates feminist analysis by replacing universalizing categories of identity with a conceptual framework that emphasizes fluidity over fixity, multiplicity over singularity, and contradictions over consistency. In practical terms, this means that third wave feminism advocates working with the particular differences that constitute women's positions at the local level, inviting the expression of hybrid identities, while developing strategies for working productively across differences based on a coalitional politics of affinity rather than equivalence. Krolokke and Sorensen (2005: 15), for instance, hold that third wave feminism is motivated by the need to develop a feminist theory and politics that is able to honour the contradictions that constitute women's identities; and achieving this necessitates embracing ambiguity while maintaining a commitment to work inclusively with those particular differences.

The language of inclusivity that is deployed in third wave discourse represents one of its defining rhetorical devices and it is used, often controversially, to define its establishment as separate from second wave feminism. This distinction relies upon representing second wave feminism as ethnocentric and overly concerned with imposing similarity upon women's difference, as for example in the use of the metaphor 'universal sisterhood' to describe women's similar social position. The adequacy of this contentious construction of feminism as divided into distinct waves is questionable on two fronts. Firstly, as Bailey (1997) argues, the significance of invoking the imagery of a wave to represent how feminism materializes across time and place is not entirely clear.

> When we speak of a wave, we typically mean 'one among others.' 'Wave' just doesn't sound like the right word for the lone occurrence of something. Waves that arise in social political milieus, like waves that arise in water, become defined only in context, relative to the waves that have come and gone before. (Bailey, 1997: 18)

Waves suggest a relationship of both continuity and discontinuity with a greater whole. The exact nature of these relations is determined by knowing where one wave ends and another one begins; but that point is often imperceptible, becoming clearer perhaps only in retrospect, with the benefit of time. To claim, therefore, that a third wave now exists not only begs questions about how the second wave might best be defined, given its diversity and complexity, but also, provokes debates about whether it is accurate to deem its time as wholly in the past. To establish a new, third wave requires a break with, and a relegation of, second wave feminism to the past, and therefore an investment in that wave having been displaced (Orr, 1997). In this construal, second wave feminism is depicted as a 'definable phenomenon, as embodying a more or less coherent set of values and ideas that can be recognized and transcended' (Bailey, 1997: 23).

The language of discontinuity deployed in third wave discourse sets up a particularly difficult relationship with second wave feminism, because there is a temporal overlap between these two waves, one that did not exist between the second wave feminism of the 1970s and the first wave of feminism associated with late nineteenth and early twentieth centuries. Therefore in the present context, women who advanced the politics and scholarship now designated as part of the second wave of feminism continue to identify with those practices and to advocate their significance. This overlap often results in the second and the third wave being interpreted as representative of different *generations* that temporally co-exist, and this generational trope has become a recurring characteristic of third wave discourse.[2] As Bailey (1997: 21) argues, many of the young writers who first heralded the third wave did so by conveying 'the sense that the feminism of their mother's generation is naive, obsolete, or otherwise somehow lacking in relevance to their lives'. Strategies used to define the third wave often involve 'perpetuating the idea that older feminists have distorted the truth about difficult issues, either through ignorance or narrowness' (p. 23).

Generational metaphors have proven to be a major hindrance as this way of constructing difference between feminist positions has produced antagonism and antipathy more often than co-operation and collaboration (Detloff, 1997; Henry, 2004; Looser and Kaplan, 1997). It has been suggested, therefore, that the language of the different waves of feminism should be used more reflexively, so as to undermine the generational paradigm, which too often slips into usage and causes debates to get 'stuck' in a place that is unproductive. Instead the aim should be to generate a more radical and open-ended figuration of the third wave (Dean, 2009). Many have argued that, if the term 'generation' is going to be used, it should be qualified by adding the term 'political' (Alfonso and Trigilio, 1997; Arneil, 1999; Kinser, 2004; Siegel, 1997a). The concept of a political generation is defined by Whittier (1995: 180) as designating 'a group of people (not necessarily of the same age) that experiences shared formative social conditions at approximately the same point in their lives, and that holds a common interpretive framework shaped by historical circumstances' (quoted in Alfonso and Trigilio, 1997: 3). From this perspective, diversity within feminism has more to do with variations in climate than with inherent differences in politics. 'Second wave' feminism, therefore, may be used to 'suggest the *era of feminism rooted in and shaped by the 1960s–1980s political climate* and "third wave" to suggest the *era of feminism rooted in and shaped by the mid "80s-new millennium political climate"*' (Kinser, 2004: 132, emphasis original). Situating feminism within this framework moves our concern away from demanding the development of commonly held, historically constant, unifying beliefs and values towards a 'common exposure to the pressure of some of the same (material, theoretical) problems' that emerge at specific times and in specific places (Siegel, 1997a: 56). Third wave feminism is thereby invoked as a political delineation, and not as an inevitable phase in the evolutionary progression of feminism. This perspective requires the critical interrogation of the social and political milieus that have made possible the emergence of third wave feminism. As Bailey (1997: 19) persuasively argues, given the uncertainty of drawing a terminal boundary around the second wave, the political motivations behind christening the beginning of a new wave stand out. In other words, the lack of any natural or obvious boundaries makes the motivations for asserting the beginning of a new wave more clearly political ones.

While in the 1990s the phrase 'third wave' was often harnessed by young writers who declared themselves a 'new generation' of feminists setting out to 'reclaim' feminism (Findlen, 1995; Walker, 1995), many critics have pointed out that, prior to the construction of difference along generational lines, black and lesbian feminists deployed the language of difference to assert their own feminist identities and to lay claim to their unique experiences, differing as they did from dominant feminist discourses of the time. Third wave feminism, therefore, is rooted in 'the questions raised by feminists of colour and lesbian and queer theorists about the nature of identity, the meaning of "gender" and working through some of the contradictions elicited by such questions' (Arneil, 1999: 192). Orr (1997) similarly traces the 'definitional moment' of third wave back to the terrain of 'race' in early 1980s rather than to the terrain of age in the mid-1990s. Hence the complex character of third wave feminism owes a large debt to the critiques of feminists of colour, who called for a 'new subjectivity' in 'what was, up to that point, white, middle-class, first world feminism' (Orr, 1997: 37). Dean (2009: 336) also locates the origins of third wave feminism within these critiques and their convergence with those being launched from post-modernist and post-structuralist quarters. From these historical events questions about the formation of women's subjectivities and their relationship to feminism came to occupy a central concern in the development of the third wave.

> The notion of a 'third wave' within feminist theory originally gained currency in the late 1980s at a time when poststructuralist and postmodernist critiques of hegemonic feminist conceptions of womanhood and subjectivity were becoming increasingly prevalent. These theoretical developments also coincided with, and to a large extent overlapped with, critiques from black, 'third world' and postcolonial perspectives of the parochialism of dominant conceptions of feminist politics and subjectivity. (Dean, 2009:336)

Challenging the foundational assumptions of existing feminist frameworks – such as a unified feminist subject – has resulted in a form of feminism that focuses more upon how individual women understand and claim their own feminist identities. Many of the early texts set out to explore what third wave feminism meant to those women who claimed membership were organized around autobiographical essays (Findlen, 1995; Walker, 1995). While these different personal narratives cluster under the umbrella of 'third wave', it is made clear that 'there's no singular "young feminist" take on the world' (Findlen, 1995: xv). These essays highlight the different ways in which women understand what it means to be feminist, and they advance the third wave message that there are many ways of being one. Themes of self-expression and self-determination run through the literature, and this dimension of third wave feminism is one of its defining features. These narratives may be read as 'rhetorical projects embedded in concrete material situations', which can lend insight into 'how the third wave emerges out of a series of historically specific contradictions' (Siegel, 1997a: 57). In the view of some commentators, the desire to deconstruct a feminist 'we' to create a more open-ended and fluid feminism, constituted by a series of individual experiences, means that third wave feminism lacks sufficient coherence to have any political force. The individualistic tendencies that third wave feminism displays are at the heart of many of its contradictions, but to understand why this is so it is necessary to consider how third wave feminism emerges as the product of a set of historical circumstances. As explained by Krolokke and Sorensen (2005: 15), the third wave has been embraced by women who were born with the privileges that first and second wave feminists fought for and, therefore, these women generally 'see themselves as capable, strong, and assertive social agents'. This individualism therefore imparts a sense of entitlement and confidence that is owed to the establishment of feminism, although it is not always harnessed in the service of aims associated with earlier waves.

In this book, 'third wave' feminism is not approached as 'if it were a discreet, clearly identifiable entity that can be described in a simple referential fashion', but as an 'essentially contestable signifier', taken up and used by different feminists in a variety of ways (Dean, 2009: 335). However, bearing that caveat in mind, the aim is to examine some of the key contradictions and claims associated with third wave feminism and to offer a critical account of those claims by linking them to a specific set of historical conditions constitutive of late modernity. This account will centre upon three main features of the contemporary gender order that, in tandem, produce a series of historically unique contradictions.

The establishment and social recognition of feminism is the first key feature. The mainstreaming of many basic feminist aims has converted gender equality into a recognized social good, and yet this phenomenon is taken by some to mean that gender relations no longer constitute an area of concern. The dismissal of feminism is, however, selective and in this context feminist values are often strategically deployed to support political aims that are not consistent with feminist objectives. Secondly, set against the backdrop of increased individualized conservatism and neoliberal depoliticization, feminist values and goals are at the risk of dilution and co-optation. Thirdly, within the context of increased equality and of the celebration of individualized identities, new forms of femininity have emerged, constituted through a discourse of 'female success' and achievement. The often cited phrase 'the future is female' references these new femininities and is used to describe gender transformations in the areas of educational attainment, workplace organization and employment status, political power, and family and reproductive practices.

The establishment and death of feminism

Third wave feminism has been made possible through the establishment of feminism and its widespread social and cultural presence. The movement of feminist values and practices into mainstream social institutions and popular consciousness has provided an important platform for the development of a distinct third wave feminist identity and has created new problems and issues for the study of gender, particularly with regards to how we might critically evaluate the successes that are attributed to feminism. The 'modernization' of gender relations means that equality and women's empowerment have become accepted in theory, if not consistently in practice, as a social good, while the levels of success that many women currently enjoy in educational attainment, employment status, and personal relationships are all convincing confirmations that feminism has profoundly changed the position of women in Western societies now dominated by neoliberal and individualized values. Yet it is these achievements that confirm feminism and at the same time close the door on its future. Who needs feminism now that women have it so good?

Narratives about the 'death of feminism' are not a new phenomenon. Proclamations of feminism's end have long been part of the context within which feminism has been practiced. For instance, in 1976, the cover story of an issue of Harper's magazine announced a 'Requiem for the Women's Movement' (Geng, 1976, cited in Hawkesworth, 2004: 963).³ The plot of this story, which continues to circulate in various discourses even today, conveyed that feminism had undergone a 'natural demise', caused by a loss of direction, internal factionalism, and disconnection from women's everyday lives. Feminism, it was argued, had become characterized by 'highly specialized individuals and cliques, each cultivating its arcane little patch of ground in such depth as to mystify and rebuff any interested generalists who wander by in search of a way to aid the larger goals of the women's liberation' (Geng, 1976: 53, quoted in Hawkesworth, 2004: 964). According to this characterization, feminism's viability had been undermined by troubles that were largely self-inflicted and, as such, it was insinuated not only that feminism was fundamentally and internally flawed, but also that sympathy was an inappropriate response to its inevitable failure. This has become a remarkably familiar narrative, and it is regularly offered as a reply to questions about feminism's contemporary relevance. However, it is also a characterization that runs counter to evidence confirming that feminism has been tremendously effective in the pursuit of many of its aims and has established the foundations for an ongoing political and social agenda.

Far from 'dying off' over the past four decades, feminism has undergone unprecedented growth, and its widespread establishment within cultural, social, and political realms is readily evident. As Freedman states (2006: 85), 'contrary to the views of contemporary pundits, feminism has never been more widespread or politically influential than at this point in history', and it has 'moved from the margins of alternative culture to infiltrate mainstream politics' in many countries. Hawkesworth (2004), for instance, compiles a long list of examples of feminism's global presence: the mainstreaming of feminist projects within official state institutions and the creation of ministries for women, women's bureaux, and gender equality commissions; the establishment of the feminist arm of the United Nations (UNIFEM); the inclusion of gender equity in the foreign policy initiatives of several countries; the ratification of the Convention to Eliminate All Forms of Discrimination against Women (CEDAW); and the proliferation of feminist NGOs, which have contributed to a healthy feminist civil society. This extensive presence has put, and kept, a wide range of feminist issues at the centre of political life and civil society.

> The substantive scope of such feminist work includes subsistence struggles; the politics of food, fuel, and firewood; women's health and reproductive freedom; education for women and girls; employment opportunity; equal pay, safe working conditions, and protection against sexual harassment; rape and domestic violence; sexual trafficking; women's rights as human rights; militarization; peacemaking; environmentalism; sustainable development; democratization; welfare rights; AIDS; parity in public office; women's e-news; feminist journals and presses; and curriculum revision, feminist pedagogy, and feminist scholarship.
> (Hawkesworth, 2004: 962)

Over the past 30 years, gender equality has moved to the centre of the global political agenda and has become institutionalized through a range of state sanctioned strategies that include gender quotas and the development of women's political agencies. Squires (2007: 1) observes that 'gender equality is increasingly framed as central to the realization of both modernization and economic efficiency and its achievement is presented as a key to good governance'. The most recent manifestation of the endorsement of gender equality as a social good is found in the extensive adoption of 'gender mainstreaming' strategies. This approach 'seeks to institutionalize equality by embedding gender-sensitive practices and norms in the structures, processes, and environment of public policy' and, because it requires the expansion of responsibility for gender issues across organizational structures rather than centralizing these matters as a specialist field of policy, this approach is often viewed as representing a widespread commitment to gender equality (Daly, 2005: 435). Gender mainstreaming is conceived of as a way of updating or 'modernizing' gender policies and has become 'part of the accepted wisdom about what modern gender equality architecture should look like – it has become a symbol of modernity' (p. 441).

The endorsement of gender equality implies that feminism, too, has become institutionalized and 'mainstreamed'; however, critical assessments of this development often reveal that gender mainstreaming may signal an explicit move away from 'women's issues' to gender issues, and therefore involves the loss of recognizable feminist oppositional politics (Daly, 2005; Squires, 2007; Walby, 2005a, 2005b). With this shift away from the space of an 'autonomous, radical opposition based on anti-system outrage at oppression', feminism has moved into another space, which is framed as accessible and inclusionary (Walby, 2002: 533). For those who are supportive of mainstreaming, this shift does not signal the end of feminist political activity; it only signals its reorientation; an adjustment in 'repertoire and form', effected by social structural changes; women's access to educational and employment resources; and the opening up of new political opportunity structures (Walby, 2002).

'Post-feminist' backlash and co-optation

For critics, gender mainstreaming presents fundamental challenges to feminism, particularly with regards to the multiple threats presented by co-optation. Mc Robbie (2009), for example, expresses deep scepticism towards gender mainstreaming; in particular, she is critical of Walby's (2005b) defence of gender mainstreaming as a new, modernized form of feminist practice. Moving away from autonomous feminist activity towards activities more centrally located within the state and civil society can lead to a 'kind of re-worked equal rights feminism which is compatible with liberal democracy' and is consistent with the modernizing agenda of British party politics and the incorporation of feminist demands (McRobbie, 2009: 152). From this perspective, gender equality initiatives have become part of governance structures organized through the normalization and institutionalization of a neoliberal economic paradigm, which has ultimately contributed to a de-democratization of policy-making. As Squires explains:

> The coincidence of the normalization of neo-liberalism and the emergence of feminist engagements with the state suggest that these recent feminist strategies may be more complicit in the

pursuit of neo-liberal agendas than its feminist advocates have liked to acknowledge. (Squires, 2007: 8)

In practice, gender mainstreaming translates into 'a technocratic process reduced to a series of procedures, such as impact assessments, that eschew both political participation and normative contestation in their reliance upon professionalized expertise and evidence-based indicators' (pp. 14–15). Modernized and incorporated into official governance structures, feminism has 'matured' and has become a more respectable 'professional top-down technocratic advocacy on behalf of women's issues on the national and global stage' (McRobbie, 2009: 153). With this status comes the loss of practising feminism from an autonomous, publicly visible, and oppositional stance. Controversially, feminism has transformed from an overtly critical practice into a professional and managerial execution of feminist aims located within an audit culture characterized by the imperatives of evaluation, measurement of outcomes, and identification of 'best practice'. Scepticism towards gender mainstreaming may indeed be warranted; for, amongst the key political equality mechanisms currently in operation, 'evaluations of gender mainstreaming have generated the least conclusive evidence regarding effective implementation, with many studies finding that its impact is limited to rhetorical change only' (Squires, 2007: 12). Furthermore, as Daly (2005: 44) argues, the adoption of equality initiatives is not always commensurate with a feminist agenda but is often driven by other imperatives.

> [T]he introduction of gender mainstreaming, rather than emerging out of or being embedded in a philosophy about gender inequality as a structural phenomenon, tends to stem from policy making exigencies or current styles or fashions... countries see it as in their interests to update. Often, there is an instrumental reason for this...

Moreover, the phrase 'gender mainstreaming' seems to imply that there is an unproblematic and transparent understanding of what the terms 'gender' and 'equality' mean. When Eveline and Bacchi (2005: 497) question what it is that is being mainstreamed when gender is mainstreamed, they effectively highlight that different conceptualizations of gender are linked to different feminist political strategies. To ask such a question brings to bear the consideration that 'meanings can congeal in ways that perpetuate established forms of seeing, or of representing problems in ways that instantiate the social status quo' (Bacchi, 1999, cited in Eveline and Bacchi, 2005: 497). While appearing to symbolize the acceptance of feminist aims, gender mainstreaming is in practice a multifaceted phenomenon, whose innocuous appearance seems to 'solve' the problem of gender but which runs the risk of glossing over the debates that characterize feminist theory and practice, at a time when the very need for feminism itself is being questioned.

From the perspective of third wave feminism, the incorporation of feminism – and indeed the currency now given to the value of gender equality – suggests the need to rethink the relationship between feminism and women's lives and experiences. The location from which this is done is defined on the one hand by the significant social impact of second wave feminism and by the coming of age of women for whom feminism and the value of gender equality has been established as part of the mainstream. On the other hand, third wave feminism interfaces with conservative, 'post-feminist' claims that feminism disempowers women by encouraging a 'victim identity' and that women should therefore reject feminism in favour of embracing power, in the pursuit of individual goals. This is a context constituted in powerful ways, by depoliticizing and individualizing discourses.

> Third wavers came of age in a world where feminist *language* is part of the public dialogue, but authentic feminist *struggles* are not accounted for in that dialogue except in terms articulated by the mainstream, which still perpetuates a conservative and sexist status quo. Young women have to have a feminism that can counter the dangerously sophisticated pronouncements of the failure and inadequacies of feminism coming out of postfeminism. (Kinser, 2004: 135)

Third wave feminism exists in tension with both second wave feminism and post-feminism, and it attempts to manage this tension by working with the influence of both. Arneil (1999) explains that the influence of these competing discourses is evident in the way third wave feminism rejects and incorporates elements from both positions. The latter position is 'rejected, in part, for being too conservative and status quo', but the 'notions of individuality, strength and female power' are accepted as having purchase (Arneil, 1999: 190). The individualism exhibited in third wave assertions that young women now experience a sense of self-empowerment, not available to previous generations of women, may be historicized in this way. Third wave feminists declare that feminism continues to be an active and important force in contemporary society but is one that often materializes in identities and practices not immediately associated with previously established forms of feminism. It is accepted that feminism has been fundamentally challenged by both the loss of a unified subject 'woman' and a perceived lack of relevance to women's lives, but that it is possible to develop ways of rethinking gender from a perspective that may still be identified as feminist in nature. Indeed third wave writers view the uncertainty that contemporary social change has brought to an analysis of gender relations as an opportunity to move beyond a post-feminist impasse to engage in the creation of a revitalized feminist project.

Female empowerment and success

Studying third wave feminism and grappling with its significance necessitates working with a definition of 'feminism' based more on difference than on commonality and upon contradiction rather than upon coherence. Third wave feminism prioritizes an analysis of individual subjectivities rather than the formation of group identity. With women's collective right to equality more firmly established, third wave feminism shifts attention to the subjective and individualized experiences of women as they develop their own relationship to feminism. Thus, third wave feminism seeks to develop a more individualized form of feminism, which can respond to diversity and ambiguity. By advocating an analytical move away from understanding gender in collective terms, third wave feminism often promotes instead a 'politics of difference', starting from the specificity of individual experience. The aim is not to develop a feminism that makes representational claims on behalf of women, but to advance a politics based upon *self-definition* and a concern with how women define their personal relationship with feminism. This is what may be understood as a 'feminism from inside' – in at least two senses. In the first instance, as discussed above, late modernity is constituted by a liberal politics of gender equality, which means that gender issues have become incorporated into mainstream systems of governance. This creates a situation in which feminism is accepted as relevant, but primarily as a social phenomenon that has achieved its aims and therefore no longer has a clear purpose. In the second instance, a popularized version of feminism that circulates throughout the dominant culture is manifest in representations of women as powerful, liberated, and highly individualized. As argued by Harris (2004a: 16), the idealized subject of late modernity is one who is 'flexible, individualized, resilient, self driven and self made and who easily follows nonlinear trajectories to fulfilment and success'. Increasingly, these are the characteristics that are demanded of young women, because they are perceived to be the 'most confident, resilient, and empowered of all the demographic groups affected by risk' (Harris, 2004a: 16). Young women are often held to be key beneficiaries of a range of socio-economic changes that now characterize Western societies, while the neoliberal tropes of freedom and choice are increasingly associated with the category 'young women' (McRobbie, 2004a: 255). Feminist ideals of autonomy, choice, and self-determination have become key normative features of 'modernized' femininity, and women are encouraged to internalize these values not as 'feminists' but as liberated individuals.

Third wave feminism does not seek to occupy an oppositional place outside of the structures and relations that feminism has become incorporated into. Indeed it is maintained that in late modernity there is no 'pure' definition either of the category 'woman' or of the category 'feminist', and, as such, there is no 'real' feminist identity that transcends the culture within which it is produced. By refusing to deploy straightforward codes to designate contemporary gender ideals in terms of simple binaries such as 'good' or 'bad', third wave feminism insists on the necessity of straddling binaries and working with the contradictions that result. Feminism must be able to respond to the development of new contradictions by acknowledging their manifestation within individual subjectivities and those contradictions that emanate from the differences that constitute women's lives. This involves expanding the range of meanings and practices that can constitute a feminist identity and contribute to a politics of subjectivity. Gendered identity is inherently contradictory and complex, especially as new forms of empowered female identities have emerged. Therefore, from the vantage point of the third wave, feminism must be able to accommodate behaviours and desires that may not be immediately recognized as feminist within established perspectives.

Summary of chapters

The solutions offered by the third wave to the challenges feminism faces in late modernity have been discussed and contested both by those who identify themselves as third wavers and by those who are more sceptical of what that identity entails. In this book it is argued that, because the label is contested, third wave feminism acts as a useful site for examining current debates about the role that gender plays in the constitution of contemporary society. Some of these issues indicate continuity with feminist emancipatory concerns of the past, while others reveal the emergence of new problems, associated with greater gender equality and levels of female success. Criticisms have been levelled at third wave feminism for being overly ahistorical and atheoretical. This necessitates a more historically situated and systematic engagement with the claims made about gender and feminism within the third wave literature. The aim of the present book, therefore, is to offer a critical assessment of the strategies third wave feminism promotes for linking feminism to a reconstituted postfeminist gender order, to new forms of femininity, to a proliferation of feminisms, and to the significant consequences these factors have for thinking about gender as it relates to the areas of gendered subjectivity, identity, politics, knowledge, and critique. Key questions that are explored in the following chapters include: How has femininity changed over the past 40 years and what is the impact of these transformations on the formation of gendered subjects? What role does feminist discourse play in the formation of gendered identities? What relationships exist between different feminisms? Can feminist politics be founded upon individual difference?

In Chapter 2 the kinds of questions third wave feminism poses will be contextualized by examining how feminism has been made manifest through various practices and different conceptual frameworks at specific times and places. This genealogical analysis of feminism draws attention to the contingent factors that define the contexts that differing forms of feminism have responded to historically. Feminism does not fit into a unitary form, which is consistent across time, but it develops in relation to specific socio-historical demands, and at this particular juncture this context can be described as post-feminist. A post-feminist social constellation is made up of contradictory and competing forces such as neoliberalism and individualism, which overlap with feminism particularly in its mainstreamed and popular forms. Feminism does not occupy a separate space outside of this convergence of forces, but instead it affects and is affected by them, often drawing upon similar but contested values such as choice and autonomy.

The aim of historicizing third wave feminism continues to be pursued in Chapter 3 through the examination of newly emerging feminine subject positions. In particular, this chapter explores the ways in which femininity has increasingly been reconstructed through discourses of individuality, such that the cultural ideals of choice, independence, and self-determination have not only become possible for women to pursue but are increasingly operating in a normative and regulative fashion, so as to define an ideal femininity. While feminism has significantly impacted upon the empowerment of female subjectivity, this new discourse of success must also be located within a wider 'culture of the self' permeated by the logic of neoliberal self-governance. The overlap in feminist and neoliberal discourses creates a series of contradictions for young women, who are attempting to negotiate their positioning by adopting ideals that current social arrangements make difficult to realize. Third wave discourses tend to focus on individualized notions of female empowerment and autonomy but attempt to retrieve this form of selfhood for a feminist politics of the self, in which individual women are granted the space and autonomy to define their own relationship to feminism.

In Chapter 4 the significance of individual experience for third wave identities and politics is examined. The emphasis placed upon women's individual differences and the caution which third wave feminism expresses towards collective representation are highlighted through autobiographical writings, which are used to communicate a third wave feminist politics of location. Autobiography is defended in third wave discourses as a vehicle for articulating how women come to incorporate feminism into their lives on their own terms. Therefore these stories situate third wave politics within the experiences associated with doing gender in the context of late modernity. A striking feature of this context is the structurally ambivalent nature of contemporary femininity, which often makes occupying idealized femininity a difficult undertaking. The discussion of experience will be grounded in an analysis of several studies that have explored how young women encounter and attempt to resolve the contradictory aspects of late modern femininity, and also the ambivalences that result as they attempt to make themselves into idealized feminine subjects. Within this context personal theorizing requires us to ask after the conditions that produce particular experiences. Third wave feminism, in advocating for a personalized feminism that recognizes the validity of women's experiences, must also engage in critical evaluation of how particular experiences come into being and question why some experiences acquire cultural value over others.

Further analysis of the contradictory nature of femininity is undertaken in Chapter 5, with a specific emphasis placed upon the connection that third wave feminism makes between contradictory experiences and a politics of the self that is founded largely upon the claim that women need to work within those contradictions to pursue autonomy and self-definition and to resist hegemonic definitions of femininity. Situated within popular culture, the strategies of resistance promoted by third wave feminism often rely upon re-appropriating negative terms and recoding them, in acts of self-determination. However, in a politics that relies upon the appropriation of dominant logics and their resignification, it may be the case that not all terms are equally open to appropriation and reversal. The context of any particular re-appropriation will influence the efficacy of that re-appropriation as a form of counter-hegemonic practice. Moreover, the intention that drives an act of resignification cannot guarantee the *particular effect* of that act of re-appropriation.

The discussion in Chapter 5 raises questions about the extent to which women's agency is enhanced in a culture where idealized femininity has been linked to neoliberal discourses of self-empowerment and individual success. Late modern feminities are constituted significantly through a language of choice; therefore in Chapter 6 the conceptualization of autonomy from a feminist perspective is considered. Third wave discourses tend to emphasize agentic choice but fall short of offering a standard against which acts of choice may be evaluated. Transformed social conditions have opened up choices to women, but it is also the case that the choices that are available, the meaning that attaches to particular choices, and the relations that are resisted or reproduced in the act of making choices can only be understood by their conditioning within social relations. It is, therefore, useful to rethink autonomy by recasting it as a fully social phenomenon and to reconceptualize choice from the perspective of social interdependence. This strategy complicates the language of choice, requiring that choices are critically evaluated, both in terms of the relations that make particular choices possible and in terms of the reciprocal effects those choices have on the relations within which they are embedded.

In Chapter 7 themes raised in this introduction will be revisited by examining how third wave feminism attempts to promote a feminism that can transcend claims that feminism is no longer viable or necessary. In service of this aim, third wave feminism often constructs feminist waves through the lens of generational difference. In this construction the third wave is positioned as a successor to second wave feminism; one that is able to provide an antidote to the failure, attributed to its predecessor, to deal adequately with conditions that demand feminism to encompass contradiction, multiplicity, and non-unitary identities. Third wave feminism seeks to establish a radical figuration of feminist subjectivity that is *not reducible* to second wave principles and problematics. The logic underlying this strategy requires recognition of multiple differences that cannot be contained within a binary relation, where the meaning of terms relies upon the negation of one term by the other. However, a serious incongruity is at work in this position. By invoking a *reproductive* temporality, many third wave feminists remain lodged within a negative conception of difference; one that disavows a feminist past and limits the possibilities for conceptualizing feminism in more radical and open-ended ways.

2
A Post-Feminist Gender Order

The formal currency granted to gender equality as an *ideal* is often popularly assumed, almost as a form of 'common sense', to constitute evidence of its *actual* existence. The general acceptance of women's rights to equality often obscures the ways in which current discursive and material practices operate to produce differential social outcomes for women and men. This obfuscation is one of the defining features of a social context increasingly characterized as post-feminist in nature. Although there is much debate about what post-feminism signifies and what accepting it as a descriptor of the contemporary social order might imply, its usage has become ubiquitous in current discussions of feminism (Hawkesworth, 2004). The burgeoning literature on post-feminism is indicative of a growing concern with the state of gender relations in late modernity, which in turn has given rise to a strong interest in analysing what is happening to feminism (Genz, 2009; Genz and Brabon, 2009; McRobbie, 2004b; Negra, 2009; Tasker and Negra, 2007). As Gill explains, 'in recent years debates about everything from the history and exclusions of feminism to the gender consciousness (or otherwise) of young women and the ideological nature of contemporary media, have crystallized in disagreements about postfeminism' (2007a: 147). The aim of this chapter is to provide a detailed account of post-feminism, which is used in the context of this book to describe the contemporary Western gender order. Outlining the main features of post-feminism aids in situating third wave feminism within this specific set of social conditions and helps to explain how third wave feminism has manifested within a genealogy of feminism.

Features of post-feminism

Post-feminism is a complicated phenomenon, associated with a number of meanings that allow the term to be deployed in multiple and often contradictory ways. However, despite lacking a 'pure' definition, post-feminism represents a general set of features associated with the particular gender regime characteristic of late modernity – features that are coherent enough to justify its usage. Firstly, post-feminism refers to an anti-feminist stance associated with a general social backlash against feminism, driven largely by the belief that gender equality has been achieved. Secondly, post-feminism is often used to characterize a type of feminism that followed on from second wave feminism and sought to focus on women's diversity. Thirdly, post-feminism is used at times to describe a theoretical position influenced by post-modernism (see Gill, 2007a; Kavka, 2001). Within each of these manifestations, debates ensue over whether post-feminism represents the demise of feminist goals or a phase of feminist reinvention.

Backlash

Within post-feminist culture, feminism is often popularly portrayed as an outmoded, redundant 'unwelcome, implicitly censorious presence' (Tasker and Negra, 2007: 3). This dismissal of feminism's relevance is underpinned by the claim that feminism has achieved its primary goals and, since gender oppression has been dismantled, women no longer need a feminist perspective to inform the choices they make in their lives. As Orr states, 'put this way, "feminist" practices become matters of personal style or choice and any emphasis on organized intervention is regarded as naive and even oppressive to women' (1997: 3). The target for this backlash is second wave feminism, which is characterized as having overstayed its welcome only to become 'anachronistic, completely unfashionable and totally lacking in fun' (Braithwaite, 2002: 338). Feminism is not being rejected here *per se*; rather the prefix 'post' is deployed to demarcate a boundary between 'retrograde' second wave and an ostensibly more progressive type of 'power' feminism, which allows women to take full advantage of the opportunities available to them. This position is espoused in the libertarian form of feminism promoted by early post-feminists, including Rene Denfeld, Katie Roiphe, Christina Hoff Sommers, and

Naomi Wolf, who advocated a woman-centred stance that conflated female autonomy with individualism (Parkins, 1999). These authors launched a derisive attack on second wave feminism, proclaiming that the biggest obstacle standing in the way of women's achieving their individual goals was feminism itself – because it encouraged women to identify with a collective position of victimhood. As a solution to this feminism-induced dependency, women are encouraged to adopt a view of themselves as fully autonomous individuals, free to wield power in the pursuit of personal goals.

Post-feminist accounts of gender relations tend to invoke liberal notions of the formal equality between men and women, as the latter is enshrined in law, while ignoring the enduring effects of historical power asymmetries (Modleski, 1991). Critics of post-feminism view this as an inherently conservative, anti-feminist, and reactionary stance, which results in 'the simultaneous incorporation, revision, and depoliticisation of many of the central goals of second wave feminism' (Stacey, 1990, quoted in Orr, 1997: 34). By positing gender issues as matters to be dealt with by individuals in whatever way they may choose, this manifestation of post-feminism encourages the expulsion of the feminist agenda from public debates and removes feminist issues from view. Privatizing gender issues in this way reaffirms the *status quo* and works to create the appearance that the current social order is as it should be, because feminism has been transcended. Post-feminism from this perspective is closely aligned with, and bolstered by, patriarchal interests.

> Invocations of postfeminism, then, could be read as banishments, commanding us to imagine gender relations, higher education, individual psyches, and contemporary culture at large as spatial and temporal zones in which feminism has been eclipsed. Much like the obituaries in the popular media, assertions about postfeminism proclaim that feminism is gone, departed, dead. (Hawkesworth, 2004: 969)

The most troublesome effect produced by post-feminism is a misguided understanding of feminist achievements, namely that *particular* advancements made by *some* women are taken as being representative of success writ large. The result is a contradictory dynamic, by which feminism erases 'itself out of existence by its very success' (Kavka, 2001: xi).

In response to the proclamation that feminism has died out, we can often trace a desire to regain a 'proper' feminist vision that can reliably guide women's agency; however, setting up oppositional categories such as 'power feminism' versus 'victim feminism' problematically constructs a 'real' or authentic feminism, which belies the contradictions that inescapably constitute feminism (Orr, 1997). This dichotomy relies upon rejecting established forms of feminism, namely an entity imagined as singular and uniform, as 'bad', in favour of a 'new' feminism – again, singular and uniform, but one that can be labelled 'good' because it has replaced the former, outdated variety (Siegel, 1997b).

After the second wave: Internal debates

Post-feminism may also be used to describe the phase that followed second wave feminism. This implies a continuation of feminism; however, due to a more reflexive engagement with feminism's own assumptions, the prefix 'post' is used to reference a historical shift in the understanding of feminism's subject and associated goals. As described by Kavka (2001: x): '"Post-feminism" implies, first and foremost, that there was a time when feminists could say "we" and that that time is now gone.' That 'we' is acknowledged retrospectively, as an imagined entity, and it is that very recognition that marks the transition into post-feminism – a complication brought to the category of 'woman' by the acceptance of women's actual differences and diversity along the lines of class, nationality, sexuality, 'race', and ethnicity.

The commonality once thought to constitute 'women's experience' has been replaced by an understanding that that category is more contingent and variable than was previously assumed in approaches that took feminist consensus as the starting point for a feminist politics. White solipsism and ethnocentric tendencies present in some second wave approaches have been countered with an emphasis on the analysis of interlocking, multiple, and simultaneous oppressions, which ultimately undermine the assumption that a shared feminist political platform could be founded upon the claim of a common female oppression (Collins, 2000; Hooks, 1981). This critique not only effected a reformulation of feminism's subject, but drew attention to the ways in which feminism itself had become implicated in perpetuating social inequality, despite its aim of addressing social injustices. When it is used to refer to this shift, post-feminism represents a demand for a more complex and more inclusive feminism (Zack, 2005).

> Linked with an earlier moment in feminism and indebted to it, the term postfeminism simply suggests that the breadth of feminist issues is now much broader than ever before and intersects with a number of theories about gender, race and ethnicity, sexuality, class, corporeality and popular culture, to name just some of the areas of current complex feminist discussion. (Braithwaite, 2002: 341)

A post-feminist socio-historical context requires the negotiation of a series of tensions that have been produced through a reflexive reformulation of the assumptions feminism makes, particularly with regard to the subject which feminism seeks to represent. Acceptance of heterogeneity has challenged the feasibility of identity politics and has raised questions about how feminism might retain some degree of collectivity in its categories while simultaneously avoiding essentializing tendencies.

Post-feminist heterogeneity is often linked to the greater importance placed upon cross-generational dynamics in the constitution of debates internal to feminism (Budgeon, 2001; Henry, 2004; Looser and Kaplan, 1997). When operationalized as 'generational difference', post-feminism indicates a relationship between two entities – second wave feminism and its successor. Far from this relationship being straightforward, its nature often raises challenging questions about feminism's existence over time. It has been argued, for instance, that generational metaphors imply the handing down of a tradition that, if respected, will be left intact (Adkins, 2004; Elam, 1997; Roof, 1997). This exchange is commonly characterized as one fraught with Oedipal tensions, anxiety, and ambivalence, given that the act of inheriting can be laden with notions of debt, duty, and obligation. For those who view the intergenerational hand-over as unsuccessful, post-feminism represents a profound disappointment in the failure of the next generation of feminists to carry on previously established feminist aims and strategies.

On the other hand, generational paradigms have been claimed to offer a different vantage point, from which younger women are able to profess a feminism that has continuity with the second wave but is incorporated into the younger women's identities on their own terms. Third wave feminism is frequently understood in terms of generational differences. While a debt to feminism's past is acknowledged, gender relations are understood to have undergone sufficient restructuring to make generational difference centrally involved in the production of different feminist subject positions. These identities are claimed on the basis of a set of experiences that demand an alternative to second wave feminism but share with second wave the category of experience as a crucial starting point in generating feminist politics. For a younger generation, whose members came of age when feminism was already established as part of their cultural imaginary and have benefited enormously from previous feminist successes, post-feminism represents an opportunity for a more self-defined politics – one that is individually oriented to the existence of multiple social differences, which constitute women's lives, but may also give rise to activist politics. While some of the concerns identified with this new generation are shared with the second wave of feminism, it is also the case that members of the new generation 'face differently configured problems, issues and ideologies – however subtly or radically changed. Secondwave feminists – like it or not – are destined to fail in their mission to "pass on" feminist knowledge' (Looser, 1997: 34). Chapter 7 will examine these issues further and analyse the debates associated with the construction of feminist generational differences by looking at how third wave feminism might envision feminist subjectivities not reducible to generational difference.

Post-modernism and post-structuralism

In contrast to the usage of 'post-feminism' in popular culture, as shorthand for 'the death of feminism', in academic circles the term has been used more optimistically, to describe feminist engagement with deconstructive critiques of modernist paradigms and of their reliance upon grand narratives, universalizing categories, truth claims, and humanist conceptualizations of the subject. Debates internal to feminism about the significance of women's differences have carried through into the analysis of feminism's external relationship with post-modernism and post-structuralism. Given that categories such as 'women's experience' had been destabilized through the recognition of difference, feminism was already grappling with a range of ontological, epistemological, and ethical challenges also raised by post-modernism and post-structuralism. By offering a range of conceptual and critical tools designed to aid in the interrogation of identity and social difference, post-modern and post-structuralist theory presented to feminism both a challenge and an opportunity.

> Despite their own indebtedness to the Enlightenment, feminists have come to recognize the masculinist assumptions embedded in its conception of rational individuals and its aspirations for equality. This has affected their understanding of their own history. The women's movement's lived and willing participation in modernity's rationalist project, subsequently recounted in grand narrative terms (as a single story of progress and continuity in pursuit of a specific emancipatory goal), begins to look problematic. Its familiar history might unwittingly sustain deeper structures of oppression while its monolithic recounting might perpetuate an exclusionary logic. (Coole, 2000: 36–37)

In her account, Brooks (1997: 1–2) argues that the 'post' in post-feminism implies a 'process of ongoing transformation and change', but she does not assume that patriarchal or modernist frames of reference have been overcome. Rather the advent of post-feminism indicates that feminism has reached a point of development that brings into perspective a view of 'earlier feminist frameworks at the same time as critically engaging with patriarchal and imperialist discourses' (Brooks, 1997). Coole (2000: 36) similarly points out that, in comparison to other ideological movements, feminism has been particularly 'self-critical in reflecting upon its own foundations and values since it must constantly elicit, criticize and deconstruct unexpurgated patriarchal or phallocentric assumptions there'. As a consequence of this tendency towards auto-critique, the assumptions that underpin feminist positions are interrogated as robustly as those associated with the male-dominated society within which they operate. The result is a 'post-feminism' that avoids the essentializing tendencies of earlier feminist positions, accepts a more contingent understanding of the subject, and promotes a more open-ended feminism.

The optimism associated with this manifestation of post-feminism is not shared by all, and many feminists contend that the incorporation of post-modernist and post-structuralist principles seriously detracts feminism from its proper aims and objectives. As Murray (1997: 37) protests,

> postfeminist theory has disconnected women from activism in the name of difference; their idea of difference admirably recognizes that women have different needs but then deprives them of a common commitment to end female oppression. Postfeminist difference means that as women we have no voice because we speak for no one.

Post-feminism, therefore, is criticized for encouraging relativism, for generating scepticism, and for promoting a 'politics of retreat'. Segal (1999), for instance, observes that the reorientation of feminism around the task of theorizing subjectivities, analysing formations of selfhood, and advocating non-identity has directed attention away from the more fundamental issues of distributive justice and social restructuring. This shift away from what is conceived of as broad social concerns has placed abstract cultural concerns at the centre of feminism (Segal, 1999: 35). For those who view this reorientation as a serious error, post-feminism represents a turning inwards, away from feminism's proper object.

A post-feminist social order is one in which the need for feminism is continually questioned and faced with the challenges that heterogeneity, difference, and a self-reflexive engagement with its own categories and representational practices present. The phenomenon of post-feminism generates a high level of interest because, with all of its intricacies and contradictions, the questions it poses reveal that *something* compelling is happening to gender relations at this particular historical juncture and that a feminist response is necessarily difficult – but necessary nonetheless. As examined here, the term 'post-feminism' can be usefully deployed as a descriptor of the contemporary gender order, in which feminism cannot be reduced to a singular set of effects or restricted to any particular site of operation. Nor should definitive judgements be made about either the success or the failure of feminism. Instead it is more useful to conceptualize feminism as a dynamic and variable set of forces and relations.

> 'Postfeminism' is assumed to be anti-feminist, the successor to a surpassed prior, but now discarded, feminism. Of course, this understanding of the term only makes sense if one believes that

> there ever was only one stable meaning of feminism that could then be surpassed. The insistence that something is anti-feminist too often reflects an equally problematic belief in and desire for a definitional stability to the term feminism itself, for that time when feminism supposedly had a stable meaning – and, one presumes, a stable agenda [...]. (Braithwaite, 2002: 337)

The recognition given to diversity has undermined the belief that feminism can be rendered intelligible through a single lens. Increasingly it has become understood as a diverse set of ambitions, goals, and practices that involve a range of both local and distant constituencies. Accepting that feminism is a diverse set of practices that exceed a single definition has been seen as an effective strategy for countering claims that feminism has overreached its own goal. Rather, 'the problem is not that the project has been completed. On the contrary, given that feminism lacks a single definition, it can also have no single moment of ending' (Kavka, 2001: xi).

These debates surrounding post-feminism illustrate that feminism is modified and adjusted through its relation to the social forms in which it is located. At certain times and in particular places feminist activity will impact upon social relations and forces in such a way as to foster further feminist projects; but this impact will also occur alongside forces that sustain and encourage further social retrenchment. The post-feminist gender order does not assume a coherent form as much as it operates as a series of interwoven social relations and dynamic tensions across a range of social, cultural, academic, and discursive fields (Genz and Brabon, 2009: 5). These dynamics produce multiple and inconsistent effects at 'the intersections and hybridization of mainstream media, consumer culture, neo-liberal politics, postmodern theory and, significantly, feminism' (ibid.). Despite the controversies, anxieties, and difficulties that constitute the post-feminist gender order and despite a desire and longing for more certainty, feminism continues to operate.

> [T]he notion of a collective project with a singular history makes up both the nostalgized past and the utopian future of feminism, kept in suspense by a present that consists of multiple, ongoing kinds of feminist activity. The change marked by 'post' thus happened while we were *doing* feminism; the change happened

because we were doing feminism. The problem is not the death or end of feminism but, rather, coming to terms with the fact that its political, strategic, and interpretive power has been so great as to produce innumerable modes of doing – whether activist, practical, theoretical, or just 'quiet' – that moved well beyond the mother term, already fractured at its origin. (Kavka, 2001: xi)

A genealogy of post-feminism

This outline of the main features of a post-feminist gender order provides a sketch of the conditions that third wave feminism operates in and lends insight into why third wave feminism is characterized by particular tendencies. Siegel (1997a: 52) points out that the third wave 'is a response to what one might call the cultural dominance of "postfeminism," a word that itself has a different meaning depending on the site of its invocation'. That post-feminism can simultaneously reference a negative response to the diffusion of feminist aims *and* a positive perspective – which, when occupied strategically, allows for that diffusion to be interpreted as a productive splintering into disparate but nonetheless progressive activities – illustrates that, in late modernity, third wave feminism is situated within a series of complex contradictions. Strategies are required to engage with these tensions productively and to open up ways of resisting the claim that feminism has been immobilized or brought to its conclusion. Foremost to the debates surrounding post-feminism is the suggestion that a significant shift has occurred in feminism's relationship to its object of critique, and perhaps an even more significant shift has occurred in how feminism's self-defined project may be constructed.

In Adkins' (2004: 431) analysis of the anxiety post-feminism induces, it is argued that the fear that feminism has passed away relies upon 'hidden claims and assumptions regarding what the proper objects of feminism are, and should be, and the relationship of these objects to feminist subjectivity, and feminist consciousness'. To illustrate her argument, Adkins analyses Segal's (2000, 2003) critique of contemporary feminism, in which a sense of loss and disappointment is expressed. Segal is clear in her analysis of the problem that post-feminism poses: post-feminist culture is constituted by a depoliticization of gender relations, as witnessed in the failure of many women to identify positively with feminism. For Segal, this is a failure to reproduce a feminist consciousness – a failure that results in the loss of political subjectivity and of political agency. According to Segal's depiction of feminism, this loss can be recuperated if feminism's proper object were to be recovered.

> While political elites mouth post-feminist and neo-liberal feminist rhetoric to further their goals [...] the specter of a more politically authentic feminism lives on, always threatening to expose the erasure of those earlier feminist struggles – whether around the workplace, domesticity or access to democratically run, shared community resources. (Segal, 2003: 155, quoted in Adkins, 2004: 431)

In this characterization, feminism's proper object is a socio-empirical 'out-there-in-the-world' reality. An authentic feminist political consciousness is brought into being by reflecting upon this exterior socio-structural formation. Here a clear demarcation is made between the knower and the object that is known; however, according to Adkins, the problem with this position is that, in the shift from industrial to post-industrial society, this distance contracts such that contemporary society can no longer be characterized by 'stable distinctions between subject and object, culture and nature, history and consciousness but by a reworking (and even collapse) of these divisions' (2004: 438). The distinction between exteriority and interiority, upon which the production of feminist consciousness depends in Segal's account, has eroded in the post-social structural formation characteristic of late modernity.

Adkins cites a number of analyses of the contemporary social realm, which all undermine the view that society is organized primarily by socio-structural imperatives. In these accounts the dynamics of socio-structural reproduction have been destabilized by the greater exercise of experimentation and reflexivity. For example, theories of reflexive modernization maintain that late modern societies are characterized by a progressive freeing of agency from structure and by the lessening influence of those structures, which is achieved through enhanced levels of both structural and self-reflexivity (Adkins, 2002; Beck, 1992; Beck, Giddens and Lash, 1994). Social action, in these accounts, is shaped by an increasingly critical reflection upon the rules, norms, traditions, and expectations that govern social life

(Adkins, 2004: 437). The result is that, within specific spheres such as the economy, 'gender is being rewritten from a relatively fixed naturally or socially determined characteristic of people – constituted by sociostructural arrangements such as gender segregation – to a cultural style or genre' (Adkins, 2004: 437). The impact of the shift towards a post-social structural order for feminism is twofold. Firstly, feminism's primary focus on an external object of critique has shifted towards greater critical engagement with its own assumptions and categories (Elam and Wiegman, 1995). This represents a shift from external reflection (and political consciousness) to internal reflection and critique (and self-consciousness). This is a key characteristic of post-feminism – heightened levels of auto-critique, self-referentiality, and intensified self-reflexivity, which collapses the subject–object duality. For Segal, it is in that gap between reflection and the everyday that the development of a feminist political consciousness is produced, hence a turning inwards signals a failure on the part of contemporary feminism to secure knowledge of its proper object. Adkins explains the structure of this narrative:

> The proper objects of feminism are external, out, in-the-world socioempirical phenomena such as 'women' and/or femininity; these phenomena are ordered via sociostructural imperatives; feminist consciousness and feminist political agency are constituted in the reflection on these objects; and that contemporary forms of feminism are characterized by an inward lookingness which negates reflections on the external socioempirical world. Consequently, according to this narrative, contemporary forms of feminism are not feminist at all as they fail fundamentally to secure feminist consciousness and political agency. (Adkins, 2004: 440)

Secondly, because of the shifting relation between subject and object, feminism itself has increasingly been incorporated into its own object of critique. This merger problematizes Segal's insistence that feminism can reflect on an external reality as its proper object of critique. For example, within the context of post-feminist culture, femininity – the object of feminist critique – is often constructed in ways that knowingly reference and assimilate aspects of that critique (Gill, 2007a; McRobbie, 2004b). The dynamics of incorporation challenge the assumption that feminism can stand apart from its object of critique within contemporary social conditions.

The interrogation of feminism's own categories and of the role these play in constructing the subject that feminism seeks to represent has also extended to a critical analysis of the various strategies that feminism has deployed in representing itself as a political movement. For example, feminism has been narrated as a continuous project, which has unfolded from the point of a single origin into a series of progressive stages, in which each successive stage has addressed challenges associated with a particular time and place. In some versions of feminist history, these particularities are seen to draw together under a *common continuous cause*: that of advancing the *unified interest of a collective*. This narrative demands a level of ongoing agreement and commonality that current debates belie. Thus, when the project of feminism is constructed according to this logic, discord between different feminist positions can only be interpreted as a threatening divergence from the path of progress.

To counteract this reaction and the political stalemate that may occur as positions become further entrenched, it is useful to recognize that feminism is composed of two elements, which are closely yet contingently related: a women's political movement and a feminist ideology that enables the identification of political goals and of strategies for bringing these goals to fruition (Coole, 2000: 35). In accounts of the history of feminism, this relationship between theory and practice is conventionally traced through three waves. The first wave of feminism is often portrayed as an emancipatory project, driven by the feminist appropriation of liberal political thought to secure universal autonomy, equality, and liberty for all citizens, regardless of gender. In this first phase feminism successfully deployed liberal ideology to claim its place within the progressive development of modernity and the achievement of a just society. In the second wave, feminism materialized primarily as a liberation movement with an agenda informed by radical and socialist ideologies, which allowed feminism to extend the borders of political engagement and to enlarge the political agenda by calling into question, more fundamentally, the structures of capitalism and of patriarchy. In these two phases it was possible for feminism to operate as a mass-based political movement driven by a liberal grand narrative, which endorsed modern progress.

3. However, in a further third stage, which corresponds to Adkins' description of self-reflexive engagement, feminism's achievements and the progressive narrative that has been central to its ideological project have been subject to sustained questioning from within feminism itself.

> Where feminists previously saw themselves participating in modernity's progressive unfolding, pursuing its promises of personal autonomy and liberty on all women's behalf, both this project and its self-perception have subsequently been subjected to widespread criticism. This has arisen as part of a more general antipathy toward the Enlightenment with its rationalist and universalist orientations. Despite their indebtedness to the Enlightenment, feminists have come to recognize the masculinist assumptions embedded in its conception of rational individuals and its aspirations for equality. (Coole, 2000: 36)

Feminist discourse has tended to incorporate particular 'apocalyptic' features, 'namely claims for universal truth about man and woman, its arguments for a single origin of patriarchal oppression, its versions of anatomy as innate character, and its utopian visions of a harmonious matriarchal past and a future free from all oppression' (Quinby, 1997: 147), but the narration of feminism's ideological project as 'a single story of progress and continuity in pursuit of a specific emancipatory goal' has not been sustainable (Coole, 2000: 37).

The rhetorical power of a narrative of progress has been a key force that, at various times and in various places, helped to organize a mass-based feminist political movement forged on a shared identity, in pursuit of a collective purpose. Through this narrative, 'feminism has often dreamed the possibility of an absolute defeat of the patriarchy and a utopia of human harmony' (Quinby, 1997: 147), to be brought into being through the formation of political subjectivities able to offer 'futurity in the present' and the promise of revolutionary social change (Wiegman, 2002: 20). Adherence to this ideological construction of feminism's time has increasingly been recognized as a particularly problematic element in feminist self-presentation. This has been due, in part, to recognizing that, as feminism has become institutionalized, its presence as an oppositional social movement has waned.

> Positioned outside and against both disciplines and institutional economies, academic feminism was renegade knowledge, one whose illegitimacy demonstrated the movement's central political claim concerning women's oppression and systematic exclusion [...] Today, it is surely safe to say, much has changed [...]. (Wiegman, 2002: 18)

For many, this dynamic of incorporation has halted the progress of feminism as a world-transforming force and has become a cause of concern for the future of feminist politics. Placing the narrative of progressive emancipation and the representation of feminism as a collective movement under question has provoked a rupture in feminism's own story and ushered in an era of post-feminism characterized by a lack of consensus.

The significance of this moment is open to various interpretations that depend upon how feminism's past is recounted. Variations in these accounts go some way towards explaining whether a post-feminist gender order is interpreted as a threat to the advancement of feminist goals, or it potentially offers a productive perspective, from which it is possible to address limitations built into feminism's political strategies. As Coole (2000: 38) explains, two accounts of the history of feminism are available. In the first account, feminism is construed as an unfinished emancipatory project that is consistent with the grand narratives of modernity. However, in light of the rupturing of this singular progress narrative, this representation also 'courts the triple dangers of nostalgia, reification and political pessimism' and instills a fear that the present is characterized by failure (ibid.). This response to post-feminism is readily evident in many feminist critiques that view contemporary feminism as a site of disappointment. The post-feminist present is judged against a feminist past imagined through the lens of harmony, coherence, and unified political action, and is found to be lacking.

In the alternative account, 'a more pluralistic, heterogeneous and contingent history' is offered (Coole, 2000:38). This understanding of feminism is derived from deploying a genealogical analysis, which traces how power operates discontinuously in different ways, at different times, in relation to gender. Rethinking both feminism and its object of analysis – femininity – through a genealogical lens has been very productive (Stone, 2005). A genealogical history draws attention to the complex interplay of socio-cultural forces and diverse relations of power that constitute feminist practices in particular ways. These diverse sets of practices and beliefs, which we recognize as feminist, are comprehended as such not because feminism has an essential identity or unity over time, but because these varied practices and beliefs can be located within a historical chain, in which later forms of practice successively reinterpret earlier ones (Stone, 2005: 7). Some elements of the earlier meanings become incorporated into new formulations, while other elements drop away.

> [P]re-existing meanings that succumb to reinterpretation have already taken shape as reinterpretations of still earlier layers of meaning, from which, in turn, they preserve some elements, while transforming and erasing others. Over time, therefore, a gradual shift takes place in the meaning of a practice, as earlier layers of meaning eventually get eroded away through successive waves of reinterpretation. Consequently, no common core of meanings endures across all these waves of interpretation. (Stone, 2005: 8)

This mode of analysis allows for both continuity and fluctuation. On the one hand, while no core meanings endure that would allow for the identification of an authentic or 'real' feminism, it is possible to recognize feminism as a meaningful entity over time because different reinterpretations always involve partial overlaps within complex historical chains. On the other hand, acts of reinterpretation are the unpredictable result of a complex balance of forces, therefore prospective feminist struggles may be expected to be 'contingent and diverse in nature responding to context specific demands' (Coole, 2000: 35), as gender itself 'has a contingent and historically defined content which evolves within relations of power' (Coole, 1998: 111).

Coole (2000) uses the term 'constellation' to describe the combination of various forces, structures, relations, and activities that form the diverse contexts within which feminism has historically emerged.

> [T]he kind of interventions made at each stage were those appropriate to the specific situation in which they engaged, rather than phases of one continuous project. This means that the historical force field; a particular way of understanding politics; the sites of contestation deemed relevant; the kind of acts and agency that

are summoned; the identity and identification of participants: all these form a *constellation* that is historically specific. (Coole, 2000: 38)

The formation of political subjectivities, the shaping of political consciousness, the formulation of political objectives, and the exercise of political agency occur within specific socio-historical sites. Rather than posit that feminism in its current state is an unfinished emancipatory project, the different phases of feminism reveal a 'more pluralistic, heterogeneous and contingent history', which is better understood by applying a genealogical 'understanding of the shifting permutations of power in relation to gender' (Coole, 2000: 38). Feminism is rethought here as a loosely related set of objectives, critical positions, and political practices upon which a narrative of coherence has been imposed. The issue, then, is not that feminism has fragmented, but that practices of self-reflexivity have uncovered that a self-narrative based upon notions of continuous linear progress is illusory.

Squires (1999, 2007) outlines three different strategies of political engagement that feminism has deployed to counteract gendered power relations: 'adding women in', 'extending the boundaries', and 'reconceptualizing the core concepts'. These strategies correspond to different feminist political objectives, which depend largely upon how power dynamics are conceptualized. 'Adding women in' promotes a politics of inclusion where the gender differences that have been used in a patriarchal social order to justify women's exclusion from social institutions are challenged as a legitimate basis for assigning rights. 'Extending the boundaries' is a strategy for widening the remit of feminism by expanding our understanding of the political field. This has been enacted through demands that the current system be reconfigured to recognize the legitimacy of gender-specific needs. The final strategy puts both of these objectives into question and deploys instead a genealogical method designed 'to deconstruct those discursive regimes that engender the subject' (Squires, 1999: 3).

The normative task for the theorist aiming at inclusion is to argue that gender ought to be non-pertinent to politics. The normative task for the theorist aiming at reversal is to argue that politics ought to be reconstructed to manifest the distinctive perspective of non-hegemonic gender identities (usually female). The normative task for the theorist aiming at displacement is to reveal the extent to which gendered identities are themselves products of particular political discourses. (Squires, 1999: 4)

In a genealogical account of feminism's history, continuity is disrupted by acknowledging that different feminist struggles have been formed in relation to particular configurations of power that organize gender relations in particular ways, thus demanding the development of varied strategies for counteracting these relations. By drawing upon a Foucauldian framework, Coole (2000: 42) identifies a series of historically specific constellations in which gender relations are organized through distinct power relations: domination, exploitation, and the management of subjectivity. These correspond to Squires' typology of three normative positions explained above. Understanding how these different force fields operate so as to constitute gender relations is key to comprehending both the overlaps and the discontinuities that characterize feminism. According to this analysis, at the beginning of the twentieth century feminist struggles were fought in what can be described as a state of domination, defined by asymmetrical gendered power relations, which were largely universal in nature and relatively immobile. In response to these conditions, struggles were organized around specific goals, which were concerned principally (but not exclusively) with securing rights for all women.

> [H]undreds of thousands of women were motivated by a common cause because they shared a common situation of disenfranchisement and second-class citizenship. Their identification did not arise from some shared ontological status, experiential homogeneity or essentialist belief that all women are the same, but from the fact that the law defined them as an excluded, inferior category regardless of their differences. (Coole, 2000: 45–46)

Being uniformly and universally subjected to a position of disenfranchisement allowed for the strategic deployment of a collective identification, based upon a social status shared by women. In this instance, the totalizing logic of relations of domination summoned a united political reaction from women. This relative unity and coherence reflected an appropriate response to the specific political context, not because 'women already existed as a latently political group with definite interests, merely awaiting a voice', but because the imposition of a common unilateral status created 'women's interests' (Coole, 2000: 46). The dynamics that constituted this constellation also influenced the points where parameters of the political realm could be drawn – primarily around formal government and state activities. Given this understanding, feminist aims and strategies of the time tended to concentrate on effecting change within those particular areas by making universalist demands for the right to formal social and political inclusion.

Other feminist struggles, notably those associated with the late 1960s, emerged within a distinctly different power formation. In contrast to the totalizing dominance of patriarchal interests that feminism struggled against at the turn of the twentieth century, in the latter part of that century feminism emerged as 'something qualitatively different from its predecessors: as participation in a dense fabric of shifting gender relations that involve piecemeal, contingent and multiple resistances coupled with a more affirmative experimentation with (differently-gendered) "practices of liberty"' (Coole, 2000: 43). While continuities with previous struggles against patriarchal domination were evident, a shift in gendered power relations had taken place. Through greater access to the public sphere, the acquisition of citizenship rights, changed economic conditions, and enhanced political opportunities, women had not dismantled patriarchal domination in some final sense, but had significantly gained entry into the agonistic game of power in which power cannot necessarily be overcome but can be accessed more readily and deployed to reverse the system, in recognition of women's specific experiences (Coole, 2000: 43).

Within this particular historical constellation, liberation from exploitation – rather than emancipation – emerged as a key focus. Pursuit of this goal involved a more comprehensive, far-reaching analysis and political agenda to effect a radical transformation of gender relations. This concern was reflected in critiques directed towards a wide range of sites, including relationships in civil society, personal and sexual relationships, the structuring of socio-economic institutions, and the formation of gendered subjectivity (Coole, 2000: 48). By expanding the feminist analysis of gender relations beyond formal legal and political structures, radical and socialist feminists impacted upon existing understandings of political agency. Mass-based collective action in the form of the Women's Liberation Movement continued to form an important platform for social change; however, concerns with the micro-politics of personal and cultural life also emerged and, as the collective movement fractured and the possibilities for unified action were increasingly put into question, these areas took on greater significance as sites for feminist intervention.

The questioning of a mass-based politics and an increasing focus upon previously unquestioned aspects of women's identities continued as feminism engaged with post-structuralist and post-modern analyses of social change. The reconceptualization of the category 'woman' as an effect of power rather than as a pre-existing constituency with shared essential interests profoundly challenged feminism's representative claims and marked a more reflexive engagement on the part of feminism, with its own categories. This has occurred within a more mobile and fluid field, 'where power, freedom, and resistance circulate and incite one another' (Coole, 2000: 43). Analysing the dynamics of gendered power from this perspective locates political struggle at the sites where gender is created. Power is 'now discerned in processes of privileging, excluding, marginalizing, constructing and distorting on the level of meaning [...] Politically it has meant an emphasis on a politics of the subject' (Coole, 1998: 118).

Within this particular constellation, the production of gendered subjectivity has been positioned as one of the primary sites where feminist politics occurs. This is a 'politics of subjectivity' that, instead of regarding 'women' as an ontological category awaiting mobilization or a socio-empirical reality requiring representation, engages with the discursive and material practices which constitute that category in particular ways. This analysis has implications for how political agency may be rethought.

> [I]t can be plausibly argued that the challenge for twenty-first feminism is to adjust to this new social and discursive context, continuing its task of exploring the convolution of gender power and inventing new political strategies for intervening effectively. To this extent this 'third wave' marks both continuity *and* rupture with the past. (Coole, 2000: 42)

A 'politics of subjectivity' refocuses third wave feminism on the possibilities for reworking or subverting power through deconstructive strategies, which reveal the radically constructed nature of gender identity. The multiplication of sites in which this occurs, moreover, exceeds what can be addressed by a coherent theoretical strategy or a centralized programme of action. As Quinby (1997: 156) argues, 'against multiple force relations, coherence in theory and centralization of practice make a social movement irrelevant or, worse, vulnerable, or – even more dangerous – participatory with forces of domination'. The play of power brings particular identities into being, both in terms of the relations of power that feminism seeks to destabilize and through its very own claims to represent 'women's interests'. However, there is a crucial difference between a female 'we' imposed by oppressive hegemonic discourses and a 'historically specific *we* of political identity and alliance', which is invoked strategically and does not presume that women share an essential set of attributes or experiences (Squires, 1999: 73). When sameness is invoked as a political strategy, this is done contingently, so that the identity that comes into being exists only as a product of those specific conditions.

In summary this discussion sensitizes us to the need to understand third wave feminism as a historically particular reinterpretation of feminism, which has elements consistent with feminism concerns of the past, but which is also constituted as a unique response to a specific socio-historical context; and, insofar as the dynamics that structure this context produce new configurations of gender relations, third wave feminism responds to challenges not previously encountered. It will be argued in this book that this context is a 'post-feminist constellation' that effects the understanding of third wave feminist politics, of the sites where political practices take place, of the kinds agency called forth, and of the formulation of third wave feminist identifications. Firstly, post-feminism affects the ways in which feminist politics might be understood within the late modern gender order, particularly with regards to how political subjectivities are formulated within that order, configured as it is by an increased awareness of gender issues and by improved levels of gender equality. It is one of the central defining contradictions of a post-feminist constellation that feminism is simultaneously taken as successful in establishing gender inequality as a mainstream social

Ques. raised by genealogical analysis?

problem and as having failed in its aims, hence resulting in its own dismissal.

The second set of issues to be considered pertains to the kinds of acts and agency deemed necessary if one is to fulfil feminist political objectives. This set involves an analysis of where and how feminist agency is enabled or constrained by new convolutions of gender power and by the associated political interventions that these power relations call forth. What kinds of relations are being produced by contemporary gender power dynamics? How is feminism located within this field, where gender is negotiated? As gender is being re-negotiated, how is feminism being reinterpreted within this complex balance of forces? All of these questions are central to challenges that third wave feminism should address.

Thirdly, questions about gendered agency link into an examination of how gendered identities are formulated and, in particular, how feminist identifications are made. Third wave feminism is concerned with a politics of subjectivity that critically engages with the meanings that attach to feminine subject positions and with the possibility that alternative gendered subjectivities might be created by women in the context of everyday life.

> Women ask: who are we? How have we been constituted as gendered subjects and how might we be different? This cannot be all of politics but without it, women are always in danger of reproducing identities and pursuing interests that are already effects of phallic power. (Coole, 2000: 43)

Finally, a genealogical analysis of post-feminism draws attention to the relevant sites of contestation where gender politics are played out. Genz and Brabon (2009: 5) usefully define post-feminism 'in terms of a network of possible relations that allows for a variety of permutations and readings'. They identify three primary but non-unitary, overlapping sites where the dynamic forces that constitute post-feminism are particularly evident. Here they identify popular culture, academic debates, and a reworked political sphere as key manifestations of post-feminist relations (Genz and Brabon, 2009: 17). Close examination of each of these sites reveals that feminism has been incorporated into the very institutions, relations, identities, and representations that once stood apart as objects of its critique. As Adkins

(2004) has stated, this marks a move from feminist consciousness to feminist self-reflexivity and, with that move, the dissolution of a feminist 'outside', from which to assert an authentic feminist voice.

Popular culture

Analysing the sphere of popular culture has been central to second wave feminist critiques of the cultural constructions of femininity and of the limits that dominant constructions have imposed upon women's lives. Through a variety of popular practices and forms of cultural consumption, femininity and its associations with passivity, dependency, domesticity, and investment in physical attractiveness have been seen to contribute to the production of a feminine identity that makes women blind to their participation in their own oppression (Hollows, 2000: 20). Critiques of these practices have tended to rely upon a binary in which a knowing feminism is counter-posed to a fictitious, oppressive femininity. Feminist critique, construed as means of cultivating a feminist consciousness, has been promoted as a strategy for liberating women from the constraints of a 'false' femininity, by putting in its place the adoption of more authentic female values, awaiting beneath the artificial mask of femininity. The guarantee of the objectivity of this critique and of the truth of the claims made have rested upon the belief that second wave feminism could occupy a separate, counter-hegemonic space, untainted by ideological contamination, from which it would be possible to analyse the workings of stereotypical representations of femininity.

The focus on authenticity and on the production of practices that could allow women access to representations of 'real' women have ultimately become problematic as critical analyses of representational practices have revealed that what it means to be a woman is far from self-evident. Representations of femininity cannot simply reflect a stable, 'real' femininity, waiting to be uncovered; nor is it possible for particular cultural forms, such as feminist avant-garde film or 'authentic' feminine 'folk' culture, to access a 'proper' feminist femininity and thereby to overcome the distortions of femininity apparent in popular or mass produced cultural forms (Hollows, 2000). Conceptualizing femininity as an ongoing discursive construction has meant that popular culture has been identified as a site of post-feminist contestation, where multiple feminine identities circulate and 'gendered identities and cultural forms are produced, reproduced, and negotiated in specific historical contexts within specific and shifting forms of power relations' (Hollows, 2000: 27). One of the most significant shifts that have occurred in the constitution of this site is the position that feminism now occupies within contemporary cultural practices.

> One of the things that makes [sic] the media today very different from the television, magazines, radio and press of the 1960s, 1970s, and early 1980s, is that feminism is now part of the cultural field. That is, feminist discourses are part of the media, rather than simply being outside and independent critical voices. It is a measure of the success of feminism that many ideas that once required active battles are now accepted as uncontroversial [...] Today, feminist-inspired ideas burst forth from or radios, TV screens and print media (alongside many anti-feminist ideas). (Gill, 2007b: 40)

According to Genz and Brabon (2009: 19), the outsider position that feminism occupied to critique the objects of popular culture has collapsed as an acknowledgement of feminist aims has increasingly been integrated into mainstream values and norms. Feminism can no longer assume to occupy a 'pure' outside, but has become part of the objects and representations circulating throughout the global cultural landscape. Indeed it has been argued that 'it is probably fair to say that most feminism in the West now happens in the media, and that for the majority of people their experience of feminism is an entirely mediated one' (Gill, 2007b: 40). Therefore, in late modernity, feminism cannot locate itself within any *authentic* form, 'unadulterated by the often conservative forces of cultural representation' (ibid.); however, the realm of post-feminist popular culture is seen by some to raise the possibility of a reworking of femininity from within. This dynamic assumes that popular feminism is not only possible, but is also one of the means by which feminist values are widely transmitted and made available for local appropriation.

> Unlike other critics, we do not interpret feminism's entry into the popular as necessarily a depoliticisation and dilution [...] We maintain that popular/consumer culture should be reconceived as a site of struggle over the meanings of feminism and the reconceptualization of a post-feminist political practice that, unlike second wave feminism, does not rely upon separatism and

collectivism [...] and instead highlights the multiple agency and subject positions of individuals in the new millennium. (Genz and Brabon, 2009: 25)

From this perspective, a feminist subjectivity is formed in the active negotiation of contradictory femininities where popular culture, no longer uniformly antithetical to feminism, is seen to provide resources for the fashioning of new femininities and new sites of feminist critique.

Academia and post-feminism

Concerns about attaching the prefix 'post' to feminism, particularly with regards to theoretical and political matters, are also manifest in academic analyses. Debates often focus upon the impact that anti-foundationalist thought has had upon the representational claims made by feminism and upon the resulting questioning of identity politics. Again, within these debates the central dynamic associated with post-feminism is one of feminist reflexivity – of feminism affecting its own object of critique. The deconstruction of the foundational discourse of identity upon which feminist politics might be built means that 'feminism can no longer rely on the notion of an authentic and unanimous feminist realm or "outside" and has to renounce the idea of a detached and untainted feminist identity' (Genz and Brabon, 2009: 29). In optimistic accounts, the argument is advanced that it is possible to rethink feminist debates and to open up new theoretical spaces, where the relationship between feminism and women's lives can be re-imagined. This involves innovative conceptualizations of feminist subjectivities that recognize the multiple sites in which these subjectivities come into being.

> [I]t has now become essential to rethink (political/feminist) agency in the context of recently destabilized identity categories and gender relationships as well as the mainstreaming and commoditization of feminism in late twentieth- and twenty-first-century culture and society. (Genz and Brabon, 2009: 33)

Post-feminism and politics

A rethinking of feminist politics interacts with, and flows out of, both of these contexts, focusing upon the opportunities that a

Diff. forms of feminist agency...

non-universalizing stance presents for understanding the emergence of critical and political practices that transcend the limits of a singular women's movement. Controversially, post-feminism is characterized by dynamics that often problematize collective agency and favour individualized political agency. While for many critics such a focus leads to a narcissistic and a-political position that evacuates feminism's political efficacy and re-instates patriarchal and capitalist structures, a more sympathetic reading of post-feminism emphasizes that political agency may be reconceptualized in ways that can validate multiple and less collective forms of feminist agency, characteristic of twenty-first century culture and society. For Genz and Brabon (2009: 39–40), the social and cultural dynamics associated with post-feminism require that individualism be rethought and that greater engagement with the plurality and contradictory nature of women's and men's experiences is demonstrated. This perspective acknowledges that a transformation of the political is occurring and that a feminist position will invariably be 'impure', operating as it will between complicity and critique within a contradictory political field.

> Postfeminism responds to and is emblematic of the paradoxes of modern-day politics and culture, seeking to reconcile feminist ideas of female emancipation and equality, consumerist demands of capitalist societies and media-friendly depictions of feminine/masculine empowerment. For us, it makes more sense to examine how power functions in contradictory ways in post-feminist discourses and how engaged individuals rework notions of agency in the context of postfeminist politics. (Genz and Brabon, 2009: 41)

The challenges posed by post-feminism require that feminist political identities be rethought; that the sites in which these identities are constituted are critically analysed; and that the practices through which these identities are expressed are closely interrogated.

Conclusion

This chapter has contextualized one of the defining contradictions of the contemporary gender order – feminism has been incorporated into many aspects of everyday life and yet is also, and often, dismissed as irrelevant. The success of feminism is evident in the value placed upon gender equality as a social good and in the extent to which women's choices and opportunities across education, employment, and family life have improved significantly. On the other hand, the incorporation of feminist values into organizational practices, as is the case in gender mainstreaming, can be controversial, as incorporation can lead to co-optation, to the dilution of a critique that demands more radical social change, and to the advancement of neoliberal governance. Contradictions such as these exemplify a gender order described in this chapter as emerging in a context described as post-feminist. While post-feminist social conditions are neither wholly negative nor positive in terms of the practice of third wave feminism, it is the case that post-feminism poses a number of very important challenges for feminism, which a third wave is seeking to engage with. Foremost amongst these challenges is the questioning of whom feminism is speaking to and for, and of how this subject comes into being through hegemonic discourses; but also, in a more reflexive vein, the questioning of how feminism itself plays a part in making particular identifications possible. The dynamics of incorporation; the recognition of women's diverse experiences and social locations; and the questioning of the logic that underpins categories, deployed in feminist critique, have all complicated the project of third wave feminism. In Chapter 3 feminist subjectivities will be discussed by looking at the ways in which, within a 'culture of the self', women have been incited to construct themselves as autonomous individuals. This discussion provides a backdrop for a closer analysis of the third wave's politics of subjectivity, to be presented in Chapter 5.

3
New Femininities and Feminist Subjectivities

The self-determining, sovereign individual is a culture ideal, which features centrally in many accounts that seek to explain the core features of modernity (Felski, 1995; Marshall, 1994). To become modern is to liberate oneself from traditional sources of authority and relations of dependence, so that one may assume the position of an autonomous, self-constituting subject. Feminist critiques of the assumptions that underpin these analyses of modernity, however, have established that many of the processes that define modernity and have been seen to symbolize universal experience, such as the freeing of the individual from tradition, are in fact specific to masculinity. Furthermore, the meaning and status accorded to these symbols have been derived from their relationship to the feminine, which is positioned as the 'other' to the uniquely modern, individualized subject. As Braidotti (1994: 161) has stated, 'what is at stake is definition of woman as other-than a nonman'; not merely different from man but an inferior 'other'; a wholly negative difference. The realm of femininity has been associated with qualities and spaces untouched by processes of cultural modernization, so, while 'the place of the free-willed subject who can transcend nature's mandate is reserved exclusively for men', the association of femininity with tradition, nature, and emotion historically barred women from assuming the position of a self-determining subject (Alcoff, 1995: 434–435).

The un-interrogated concept of the autonomous, self-defining individual is implicitly gendered. Independence and autonomy, the rational mind freed from the distorting effects of the emotions and needs of the body, and the individual unrestrained by private or domestic responsibilities able to devote all his energies to public activities, represent values and characteristics historically associated with the masculine. (Johnson, 1993: 18)

In Western culture, 'woman' has been positioned as 'irrational, oversensitive, destined to be wife and mother' and associated with the body, sex, and sin (Braidotti, 1994: 235). This dominant construction of femininity has operated so as to subject all women to 'common, culturally enforced assumptions', so that, regardless of their individual differences, they appeared to share a 'natural' incompatibility with the rigours of political and intellectual life (ibid.). Through the gendered dynamics of inclusion and exclusion, particular forms of subjectivity have been denied to women, and this refusal to grant women the status of 'individual' has provided a central focus for feminist critiques of gender inequality.

Feminism is the question – the empowerment of female subjectivity in the political, epistemological, and experiential sense is the answer. By empowerment, I mean both positive affirmation (theoretical) and concrete enactment (social, juridical, political). (Braidotti, 1994: 237)

Post-feminist social conditions invite questions about the extent to which female empowerment has occurred and about the ongoing impact of feminist politics on the reconstitution of gender relations. This chapter will explore how femininity has increasingly been reconstructed through discourses of individuality, such that the pursuit of independence and self-determination has not only become more accessible to many women, but also these cultural ideals are increasingly operating in a normative and regulative fashion; as a result, women are incited to think of themselves, as liberated individuals, regardless of their immediate social context. Successful femininity now incorporates character ideals and norms previously associated with masculinity. This association, however, is complicated by the expectation that idealized femininity will also convey traditional traits, including physical beauty, heterosexual desire, and emotional proficiency. While feminist achievements have significantly impacted upon female subjectivity and expanded the possibility for self-empowerment, this success must be located within a wider 'culture of the self', in which the logic of neoliberal self-governance incites social actors to become particular kinds of subjects, able and willing to pursue their freedom through the practice of self-monitoring and through the rational calculation of individual interests. This emphasis upon empowerment and choice raises important questions for third wave feminism; for it has been argued that emerging feminine subjectivities, within the context of post-feminism, occupy a structurally ambivalent position in relation to the cultural ideals celebrated by neoliberal discourses. As analysed by Rich (2005: 496), gendered subjectivities are formulated at the point of convergence of second wave feminism, post-feminism, traditional gendered discourses, and neoliberal rationalities. The effects of this complex negotiation are not reducible to any one discourse, as each operates in a concurrent but not consistent way to orient women towards subjectivities defined by choice, empowerment, and individuality.

Feminism and the politics of subjectivity

Early second wave feminists sought to claim new modes of subjectivity for women by arguing that women were prevented from realizing their capacity for autonomy by the imposition of a distorted and stereotypical femininity, which discouraged the development of traits associated with masculinity. It was not women's natures that predisposed them to dependency, but their restricted access to opportunities for self-development. For other feminists, however, the problem was not the barring of woman from the pursuit of rationality, independence, and self-determination, but rather that the dominant ways of understanding subjecthood mistakenly assumed that masculine traits represented a superior form of subjectivity. The social devaluation of feminine qualities, rather than the nature of the qualities themselves, prevented women from acquiring socially legitimized subjectivities. The solution to this problem was seen to lay in reversing the values accorded to gender differences and to recognize women's different capacities, particularly by challenging the privileging of separation and autonomy over care and interconnection with others.

In both positions, feminism is centrally concerned with the dynamics that allow women to understand themselves as particular kinds of subjects while excluding the possibility of alternatives. Both analyses, however, have been problematized for assuming a self that is authentic but oppressed by patriarchal forces. In the first instance, this self is hidden from view and prevented from full realization, while in the latter analysis the self is fully present but undervalued. In either case, feminism aimed to create conditions that allowed women to articulate their selves in terms that validated their experiences and authorized the recognition of women's 'real' identities – the value and meaning of these identities being produced within a gendered dualism that marks socially legitimized femininity with the signs of passivity and dependence. More recently, strategies for theorizing femininity and the structuring of female subjectivity have not focused on what women 'are', but rather have sought to examine the embedded and embodied processes through which gender subjects come into being. As Johnson (1993: 18) explains, 'our individuality is produced precisely by the way in which our experiences of embodiment have been socially constructed, as well as, more generally, by the particular social and historical arrangements in which we live'. In a feminist 'politics of subjectivity' it is recognized that subjects are situated within concrete, socio-historical conditions, which structure subjectivity, and that gender is the product of 'various social technologies [...] institutionalized discourses, epistemologies, and critical practices, as well as practices of daily life' (de Lauretis, 1987: 2). The construction of gender is the product and the process of both representation and self-representation (ibid., p. 9).

The identities that women may form are not dependent on creating social arrangements that will allow for the expression of a (so far repressed) authentic femininity. Rather, what is required is an analysis that addresses the social arrangements that produce particular self-understandings. From this perspective the analysis of feminine subjectivity is concerned with the forms of identification made available to women and with the ideals that women are incited to adopt in making themselves into particular kinds of subjects. As Braidotti (1994: 99) argues, the acquisition of subjectivity is a 'process of material (institutional) and discursive (symbolic) practices, the aim of which is both positive – because they allow for forms of empowerment, and regulative – because the forms of empowerment are the site of limitations and disciplining'. A feminist politics of subjectivity, therefore, aims to critically analyse those techniques of the self through which gendered subjects come into being, acknowledging that such processes are simultaneously *empowering* and *regulatory*.

The concept of an authentic self is itself a socio-historical production rather than a pre-social entity that is merely shaped by the social process. If individuals are incited to take up modern forms of subjecthood and to constitute themselves according to particular ideals, such as authenticity and individuality, then the focus should turn to the processes through which women negotiate those ideals from their locations within networks of power.

> Women's experiences cannot be seen as a pre-given ontology that precedes its expression but is constituted through a number of often contradictory, albeit connected strands, which are not simply reflected but are constructed through the 'technologies of gender' of particular cultures and periods [...] Gender is continually in process, an identity that is performed and actualized over time within given social constraints. (Felski, 1995: 21)

The processes that effect the production of late modern forms of personhood based on independence and self-determination are now understood to have become more readily available to women. The contemporary gender order is one in which modern notions of personhood and individuality have begun to be understood as forms of identification increasingly accessible to and desirable for young women (Gonick, 2006: 3). In the logics of socio-cultural modernization, 'woman' no longer necessarily holds the place of man's inferior 'other', but she has to some extent assume a socially recognized identity, constructed through the ideals of increased levels of individualization and autonomy. New femininities emerge from the dissolution of the kinds of gendered boundaries that used to define traditional femininity and masculinity. While this dissolution does not signal the end of traditional gender norms, it is the case that many aspects of long-established norms may now co-exist with newer expectations about what constitutes legitimate femininity and masculinity. The discursive field that women negotiate as they assert their identities as individuals places them in-between the terms of binaries that, previously, were neatly and clearly gendered – such as subject/object; assertiveness/passivity; self/other; individuality/relationality; and autonomy/dependence. This is a positioning which dictates that, ideally, women must be assertive, autonomous, and self-determining, but they must also retain aspects of traditional femininity, including heterosexual desirability and emotional sensitivity to others. The reworking of gender norms and ideals has taken place within a context where notions of selfhood have undergone significant transformation, a notable emphasis being increasingly placed upon the individual and her/his capacity for self-realization.

Neoliberal subjects

The development of feminine subject positions defined through the ideals of choice, independence, and self-responsibility has occurred against the backdrop of a socio-cultural formation increasingly ordered by neoliberal principles that are based upon 'laissez-faire free market values and freedom of globalized corporations' and upon the enshrinement of the 'values of competition, entrepreneurialism, market participation, privatization, lack of state intervention, individual responsibility (e.g., employability), surveillance, assessment, and managerialism' (Phoenix, 2003: 228). The effects of neoliberal rationalities are evident in the 'pro-market restructuring of national economies into global economic competition'; 'the deregulation of financial and labour markets'; and the 'dismantling or privatization of public institutions' – all of which contribute to a thoroughgoing privatization of life (Elliott, 2002: 11). The incursion of neoliberal values into political and social spheres has meant that former notions of social goods, common interests, and the public have been superseded by the individualized pursuit of consumer choice. Kingfisher (2007: 94) draws our attention to the privatizing tendencies of neoliberalism by characterizing it as an 'approach to the world, which includes in its purview not only economics, but also politics; not only the public, but also the private; not only what kinds of institutions we should have, but also what kinds of subjects we should be'. The encroachment of market fundamentalism into non-economic areas of life, including our 'personal sense of identity, interests, happiness, hopes and even the value of life', is identified by Inoue (2007: 80) as

constitutive of a specific form of governance, which brings distinct subjectivities into being.
Governmentality is broadly concerned with the means by which behaviour may be systematically shaped and oriented towards the achievement of identifiable ends (Dean, 1999). Neoliberal governmentality, in particular, refers to strategies through which individual conduct is self-directed towards the pursuit of individual interests and personal freedoms. The emergence of a neoliberal social order cannot be accounted for by any single cause; rather a confluence of events and forces, one of which is the reworking of gender relations, constitutes this constellation.

> Neoliberal governmentality emerged from a determinate historical conjuncture that included the fiscal crisis of the state; 'deregulation' at home and 'structural adjustment' abroad; post-Fordist flexible accumulation as the dominant mode of capital accumulation globally; consumer movements and demands for corporate, professional, and government accountability; various rights movements within liberal democracies, women's movements among them; the rise of cultures of 'self-improvement,' and probably other factors, none of which are reducible to any other, but which together have served as the ground for the appearance of neoliberal techniques of the self. (Inoue, 2007: 81)

Self-government implies a process of making selves into specific kinds of subjects, who are presumed to possess the capacity for autonomy and the associated means for undertaking self-monitoring and the regulation of conduct. The presumed capacity that individuals have for the rational calculation of self-interests and the facility to formulate and enact rational strategies in pursuit of those ends is central to this mode of self-governance. This form of governance consists of a wide range of institutional practices that 'figure and produce citizens as individual entrepreneurs and consumers whose moral autonomy is measured by their capacity for "self care" – their ability to provide for their own needs and service their own ambitions' (Brown, 2006: 694). The idealized subject is imagined as 'self-governing, responsible, autonomous, self-sufficient, independent, and entrepreneurial'; a self poised to maximize quality of life and self-fulfilment (Kingfisher, 2007: 96). The shaping of conduct, furthermore, links with moral questions 'understood as the attempt to make oneself accountable for one's own actions' (Dean, 1999: 11). The analysis of governance is therefore concerned with the code of conduct of conduct, as enacted through the calculation of who we *are* and the distance between this calculation and the knowledge of who we *should* be. These calculations involve the ongoing questioning or problematization of one's conduct, undertaken in the name of taking responsibility for self-improvement. In this pursuit, 'neoliberal subjects assume responsibility for the management of personal and life-cycle risks formerly seen as social or governmental obligations' (Inoue, 2007: 85).

Understanding how conduct is self-managed in the name of particular 'truths' and social 'goods' has been a highly influential approach to the study of individual and collective identity. In making an active identification with an idealized subject, individuals are incited to recognize themselves as particular kinds of subjects. Power operates, therefore, through inciting the act of recognition.

> Regimes of government do not *determine* forms of subjectivity. They elicit, promote, facilitate, foster and attribute various capacities, qualities, and statuses to particular agents. They are successful to the extent that these agents come to experience themselves through such capacities (e.g. of rational decision making), qualities (as having a sexuality) and statuses (e.g. as being an active citizen). (Dean, 1999: 32)

Critics argue that, when individuals willingly internalize the value of self-management as a strategy for individual freedom, they mistake the availability of choice and the cultural value placed upon taking advantage of a diverse range of choices for autonomy (Rose, 1998, 1999). Neoliberal governance works through the consent of individuals, which is given freely when they pursue what is perceived as their own freedom.

> The regulation of conduct becomes a matter of each individual's desire to govern their own conduct freely in the service of the maximization of a version of their own happiness and fulfillment that they take to be their own, but such lifestyle maximization entails a relation to authority in the very moment as it pronounces

itself the outcome of free choice. (Rose, 1996, quoted in Inoue, 2007: 86)

Within the contemporary 'culture of the self', formulations of selfhood are defined through their constitutive relation to the pursuit of freedom, as expressed in the course of realizing one's desires and of creating a meaningful lifestyle through various acts of choice. Through technologies of consumption and through the pervasive circulation of psychotherapeutic knowledges, human beings are incited to constitute themselves as subjects who desire self-actualization, aspire to independence, and seek personal fulfilment and happiness. The imperative to know who 'we really are' and to realize this through the choices we make in everyday life ties us to our freedom (Rose, 1999).

> [M]odern individuals are not merely 'free to choose', but *obliged to be free*, to understand and enact their lives in terms of choice. They must interpret their past and dream their future as outcome of choices made or choices still to make. Their choices are, in turn, seen as realizations of the attributes of the choosing person – expressions of personality – and reflect back upon the person who has made them. (Rose, 1999: 87)

Reflexive modernization

Theories of reflexive modernization have also provided a framework for thinking about the changing interrelationship of autonomy, choice, and personhood in late modernity (Beck and Beck-Gernsheim, 2002; Giddens, 1991). According to theorists of reflexive modernization in late modernity, the imperative to 'become an individual', which is constitutive of modernity, has intensified, and this has resulted in the freeing of agency from structure, thereby creating a social order where individual biographies are shaped less by prescription and more by reflexively made choices. The resulting emphasis on the individual contrasts with that of neoliberalism, primarily because, unlike the individual who is imagined as freed from all external constraints to pursue self-interests, the individual of late modernity is produced in relations of interdependence and reciprocity across the central institutions of society. As the taken for granted certainties that defined the relationship of individuals to the social have disintegrated, late modern social conditions produce high levels of reflexivity and a questioning of how to live one's life not only as an individual, but also as an individual involved in relations with others.

Two features of late modernity are central to understanding processes of individualization that propel these developments. Firstly, individualization refers to a tendency for structuring categories such as 'class and social status, gender roles, family, neighbourhood etc.', which once provided a frame of reference for individual biographies, to dissolve (Beck and Beck-Gernsheim, 2002: 2). Secondly, this disintegration is accompanied by the loss of established sources of authority and traditions that had once guided social action. This produces a situation whereby the regulatory norms and prohibitions associated with those traditional guidelines no longer effectively shape people's biographies. Instead, individuals are required to supply their own guidelines, to 'import them into their own biographies through their own actions' (ibid.). They are required by modern institutions to make an active effort as an individual, to constitute themselves as *individuals*. Individualization is institutionalized – that is to say, 'central institutions of modern society – basic civil, political and social rights, but also paid employment and the training and mobility necessary for it – are geared to the individual and not to the group' (Beck and Beck-Gernsheim, 2002: xxii).

> Individualization is a compulsion, albeit a paradoxical one, to create, stage manage, not only one's own biography but the bonds and networks surrounding it and to do this amid changing preferences and at successive stages of life, while constantly adapting to the conditions of the labour market, the education system, the welfare state and so on. (Beck and Beck-Gernsheim, 2002: 4)

Individualized biographies are constituted as much by new opportunities as by levels of risk introduced by the non-linear, open-ended, highly ambivalent nature of individualizing processes. Provisional guidelines and strategies for encountering uncertainty *must* be individually generated and daily life becomes a reflexive project of often precarious self-invention. In principle, 'choice' itself is not unfettered in the sense of being freely chosen, but it is actively required on the part of individuals (Beck and Beck-Gernsheim, 2002). Choice then cannot be straightforwardly equated with freedom, as the processes of individualization that produce conditions of increased choice also bring increased responsibility and the ever present chance that, despite all the planning, adjusting, and negotiating demanded by individuals as they create their biographies, the ultimate result may be failure.

Gender and individualization

Theories of reflexive modernization are centrally concerned with how processes of individualization are bound up with transformations to gender relations. Beck and Beck-Gernsheim for example argue that individualization is characterized as a shift, in women's orientation, from 'living a life for others' to 'living a life of one's own'. This shift has considerable impact on gender norms and on the contours of what is considered a normal female biography. Structural changes have undermined traditional female norms of self-sacrifice and dependence and produced a set of conditions within which women are invited to construct their identities in more individualized terms[1] (Beck and Beck-Gernsheim, 2002: 54–55).

> The ethic of individual self-fulfilment and achievement is the most powerful in modern society. The choosing, deciding, shaping human being who aspires to be the author of his or her own life, the creator of an individual identity, is the central character of our time. It is the fundamental cause behind changes in the family and the global gender revolution in relation to work and politics. (Beck and Beck-Gernsheim, 2002: 22–23)

The ascendancy of the ideal of a 'life of one's own' is a gendered process. For women, the rise of this ideal has much greater impact on their identities as the distance they travel in taking it up is greater than that required from men, for whom modern social forms have traditionally assumed this ideal. Particularly in the latter half of the twentieth century, fundamental social changes have taken place within family life, education, work, legislation, and public life – all of which have brought the normal female biography closer to that of men. The reworking of female biographies has been greatly influenced by the expansion and equalization of educational opportunities; by the rise in female employment and the increased significance of paid employment to women; and by changes to sexuality and relationships. Individualization as a structural characteristic of late modern society demands that women *must* engage in making choices, which constitute life projects that express who they are or who they want to be (Budgeon, 2003). These objective trends, however, offer only a partial picture of how individualization reworks the female biography. The underlying 'subjective' effects that accompany socio-structural change are a central factor underpinning the dynamics of gender and social change in late modernity. This is because,

just as changes in society as a whole produce new developmental models of what constitutes, for example, a normal female biography, so do new normal biographies react back upon the structures of society as a whole, producing tensions and conflicts there and triggering changes in their turn. The relationship then is reciprocal. (Beck and Beck-Gernsheim, 2002: 76; emphasis in the original)

Once social conditions allow for, and even *require*, women to see themselves as individuals who are responsible for generating their own life plans; for making decisions about educational attainment and career planning; and for the organization of personal life – spaces open up that require greater levels of consciousness about the context within which these choices have to be made. In this process, Beck and Beck-Gernsheim (2002: 58) argue, women's capacity to recognize 'the specificities and restrictions of the context in which they live their lives' is enhanced at both the private and the political level of self-awareness. This is particularly so, given that individualization is uneven and incomplete. For example, while women have become less constrained by ties to the family and to the domestic realm, they continue to perform the majority of care work and domestic labour in the home compared to men. Therefore women must negotiate a social world in which many aspects of their lives are incongruous. They may assert their right to live a 'life of one's own', but they do so with an enhanced capacity for recognizing the constraints that characterize the contexts within which they make choices about their lives. Late modernity has not been wholly transformed by individualizing processes where gender relations are concerned. Rather this is a case of, as Beck and Beck-Gernsheim put it, 'no longer' as it once was and 'not yet' as it should be; an intermediate stage, which generates a series of ambivalences and contradictions in women's lives (2002: 56). Increased levels of autonomy and demands for the right to self-realization co-exist with traditional expectations regarding what constitutes 'proper' femininity.

As explained earlier, newly emerging feminine subject positions defined by the ideals of individuality, self-realization, and choice occur at the point of convergence of feminism, postfeminism, neoliberalism, and individualization. The production of new forms of gendered subjectivity, made possible by the freeing of women's agency from traditional social structures and by the greater emphasis placed upon autonomy in the construction of female biographies, coincides with neoliberal ideologies that regulate and govern social processes in late modernity (Blackman, 2004; Burman, 2005; Walkerdine, 2003). The idealized female subject formulated through neoliberal ideologies is one that embodies the values of self-realization and self-sufficiency and is able, in the name of maximizing these ideals, to respond to a set of socio-economic conditions that demand flexibility and the capacity for negotiating uncertainty. This system of governance both presumes and produces an autonomous subject, who is at once responsive to change and responsible for the individualized capacity to incorporate change successfully into ongoing life projects.

The convergence of individualization, neoliberalism, and postfeminism forms a complicated discursive terrain for third wave feminism. This is a terrain where words such as choice, freedom, and self-determination proliferate and operate according to the logic of what Bonnie Urciuoli (2003: 396) refers to as 'strategically deployable shifters'. These are words or expressions that are meaningfully used across multiple discursive sites; but, because these words are not denotative, their meaning is associated with the conventions that characterize those particular fields. Since the interpretation of these terms depends upon the relationship of their user to a specific audience, the meaning of each word will shift according to context. Thus people using a particular word or expression in one field may be engaged in a wholly different pragmatic activity from what those people using the *formally identical* term in another field may be engaged in. Meaning and significance shift with the context and with the location of those terms within communities of practice. Over time, with repeated usage, the meaning and significance of particular words and expressions become transparent amongst social actors co-located within a shared context. These meanings become, so to speak, 'naturalized' and uncontested. However, Urciuoli (2003: 397) argues that we often assume that words used in speech situations in one discursive field carry the same meaning, or refer to the same things, in another context, and the subsequent slippage between contexts brings disparate discursive fields into congruence, when in fact meanings are not constant but are deployed by users in very specific ways across contexts. As she explains,

> what appear to be 'the same' lexemes are distributed across a range of discursive fields and are, so to speak, naturalized (over the course of pragmatic sedimentation) into those fields in ways that make their meaning appear quite transparent among its users. In this way, 'the same' lexemes can come to mean different things in different fields. But since social actors, especially in the USA, are notoriously resistant to the idea that context shapes (or indeed, has any right to shape) the 'real' meanings of words, actors operate *as if* meanings are constant across contexts. (Urciuoli, 2003: 397)

When deployed strategically, these words may appear to reference a commonly held orientation or goal, when in fact social actors may fundamentally disagree on the meanings of those words, depending upon context and their constitutive communities. At the point of convergence between individualization, neoliberalism, post-feminism, and third wave feminism, particular words such as 'choice' and 'self-determination' are deployed, in statements and judgements that seemingly reference social goods held in common, but in practice the disjuncture between the fields and the specific histories through which these words have acquired their substance is obscured. The meaning of a word like 'choice', for example, carries a considerably different import when this word is used within a feminist context, as compared to a context organized by neoliberal ideologies, and it will orient users in each context to a completely different set of priorities and aims. Feminism has invested heavily in terms such as 'choice' and 'autonomy', for reasons discussed at the outset of this chapter; but these are also terms that are vulnerable to co-optation and to a subsequent 'emptying' of their political significance.

> The concern for critical theory is that neoliberalism as an art of (self) government threatens to align seamlessly with the individual's ethical practice of self-mastery and self-autonomy within feminist and liberal-democratic thinking, thus evacuating the critical edge of the latter. The political meaning of liberating practices of the self in the face of gender, race, and class oppression is always up for grabs, and can lead to accommodation and cooptation as easily as to resistance, and vice versa. (Inoue, 2007: 82)

Freedom is 'not outside the system of power that it would contest. Such freedom is in fact enabled, produced, and even celebrated within the regime of power that it attempts to escape. The moment women work on and claim their sovereign identity is simultaneously the moment of neoliberal governmentality' (Inoue, 2007: 88). This paradox features centrally within the post-feminist gender order and, as argued in Chapter 2, is indicative of the collapsing inwards of feminism into its object of critique – a movement that undermines the desire to 'step outside', into an autonomous feminist space that is 'uncontaminated'. The flow of power through practices of self-invention and self-understanding is one that third wave feminism is concerned with in articulating a politics of subjectivity.

The complexity of this discursive terrain is illustrated by debates surrounding the increasing visibility and value placed upon emotion in both private and public spheres. Burman (2009) argues that this 'emotionalization' of everyday life and the increasing circulation of discourses that encourage individuals to acquire and perform 'emotional intelligence' are linked to the 'feminization' of culture. While the significance of emotions as a resource in the development of a critical political practice has long been part of the feminist agenda, the importance now assigned to emotions operates as an appropriation of a pseudo-feminist discourse and can be found to pervade neoliberal governmentality. In this context, feminization references the transformations that have taken place in the structuring of labour practices and conditions, such that those practices and conditions traditionally associated with women's work have now been extended to other areas. This includes the increasing prevalence of part-time, casual labour, flexi-time, home work, and low paid, low status employment, which is often insecure in nature. In addition, this has occurred 'alongside a cultural appropriation of women's supposedly natural skills of interpersonal flexibility and conflict resolution in the service of capital' (Burman, 2009: 139). Having well-developed communication skills, emotional literacy, and the ability to reflect upon and express one's feelings are now in demand in a knowledge-based economy.

Within sites such as education, business and management, or social policy, politics, and consumption, the emotional capacities of individuals are viewed as a resource to be exploited in the service of social and economic progress. Emotion is constructed as a set of skills and competences that may be developed instrumentally, to increase one's productivity and to enhance one's social capital to ensure success within existing social and economic structures. For example, in one description of 'emotional intelligence', associated qualities include 'abilities such as being able to motivate oneself and persist in the face of frustrations; to control impulse and delay gratification; to regulate one's moods and keep distress from swamping the ability to think; to empathize and to hope' (Goldman, 1996: 43, quoted in Burman, 2009: 140). Through systematic training, these skills may be developed in programmes which enhance 'emotional literacy' – the ability to 'recognize, understand, handle, and appropriately express emotions [...] using your emotions to help yourself and others succeed' (Sharp, 2001: 1, quoted in Burman, 2009: 143). In these discourses emotions are constructed as a feature of the individual, while the significance of social relations and the historical context within which particular emotions are made meaningful are ignored. Social problems are cast as a deficit in individual capacity, such that the solution focuses upon strategies for intervening at the individual level rather than upon engaging with a sustained critique of what 'success' means and how current social arrangements either impede or promote it. Thus the increasing reference to emotional intelligence and literacy should be looked upon with scepticism, particularly with regard to the kinds of subjectivities these discourses encourage. As Burman (2005: 357) argues, these subjectivities diverge significantly from those advocated by feminism – and yet they achieve this by seemingly deploying feminist values:

Spuriously feminist versions of current discourses of female-affirmativeness currently circulate in which the terminological continuity between current managerial strategies and feminisms lies in the valuation of individual, personal experience. Thus the institutionalization of feminism (insofar as this has happened) has given rise to a co-option of the slogan 'the personal is political' and then reversed it to render the political as *only* personal.

Thus neoliberal modes of governance that celebrate autonomy coincide in important ways with transformations that have occurred to gendered relations of inequality in the latter part of the twentieth century. This convergence constitutes a socio-cultural moment in which young women are often celebrated as the successful and flourishing subjects of the neoliberal age (Harris, 2003; McRobbie, 2004a; Walkerdine, 2003). This is evident where economic conditions have altered and the nature of work has been restructured alongside the success of feminist advancements in women's equality within both education and employment. Neoliberal ideologies of choice and self-determination seemingly mirror and endorse many feminist ideals such as self-determination and self-sufficiency (Harris, 2004b). Whereas systems of governance once presumed a privileged masculine subject, neoliberal governance, with its emphasis on the values of self-reliance, choice, and self-realization, appears to be neatly compatible with the levels of female success that are now evident. McRobbie (2004a) argues that the tropes of freedom and choice are now inextricably connected with the category 'young woman' and that young women have become metaphors of social change. However, this successful subject position is structured within the new meritocracy of late modernity, such that occupying it requires the repudiation of feminism and its relegation to the past. In *The Aftermath of Feminism*, McRobbie (2009) analyses a complex set of social and cultural processes through which feminism has been discredited and subsequently cast out of contemporary political culture. In this analysis it is argued that a new sexual contract has been established, in which elements of feminism have been 'taken into account' through their incorporation into political and institutional spheres. In this process, select feminist values like autonomy, choice, and empowerment are acknowledged only insofar as they are commensurate with the values that govern highly individualized, neoliberal meritocratic social and economic structures characteristic of late modernity. Within this social arrangement, young women are increasingly rendered visible by their positioning as successful participants within these structures. This visibility is the result of young women stepping forward as 'subjects of capacity', who are willing and able subjects prepared fully to compete and thrive within conditions that demand an aptitude for flexible self-invention.

The often noted success of young women in educational attainment and labour force participation is cited as evidence of a 'democracy in good health', or as 'living testimony that social reform and legislation has been effective' (McRobbie, 2009: 57). The celebration of female success legitimizes current political and social modernization programmes and, instead of advancing women's interests *per se*, is a constituent element of a 'profound and determined attempt, undertaken by an array of political and cultural forces, to re-shape notions of womanhood so that they fit with new or emerging (neoliberalized) social and economic arrangements' (McRobbie, 2009: 57).

According to McRobbie, the positioning of young women as subjects of capacity emerges through a complex process of 'double entanglement': feminism is granted recognition and allowed to exist, but only as something that has *already happened*. On one level, feminism has seemingly gained a favourable status by being absorbed into the realm of common sense, but the dynamics of this recognition also secures the conditions that invite its disavowal and repudiation. It is as if to say that the concerns raised by feminism have been responded to, so there is no need to discuss them any more, and those who insist on doing so are living in the past. The dynamics of feminist recognition and disavowal allow young women to acquire a form of legitimated subjecthood, but these same processes also leave hegemonic gender relations intact, largely because the repudiation of feminism evacuates a critical vocabulary that might otherwise be deployed to analyse the role that newly emergent feminine subjectivities have in reproducing traditional gender relations. The taking into account of feminism produces new forms of gender regulation and gender retrenchment, which are made possible by processes described as a 'cultural politics of disarticulation' (McRobbie, 2009). Many of the institutional gains made by women in the past

30 years are now being eroded, as forms of 'empowered' femininity are offered to young women as a substitute for feminism. These new forms of highly visible and culturally endorsed femininities encourage young women to identify with their social positioning as the beneficiaries of Western freedoms, which deliver personal choice and self-gratification. Disarticulation

> is the objective of a new kind of regime of gender power, which functions to foreclose on the possibility or likelihood of various expansive intersections and inter-generational feminist transmissions. Articulations are therefore, reversed, broken off, and the idea of a new feminist political imaginary becomes increasingly inconceivable. In social and cultural life there is instead a process of unpicking the seams of connections, forcing apart and dispersing subordinate social groups who might have possibly found some common cause. (McRobbie, 2009: 26)

Alongside the disavowal of collective interests and a politics that draws its force from the recognition of a common cause, there comes a more active suppression of a feminist politics. This maligning of feminism occurs through spuriously casting feminists as hostile, male hating, embittered harridans: 'a hysterical and monstrous version of feminism' (McRobbie, 2009: 27). As a replacement for feminist solidarity, young women are offered highly individualized but supposedly newly empowered subject positions, from which to engage in practices of self-invention offered by consumer culture and rewarded recognition by neoliberal discourses that attach labels of success to those who take up these forms of subjecthood. Young women are 'called forward', on condition that feminism fades away. Gender relations that might continue to be reconfigured through feminist critique and practice are instead re-stabilized through the reassertion of traditional heterosexual gender norms that regulate and constrain contemporary gender relations.

The positioning of young women as successful recipients of this new gender order occurs within particular 'spaces of attention' or 'luminosities', in which feminism is abandoned through the taking up of culturally viable femininities that demand engagement in individualized self-production (McRobbie, 2009: 54–60). With feminism firmly in the past, young women are encouraged to construct themselves as autonomous agents who are able to take advantage of educational and occupational opportunities; to pursue successful careers, achieve economic independence, delay motherhood, and become full participants in consumer culture – all of which are defining features of contemporary modes of feminine citizenship (McRobbie, 2009: 54). To do so requires a belief in meritocratic principles of self-reliance and self-determination and a linking of these principles to a project of self-monitoring and personal development (Budgeon, 2003). McRobbie identifies four 'spaces of attention' in which new femininities are particularly visible.

The post-feminist masquerade

The incitement to take up independent femininity must at the same time be enacted in such a way that this femininity remains intelligible within patriarchal gender norms. This occurs primarily within the commercial domain, which

> provides a proliferation of interpellations directed to young women, with harsher penalties, it seems, for those who refuse or who are unable to receive its various addresses. That is, it becomes increasingly difficult to function as a female subject without subjecting oneself to those technologies of self that are constitutive of the spectacularly feminine. There are new norms of appearance and self-presentation expected not just in leisure and in everyday life but also in the workplace, and government concerns itself with this aspect of self-management through various initiatives. (McRobbie, 2009: 60)

This 'spectacular' femininity is the object of the contemporary fashion-beauty complex, which operates so as to prescribe a highly stylized femininity and to incite young women to take up this position knowingly, as an active choice. This post-feminist masquerade, because it is undertaken self-consciously, can be dissociated from the critique, made by feminism, of the constraining and disempowering nature of fashion norms and beauty rituals. In its place, this masquerade is undertaken as part of a regime of 'self-perfectibility', which defuses feminist critique and counter-balances the threat that new norms of female independence may pose to hegemonic masculinity. The post-feminist masquerade manages the disruption that female success may pose to masculine privilege by maintaining heterosexual desirability as a requirement for success. As McRobbie (2007:66) argues, the

> masquerade disavows the spectral, powerful and castrating figures of the lesbian and the feminist with whom they may conceivably be linked. It rescues women from the threat posed by these figures by triumphantly re-instating the spectacle of excessive femininity (on the basis of the independently earned wage) while also shoring up hegemonic masculinity by endorsing this public femininity which appears to undermine, or at least unsettle the new power accruing to women on the basis of this economic capacity.

The post-feminist masquerade also re-inscribes a femininity that is underpinned by the racialized dynamics of privileged femininity. This is a femininity that is implicitly white, and as such re-instates whiteness as a cultural dominant, while undoing the struggles fought for racial equality – which, like feminism, are relegated from the present, where they are deemed redundant, to a past where they are seen as having been necessary.

The well-educated working girl

A second site where young women are rendered visible as subjects of capacity is within the pursuit of qualifications and career advancement. Whereas young women were once constructed as a cause for concern due to gender inequality, their ascendance as key benefactors of modernization means that they are positioned as aspirational subjects, ready and able to respond effectively to the expectation that they will take up the opportunities made available to them. McRobbie argues that we have witnessed a shift away from the traditional areas of family and domesticity, as sites where femininity is validated and subsequently contained, towards sites where the attainment of educational qualifications and full employment are pursued. The possibility of this pursuit of success is not attributed to the efforts of feminist struggle; it is rather celebrated as evidence that governmental policies that have sought to embed meritocratic principles within schooling systems have succeeded. The celebration of the highly visible success of *some* girls, however, conceals the extent to which the modernizing agenda of the state has operated to the detriment of other girls, particularly those from lower income families

(McRobbie, 2007:74). Underachievement, recklessness, and individualized failure are attributed to girls deemed to lack the capacity to make 'good choices' that affect their life chances (Harris, 2004b; Walkerdine, 2003).

While feminine subjects of capacity are now visible in newly public ways, this does not fully destabilize gender hierarchies. The post-feminist masquerade operates here to ensure that, while young women embrace economic independence, they take up this position within the limits set by normative heterosexuality and the dictates of traditionally gendered caring responsibilities. Work/life balance is achievable, but only through the acceptance of a compromise that requires a downsizing of personal ambition and the reprivatization of relations of care back into the domestic sphere, where individualized solutions to the competing demands of work and family life are 'chosen' by women. In this scenario men may contribute to caring for children, or may offer their time and effort to meet the demands of domestic life, but this, too, is a matter of individual choice. The reprivatization of these issues marks a sharp shift away from the challenge launched by feminism against the sexual division of labour, in which greater accountability on the part of men for care work was demanded towards a post-feminist accommodation that maintains unequal gender arrangements. In McRobbie's analysis, this accommodation secures the subordinate status of women in terms of their wage-earning potential, while also providing an opportunity for the state to cut back on long-term welfare expenditure.

The phallic girl

In this figuration of femininity, young women are given license to exhibit decidedly 'unfeminine' and aggressive behaviours, traditionally associated with masculinity. It is the presumption of gender equality that allows participation in freedoms that were once the preserve of men, including 'heavy drinking, swearing, smoking, getting into fights, having casual sex, flashing her breasts in public, getting arrested by police, consumption of pornography, enjoyment of lap-dancing clubs and so on but without relinquishing her own desirability to men' (McRobbie, 2009: 83). The granting of sexual agency to young women in such a way that it undermines the traditional sexual double standard, however, is removed from previous feminist critiques of heterosexuality. Instead, the celebration of phallic femininity as a newly found female freedom emphasizes that women now can 'choose' to act like men; but, by constructing this through the lens of empowered female agency, the privilege of hegemonic masculinity is rendered invisible.

> Consumer culture, the tabloid press, the girl's [sic] and women's magazine sector, the lads' magazines and also down-market, trashy television all encourage young women, as though in the name of sexual equality, to overturn the old double standard and emulate the assertive and hedonistic lifestyles of sexuality associated with young men, particularly in holiday locations, or in the context of the UK city centre leisure culture which has developed around late night drinking. (McRobbie, 2009: 84)

The global girl

McRobbie's final feminine subject exposes the limits of the previous figurations, whose boundaries are marked as white, middle-class, Western femininities. As such, a global femininity is being reconfigured, but in ways which re-instate white, Western privilege. The post-feminist masquerade that emphasizes conventional beauty aesthetics and a passive feminine demeanour references a mode of idealized femininity that, historically, was established through the exclusion of black women. Nevertheless, young women from third-world countries are invited to aspire to membership in a global femininity defined by Western norms. In contrast to the phallic girl, the global girl is imagined as at the 'intersection of qualities which combine the natural and the authentic, with a properly feminine love of self-adornment, and the playfully seductive with the innocent, so as to suggest a sexuality which is youthful, latent and waiting to be unleashed' (McRobbie, 2009: 89). This figuration is established through a re-colonization of non-Western cultures and through the production of racial hierarchies.

McRobbie's analysis lends important insights into the dynamics of incorporation and expulsion that operate within the contemporary gender order. As young women are called upon to come forth as 'subjects of capacity' – as subjects who are the winners of the proliferation of late modern 'choices' and meritocratic social and economic structures – a series of contradictions arise. Conferring efficacy and legitimacy to feminism – that is, granting recognition – is a move done in the name of dismissing its relevance in the current context. It is acceptable to dispatch feminism if assertions that equality now exists can be defended. McRobbie's analysis, however, demonstrates that, in situations where the achievement of newly 'empowered successful' femininity requires individual women also to adhere to traditional feminine norms, the justification for feminism's dismissal only makes sense if ongoing gender inequalities are recast as the product of individual 'choice'. By initiating a 'regime of personal responsibility' (McRobbie, 2004a), neoliberal governance not only creates privileged subjects, such as young women who are seen to take advantage of the opportunities now available to them, but simultaneously produces (and requires) a new system of social inequality, in which those seen as lacking the requisite skills to capitalize on opportunities for self-development or who fail to raise sufficient motivation to perpetually undergo strategic self-invention are judged as failing to take responsibility for making good choices. Failure to succeed thereby rests squarely upon individuals (Blackman, 2004; Harris, 2003; Walkerdine, 2003). Better self-management is presented as the solution to what, Walkerdine (2003) argues, is the impossibility of illusory neoliberal subjectification. This form of subjectivity requires that individuals are impelled to make multiple choices within a context governed by uncertainty, while at the same time they are required to have a stable centre; an ego capable of resilience; and an ability to adjust successfully and to prosper with every new situation and each emerging option. The simultaneously autonomous *and* multiple self is an 'impossible fiction'; yet the failure to create life projects and the kinds of secure self-inventions that such projects presumably afford is understood and lived as an individual psychopathology, to be remedied by individual counselling and therapy.

Similarly, Blackman (2004) argues that popular discourses of idealized femininity materialize in women's magazines in such a way that readers are incited to construct themselves as self-made, autonomous women, but this regulatory ideal, which privileges independence and self-reliance, then simultaneously comes into direct conflict with other constructions, which suggest that proper femininity is also about emotional expressiveness, care, and interconnectedness. The reconciliation of these competing demands on individual women is not, however, placed within a larger context of contradictory social forces and relations, but is instead individualized through the resolution of these demands in self-help discourses. Femininity is thus constituted as inherently dilemma-ridden and encumbered by forms of psychic stress and dysfunction. Within late modern gendered processes of subjectification, the obligation to construct oneself as free is potentially enabling for women insofar as this position reflects women's ability to achieve autonomy; but this is also a form of subjectification, in the sense that women's choices are made within a socio-cultural context rife with contradictions, which are only acknowledged if responsibility for their resolution can be individualized.

Contradictions and ambivalence

This discussion highlights a number of key concerns for a third wave feminist politics of subjectivity. Newly emerging forms of femininity have been assessed in terms that suggest, on the one hand, that they are a cause for celebration because, by inciting women to make themselves into subjects of capacity, these reconstructions create opportunities for expanded agency. On the other hand, successful femininity becomes a structurally ambivalent position, presenting women with contradictions that make the realization of new ideals uncomfortable at best and impossible at worst (Gonick, 2007: 441). The significance of new forms of feminine subjectivity is debated by feminists, as are the complex implications of this significance for the contemporary gender order, because the contradictions that define newly emerging femininities are produced within a discursive field that simultaneously supports and undermines women's agency.

Despite the celebration of young women as exemplar 'choice autobiographers', anxiety is also projected onto the bodies of young women in terms of what they wear, what they think and how they act. Greer (cited in Munford, 2004: 142), for example, has criticized girls for what she views as their increasingly bad and unacceptable behaviour, citing 'aggressively randy, hard drinking young females, who have got younger with every passing year, until they are now emerging in their pre-teens' as evidence of the disappointments that femininity, released from traditional constraints, can manifest. Duits and Van Zoonen (2006: 104) argue that 'women's sexuality and girls' bodies have become the metonymic location for many a contemporary social dilemma', and that social anxiety is projected onto their bodies and onto the choices they are making. In their analysis they draw a parallel between the controversy provoked by young Muslim women's choice to wear headscarves and religious dress and by the choice of some young women to wear the kind of sexualized dress referred to as 'porno-chic'. These controversies reflect wider societal uncertainties about decency and moral decline; about the role of feminism and gender equality; about consumerism; about multicultural excess; and about the separation of church and state. Important questions are raised about women's choices within these debates, particularly as, in both examples, judgements are made that women, either by choosing to cover their body or conversely by choosing to not cover it, are making the wrong choices and not expressing their agency in appropriate ways.

The judgements made about women's exercise of agency are connected to neoliberal governance, which translates into a bifurcated female subject position, defined on the one hand by successful female individualization and on the other by failed femininity. Harris (2003: 26) describes these two normative categories as being occupied by 'can-do girls' and 'at risk girls', respectively. The idealized neoliberal subject of late modernity translates into a form of hegemonic femininity that is constituted by this regulative duality. The 'at risk' designation is assigned to those young women who are imagined as passive victims of circumstances beyond their control, or as willful risk-takers who misuse girl power to their own destructive ends. The 'can-do girls' – those who 'excel in their star careers, glamorous consumer lifestyles, and delayed motherhood' – are meanwhile celebrated for their 'optimistic, self-inventing, and success-oriented' behaviour (Harris, 2004b: 25). Young women who do not create these success stories for themselves have become the focus of wider concerns about delinquency, nihilism, and antisocial attitudes. The production of 'failed femininities' relies upon an uncritical analysis of young women's structural disadvantage as well as upon an attribution of individual incompetence (Harris, 2003: 26). Emergent forms of late modern gendered subjectivity therefore present a double bind. While autonomy is strengthened by increased educational and employment opportunities for women, so too is heteronomy, as the very choices that have been created reinforce an individualized regulatory ideal.

Debates about women's choices and exercise of agency are examined in depth in Chapter 6.

Conclusion

In this chapter it has been argued that femininity has been reworked within the context of late modernity, moving away from associations with passivity and dependence towards ideals previously reserved for hegemonic masculinity. Autonomy, independence, and self-determination are characteristics increasingly linked with young women who exercise 'good' choices within a context where vast and exciting opportunities in education, work, family life, and consumption await. Within such an imagined context, feminism occupies a precarious position. Young women are encouraged now to disregard feminism, which is seen to have done its job, and to deny that anything more needs doing. In its place, individualizing discourses draw upon feminist values such as 'choice', but they repackage them in ways that are more consistent with the principles of neoliberal governance. Freedom is valourized, and yet this very pursuit of freedom keeps individuals tied to their own regulation. This is a context in which the structure of gender relations, the flow of power through newly emerging feminine subject positions, and the possibilities for women's agency and the constraint of that agency have become exceedingly complex.

Within this contemporary gender order where the relationship between masculinity and femininity is being renegotiated, third wave feminism seeks to analyse the production of gender within particular discursive fields and the role that gender plays in producing women's own understanding of their experiences. Many third wave writers claim that femininity is lived in increasingly complicated and contradictory ways across multiple contexts. Third wave feminism emphasizes contradictions and encourages them to be part of female identity, therefore the goal is not to define female identity but to complicate it strategically to undermine processes that dictate what meanings can and cannot attach to femininity. Expressing a degree of optimism that makes some critics sceptical, third wave feminism enthusiastically advocates the opening up of new subjective spaces through performances of femininity that are at once dissonant, irreverent, and ambivalent (Reed, 1997). In Chapter 4 insights into the experience of negotiating the contradictions that constitute the post-feminist constellation will be examined in depth. This discussion will provide a backdrop to the claim, made in third wave feminist literature, that women's experiences of the contradictions and ambivalences that form the contemporary gender order are the starting place for a third wave feminist politics.

4
Experiencing Third Wave Feminism

Third wave feminism is concerned with challenging the categories used by second wave feminism to represent experience; so, while a concern for understanding women's experiences is shared with the second wave, third wave feminism returns to the category of experience to question the presumed uniformity of women's experiences. This is enacted with the hope of opening up the possibilities for a new feminist identity to be formed across multiple locations. Many third wave texts therefore emphasize the role of the personal in making claims about the meaning feminism has in women's lives. For many critics, this focus on the personal results in overprivileging the individual, who is positioned as the 'authentic' producer of knowledge and, as such, as one who cannot be challenged. When deployed critically, however, personal theorizing encourages a deconstructive view of experience, which supports an analysis of how gendered subjects are produced through particular experiences. While the category of personal experience may not be dealt with as critically and self-reflexively as it could be, within much third wave literature its presence is suggestive of epistemological and methodological strategies for engaging with the production of new femininities. This chapter examines debates concerned with the role of the personal within feminist thought and outlines the potential that deconstructive strategies have to inform the study of gendered subjectivities. The first half of the chapter focuses on the use of personal experience within third wave literature and establishes the key experiences that define third wave identities. The discussion in the second half of the chapter moves on to engage specifically with empirical studies that illuminate the experiences of young women as they seek to articulate their identities from their positioning within a post-feminist gender regime. These studies lend insight into what happens when young women attempt to make themselves into idealized, feminine subjects and reveal the complex experiences that are the result of occupying this structurally ambivalent gendered subject position. This positioning impacts upon a wide range of sites, including relationships with others, the management of sexuality, practices of embodiment, understandings of gender equality, and constructions of choice.

Theorizing experience

Personal experience has played a central role in grounding feminist epistemology. By staking a claim for the legitimacy, and indeed the necessity, of 'socially situated knowledges', feminism has been enormously influential in critiquing 'transcendental or ahistorical foundationalism' – that is, the tendency to start knowledge from the 'view from nowhere' – to generate less false stories about the social world (Haraway in Harding, 1993: 141). However, questions about how experience is formed and what status personal accounts should have in the production of feminist theory have been the source of much debate, and many of these questions remain challenging for third wave feminism. This is particularly the case as the category of 'experience' itself has been problematized as the basis for making claims about the social world. What, then, is to be made of the extensive use of autobiographical texts in third wave feminism?

It has been suggested that feminism is characterized by a conceptual trinity of experience, reality, and truth (Hughes, 2002: 173), and that connecting experience to knowledge constitutes one of feminism's central problematics (Ramazanoglu, 2002). To understand the significance of the feminist claim that the 'personal is political' is to understand that 'women's distinctive experience as women occurs within that sphere that has been socially lived as the personal – private, emotional, interiorized, particular, individuated, intimate – so that what it is to *know* the *politics* of women's situation is to know women's personal lives' (MacKinnon, 1997: 73–74, quoted in Hughes, 2002: 152; emphasis in the original). The attention given to women's experiences has provided an important starting point for developing innovative theoretical frameworks that not only critique dominant forms of knowledge and facilitate social critique, but promote the development of distinctly *feminist* theories of knowledge, subjectivity and power. Situating knowledge within the realm of the personal has inspired the use of a variety of writing techniques that foreground experience, embodiment, and social location. And the validation of female experience has been implicit in practices that write women's lives into existence and make a claim for women's epistemic authority (Bertram, 1998; Felski, 1989).

Many of the early texts that claimed the existence of a new wave of feminism did so by representing third wave feminism as a form of 'lived theory'.[1] This was achieved through the deliberate use of autobiography to write about everyday experiences associated with multiple third wave identities and about their link to politics. These personal accounts made a range of experiences visible, and in so doing they served to justify the need for a form of feminism that could engage with, and validate, these experiences as the basis for a distinctly new feminist identity. These autobiographical accounts, therefore, offer representations of particular experiences that demand a mode of *articulation* within feminism, but also operate as a specific *interpretation* of those experiences, such that what might look to some – notably those feminists aligned with second wave feminism – as firmly outside of a feminist register is made intelligible, but only through the lens of a new, third wave of feminism.

One of the earliest third wave texts, *To Be Real: Telling the Truth and Changing the Face of Feminism*, begins with the explicit claim that women's experiences are central to feminism. Walker (1995) explains that the impetus for editing an anthology on feminism and female empowerment was her desire to 'hear experiences of people attempting to live their lives envisioning or experiencing identities beyond those inscribed on them by the surrounding culture' (Walker, 1995: xxxvii). The contributions she solicited were to be 'personal, honest, and record a transformative journey taken'. The decision to begin from personal experience is justified by the explanation that personal testimonies 'build empathy and compassion, are infinitely more accessible than more academic tracts' and 'that our lives are the best basis for feminist theory and that by using the contradictions in our lives [...] we lay the groundwork for feminist theory that neither vilifies or deifies, but that accepts and respects difference' (ibid.). This claim carries an implicit critique of abstract theorizing and the often associated objection that feminism has lost its effectiveness through its institutionalization within the academy. While feminism has gained legitimacy in some quarters, the title of the text clearly suggests that it has become less connected and less relevant to the context of everyday life, and that feminist knowledge in a formal sense no longer illuminates or politicizes the experiences that constitute women's lives. Returning to women's experiences implies a strategy for producing more relevant and more complete knowledge, particularly knowledge that takes into account the different values, priorities, and understandings associated with the various locations from which women speak.

A similar position is put forward by Heywood and Drake (1997), who in their collection of essays *Third Wave Agenda: Being Feminist, Doing Feminism* draw attention to styles of writing within feminist thought and criticize the privileging of a particular form of feminist theory, which to them often seems like a 'disembodied language game'. Being critical of the abstraction that has come to characterize feminist writing led them to collect essays on third wave feminism that would demonstrate that feminism is lived as a way of being in everyday worldly encounters. The personal is validated because its inclusion grants 'an emotional life and a personal stake sometimes missing from academic writing' (1997: 2). Combining the personal mode of writing with more analytic modes performs 'a kind of hybrid thinking and writing that marks part of the critical agenda for the third wave' (Heywood and Drake, 1997: 17).

In *Listen Up! Voices from the Next Feminist Generation*, the editor, Barbara Findlen (1995), asserts that personal experience has often been and continues to be a significant point of entry into feminism, and therefore her aim was to give voice to young women's experiences and to show how these experiences are made meaningful when read from a feminist perspective. These stories are presented to the audience so that they may serve as a catalyst for consciousness and action and, ultimately, may bring about change in the lives of young women (1995: xvi). This aim reflects the view that telling stories about personal experience can function as a form of knowledge production that transcends the specificity of the location from which it is told. Third wave autobiographical texts identify particular experiences as emblematic or illustrative of women's lives in late modernity and, insofar as these experiences are shared, they support claims for recognition. Dicker and Piepmeier (2003: 13) similarly propose that essays about personal experience offer women the opportunity to reflect upon and articulate their 'process of self-discovery and identification as a feminist'.

The significance accorded to experience in the third wave literature is an orientation shared with second wave feminism, but crucial differences are apparent. The distinctiveness of third wave theorizing is associated with the location of this phenomenon in a particularly individualized ethos. For example, in a chapter entitled 'Voices and Visions: A Mother and Daughter Discuss Coming to Feminism and Being Feminist' (Harde and Harde, 2003), a conversation between a mother and daughter offers a detailed comparison of the experiences they use to define their relationship to feminism. Commonalities are found as the dialogue unfolds, but what becomes striking is the extent to which their experiences differ. For the daughter, third wave feminism is validated by what she perceives as its flexibility and malleability; it is 'messy and self-contradicting, but also encompassing, enlightening and empowering', and it allows 'women to express any ideas they have about feminism without being boxed in a category or identity' (Harde and Harde, 2003: 122). This statement implies that third wave feminism provides a means for translating complex and 'untidy' experiences into a meaningful feminist register. However, unlike the process of translation central to second wave feminism, in which experience was transformed into a collective political movement, third wave feminism tends to validate experience in and of itself. Third wave feminism is appealing because it 'helps women work on a personal level' (Harde and Harde, 2003: 119).

> [...] I believe that the emphasis on individual expression makes the third wave inviting and effective. Even though I have never declared myself a feminist, I realize that as a third waver, there is no need for radical action or strategy to support the movement. Militant action is not needed to promote the third wave; instead, the experiences of young women construct the third wave. (Harde and Harde, 2003: 119)

In the same collection of essays another woman, also involved in dialogue with an older feminist, accounts for the difference in their politics in similarly individualistic ways, by aligning third wave feminism with personal practices of self-representation.

> I'm sensing that the personal frontier is where my generation is doing most of its work [...] and that is important work. Just as important as the law-changing/tenure/first-woman-president stuff, because how we conduct our personal lives (what speaks to us, what we value) represents us directly – this is why the personal is political. (Pollitt and Baumgardner, 2003: 316)

In *The F-Word,* Kristin Rowe-Finkbeiner (2004: 91) asserts that 'there isn't just one way to be a feminist', and therefore the 'general ethos of the third wave focuses on accepting the individual, regardless of their labeled "baggage" from identity politics'. Focusing on individuals and what is significant to them is used as a strategy for recognizing that feminism is necessarily diverse. This provides the justification for using personal narratives to illuminate what otherwise might be missed or marginalized by an insistence on homogeneity. Writing about personal experience is defended as a way of opening up feminism and making it more inclusive.

> Part of this movement entails personal experiences and individual perspectives taking the place of identity politics or a monolithic theory. It is no accident that many books published about the third wave are anthologies, collecting multiple women's voices, not books of overarching theory on the future of feminism. (Rowe-Finkbeiner, 2004: 91)

The act of claiming a feminist identity, often perceived as an awkward identification to make in a post-feminist society, is a common theme that runs through many of the stories found in these anthologies. For example, in one personal narrative, we meet a young woman who, although identified with left politics, explains her long-standing aversion to the label 'feminist', which changed once the term was defined for her through the lens of third wave feminism. In this transformative encounter she was told that 'third wave feminism is about embracing individual experience and making personal stories political' and that this type of feminism was needed because, although second wave feminism had sought to empower women as 'a whole, they didn't acknowledge the varying agendas and experiences of individual women' (Wong, 2003: 295). The story ends with the confession that this author is now more comfortable with calling herself a feminist, because (in her own words) 'feminist' has 'become something to which I have given my own interpretation, and I have taken the responsibility of not letting the word feminism "name me". Instead, I believe that I can take the reins and redefine the word for myself' (Wong, 2003: 307).

The identification of diverse individual experiences as the foundation for third wave feminism has been received with scepticism in some quarters. For instance, the explicit commitment to 'multivocality', expressed in these writings, has been criticized for lacking coherence, for substituting an 'anarchic *bricolage* or autobiographical anecdote for systematic analysis', and for failing to move sufficiently beyond the personal narrative (Kelly, 2005: 3). From this perspective an interrogation of the personal, particularly of the relationship of the individual with wider structures of power, privilege, and oppression, is required for the production of feminist knowledge. Some critics warn that the 'excessive personalizing' found in third wave discourse 'can potentially obscure instead of unveil systemic problems and power structures' (Siegel, 1997a). Moreover, the claim that third wave explorations of experience produce a way of knowing that is more 'authentic' and closer to truth than other forms of knowledge production relies upon an epistemologically *naïve* understanding of how experience comes into being (Scott, 1991). For many, third wave feminists confessional writing, however, uncovers issues that have been hidden or obscured because both established feminist theory and mainstream knowledge fail to discern them adequately.

> Because people are much more interested in reading personal stories these days, third-wave feminists are weighing in to tell the truths of their lives to both mainstream and nonmainstream audiences alike; to challenge misconceptions about feminism; to use their lives as legitimate sites of theoretical production, which is still heresy in some academic circles; and also to say how feminism has shaped their lives. Furthermore, third-wave feminists are using

personal narrative to say what we think is working in feminism and what we think is not. (Jacob and Licona, 2005: 198)

Many critics remain unconvinced by this argument. Shugart et al. (2001: 99, quoted in Purvis, 2004), for instance, maintain that third wave feminism does not manage to transcend the level of the personal worlds of individuals, 'their responses to which are distinct and idiosyncratic, rather than collective'. Recognition that differences between women exist becomes problematically reduced to matters of individual choice and personal style, and a misplaced pride is invested in contradictions 'which are individual, internal and extreme' (ibid.). Third wave personal theorizing is, therefore, often viewed as a form of solipsism that advocates confession as a strategy for individual empowerment; perpetuates an unquestioning conflation of the personal and the political; and expresses a commitment to pluralism that slides into relativism. Critics often compare this use of the personal with the second wave of feminism, where personal experiences, translated through practices of consciousness raising, materialized as a shared oppression, and provided the basis for a collective politics. Without politicization, they argue, an emphasis on personal disclosure mistakenly promotes feminism as though it were merely a feminized 'therapeutic' practice and not an oppositional politics[2] (Gillis and Munford, 2004). The co-optation of the personal into self-help discourses reinforces neoliberal incitements to pursue freedom through a course of self-improvement. Therapeutic discourses invite self-narratives that are disconnected from a critical understanding of personally experienced problems connected to, and shaped by, a concrete set of social relations (Kelly, 2005). Set within this cultural context, where the values of the marketplace have achieved prominence, identity is one area amongst many that has become commodified.

Critiquing 'experience'

Despite its strategic significance, the role of women's experience in feminist theory and politics has proven to be problematic on a number of levels and, in relation to third wave feminism's advocacy of the personal as a form of 'lived theory', these problems represent challenges that need to be addressed. Firstly, the concept of experience and its relationship to subjectivity has been deconstructed, since it first formed a fundamental category for feminist politics. Historically, the creation of practices and spaces where women could be allowed to make their experiences of oppression known and shared with others was fundamental to a feminist theory of social change. Second wave feminism has often been narrated as a moment when women experienced an 'awakening', which allowed them to formulate a new relationship to the oppressive social conditions that were preventing them from realizing their 'true' selves (Johnson, 1993: 11). In these accounts the self that was revealed via this coming into consciousness was interpreted as an authentic self, unable to achieve its full potential due to the effects of imposed gender norms. As a political strategy, practices of self-disclosure generated access to previously hidden truths that had value for the speaker, for her immediate audience, and for feminism more widely (Valverde, 2004). Over time, confidence in this linkage of reality to experience and to truthful knowledge was undermined, which resulted in a questioning of feminism's epistemic authority. The status of women's experience as a direct source of knowledge has been met with increased uncertainty due to a number of complicating factors – among them being the social divisions between women, the fragmentation of grassroots feminist politics, and accusations of essentialism from the 'postmodernist and poststructuralist critics of humanism, essentialism, determinism, foundationalism and universalism' (Ramazanoglu and Holland, 1999: 381). In other words, the context within which third wave has emerged is one in which the status of the category of 'experience' has been problematized.

Secondly, this has resulted in particular attention being paid to the problems that arise when the categories of 'experience' and 'identity' are left uncontested and taken instead as transparent truths. When these terms are not problematized, first-person theorizing perpetuates 'a mystification of "women's experiences" by rendering their representations self-evident, continuous with and reflective of a "self" and a "real world"' (Bernstein, 1992: 121). The radical challenge that personal theorizing makes to the structuring of authority and knowledge and its interrogative and transformative potential may be seriously undermined by a 'critical neglect of the very categories it employs' (ibid.). The propensity to treat experience as self-evident operates as a form of 'experiential foundationalism' – the 'tendency to insist that the spontaneous consciousness of individual experience provides a uniquely legitimating criterion for identifying preferable or less false beliefs' (Harding, 1993: 141). This tendency is reflected in some instances of third wave feminist personal theorizing, where 'I' is used to express an unmediated experience of a 'real' personal truth. As Kauffman (1993: 261) argues, 'there is something fatally alluring about personal testimony', largely because, when individuals speak about their lives, the impression is given that they are granting access to that which is most deeply experienced, and therefore known. A teleological use of the 'I' relies on personal disclosure, as though it reveals the truth of 'myself as a person', and this invites a form of solipsism that encourages the viewing of an individual life story as 'inherently paradigmatic', as coherent, unified, and morally inspiring (Kauffman, 1993: 263), thus preventing sufficient attention being given to the question of what the 'I' represents and how it comes into being. The aim of feminist personal theorizing is to draw critical attention to these questions and, unlike impersonal modes of expression that obscure the conditions of its production, feminist theory is explicitly concerned with those gendered dynamics. When such questions are put aside, 'the author's personal "experience" becomes the new uncontested authority that displaces any accounting for its discursive, cultural, and ideological positioning' (Bernstein, 1992: 129). The aim of feminist 'truth-telling' practices, therefore, is not to make women's experiences visible as though they revealed a hidden truth about the 'real world', but rather to raise critical questions about the workings of the ideological system that furnishes those practices with categories of representation such as man/woman and brings particular experiences into being (Felski, 1989).

The third problem for third wave personal theorizing is the charge of gender essentialism. On the one hand, the deployment of the feminine personal as a critical foil to masculine abstractions has been an effective strategy for challenging gendered power relations as expressed in the production of privileged knowledge; yet on the other hand, this strategy can also reproduce the logic of gender essentialism. For many feminists, correlating the personal with the feminine promotes the notion that there is a distinctive 'women's way knowing', which not only challenges abstract 'masculine theory', but represents a form of knowing that is superior, as it is more 'grounded' and closer to the concrete realm of the 'real world'. As argued by

Kauffman (1993: 267), in some instances of personal theorizing the appeal of the personal is its perceived safeguard against the 'patriarchal gesture' of theory – a form of knowledge produced neither *by* women nor *for* women. Personal theorizing, with its underlying values of sincerity and authenticity, seemingly promotes a better way of understanding women's lives under patriarchy. This view, however, reasserts and locks women back into 'the very dichotomies (male intellect versus female intuition; head versus body, etc.) that so many other feminists have spent so much time trying to dismantle' (Kauffman, 1993: 267).

Finally, personal theorizing presents the risk of promoting an individualist ethos by endorsing a therapeutic approach to self-knowledge – one that encourages the individual to find the roots of their difficulties through processes of self-reflection. As argued by Kauffman (1993:269) 'it is clearly a delusion that by throwing off the straitjacket of formal repository prose, anyone will be revealing her "true," unique self. Writing about yourself does not liberate you, it just shows how ingrained the ideology of freedom through self-expression is in our thinking.' If the relevance of personal experience is not elaborated beyond the individual, to wider patterns of experience so that others, too, may recognize them as their own, the realm of the personal is privileged at the expense of generating knowledge about the economic, social, and political context that structures those experiences. Failing to locate experience critically perpetuates an ideology that casts the individual as an autonomous, self-made subject 'who always has choices and whose choices are free' (Kauffman, 1993: 269).

Experiencing contradictions

Bearing these criticisms in mind, third wave feminism promotes a return to experience that is important at this particular historical juncture. Engaging with the kinds of experiences that young women, for example, have is a valuable methodological strategy, which advances our understanding of the 'complex and changing discursive processes by which identities are ascribed, resisted, or embraced and which processes themselves are unremarked, indeed achieve their effect because they aren't noticed' (Scott, 1992: 33). In Chapter 3 it was argued that femininity has increasingly been reconstructed through discourses of individuality, such that the cultural ideals of choice, independence, and self-determination have not only become more possible for women, but also are increasingly operating in a normative and regulative fashion. Discourses associated with feminism, post-feminism, neoliberalism, and individualism all contribute to the incitement of women to make themselves into particular kinds of subjects, in a process that is far from straightforward. It has been argued that, in practice, idealized femininity cannot be pursued without encountering a series of difficult contradictions and ambivalences, and that the effects of these encounters are lived out in complex ways. Neoliberal discourses require that the 'ideal person embrace both emotional openness or flexibility and ambitions for autonomy', but the demands made by traditional gender norms, which associate femininity with care and affective ties, do not coalesce easily with processes of female individualization, which orient women towards autonomy (Gonick, 2004: 191). A wide range of empirical studies dedicated to exploring how young women are negotiating contemporary gender relations and the impact that this process has upon their identities indicate that, as young women attempt to make themselves into idealized feminine subjects, they are faced with managing a series of often irreconcilable demands (Baker, 2008; Gonick, 2006; McRobbie, 2009; Nielsen, 2004; Rich, 2005).

These studies are important to consider in relation to the category of experience as deployed in the third wave feminist literature because they make visible some of the dynamics by which particular subjects come into being, particularly with regards to an intensifying ideology of individualism and to its connection to the normative construction of successful femininity. In these studies the experiences of young women are interrogated and important questions are asked about which experiences are associated with late modern *successful* feminine subjectivities; how the construction of those experiences contributes to the practice of self-governance; and why these experiences are far from unproblematic. This critical intervention reveals that third wave feminism needs to approach gendered experience as produced by the discursive dynamics of late modernity with a critical edge and that a failure to do so leaves the category of experience at best unexamined and at worst naturalized. The link that has been made between new, culturally imagined, 'empowered femininities' and modes of governance that give rise to the experience of freedom render suspect some of the celebratory claims that have been made about experience in the third wave literature.

Negotiating femininity

Gonick (2004, 2007) has explored the strategies that young women from diverse racial and ethnic backgrounds perform within a discursive space that requires them to draw upon a range of cultural meanings currently in circulation to actively construct a feminine identity. In this analysis the modern imperative of identity to 'become somebody' places demands upon young women that, at the beginning of the twenty-first century, undermine the previously required repression of their desire and ambition (Gonick, 2004: 198). To 'become somebody' is to express a self that is separate and self-determining. However, the dynamics of identity formation are such that the self can only be established through recognition by others, and, by implication, through the bestowal of social approval. By examining a series of stories constructed by young women, Gonick was able to analyse the extent to which an awareness that contradictory discourses govern femininity was present amongst young women. Not only did they construct accounts of femininity that expressed a tension between being self-determining yet loyal to family expectations, but also they were aware of how this dilemma impacted upon their own lives.

As one of the participants explained, the narrative in her story was about a girl who does 'not know how to be good without being bad' (Gonick, 2007: 441). The self that emerges is one that is defined by the multiple tensions of self-definition and social recognition. The intersubjective nature of achieving selfhood complicates young women's lives because to be a 'good girl' places them on 'an inescapable collision course with the contradictory demands of becoming an individual through belonging' – whether the sites where young women seek to belong be family, community, school, or peer culture (Gonick, 2004: 205). Similar tensions carried into their construction of sexuality and into the pressure to reconcile the old-fashioned values of their parents and a newly emergent discourse, which incites young women to constitute themselves as active sexual agents. Agency, desire, and femininity intertwined in their narratives in such a way that new articulations of female sexuality were made possible; but these expressions were made manifest in often ambivalent ways. Whereas overt sexuality for women is no longer strictly associated with illegitimate forms of female sexuality and is regulated to a lesser extent by the use of derogatory labels such as 'slag', elements of normalizing discourses remain in circulation. The young women in this study, therefore, struggled to define the central character in their stories both in terms of traditional characteristics such as vulnerability and in relation to a more proactive approach to romance and heterosexual desire.

In a study that also reveals how tensions between old and new gender discourses circulate, Nielsen (2004) traces the features of emergent forms of female subjectivity by examining how three generations of Norwegian women construct narratives that, each, express very different forms of selfhood. This study reveals how 'becoming modern' has been a contradictory and often complex process for women. Whereas femininity in traditional gender discourses precluded the possibility of women taking up the position of individuality, in the contemporary context neoliberal discourses require young women to reflect upon their lives and to take responsibility for formulating and articulating a unique and autonomous identity. In one of the case studies, the women from the oldest generation, born in 1911, tended to orient their identities towards relationships, with family in particular occupying a central place. Responsibility, too, was defined in terms of external demands and expectations. For the middle generation, born in 1944, it was evident that a shift had begun to take place, as increasing reflexivity re-oriented these women inwardly, making them focus more upon their individual sense of self. This increasing concern with one's own identity, however, was held in tension with relationships to others. In the youngest generation, born in 1972, a very different relationship to the self was apparent. In this generation young women clearly positioned themselves as individuals, their independence being secured by practising their identities according to the adage of 'being true to oneself'.

Each generation must deal with the socio-historical contradictions that constitute femininity, but the content and form of those contradictions varies across each generation. This is illustrated by Nielsen's analysis of sexuality. The shift that Nielsen describes is largely about the ways in which women have been able to become active subjects of desire. As Nielsen argues (2004: 14), 'being positioned as an individual is not only a question of more or less; it is rather a brand new identity form seen in relation to the nineteenth-century gender dualism that framed men as individuals and women as a members of gender'. For the oldest generation in this study, sexual morality was practised through the management of reputation, in accordance with rules of respectability defined by external authorities. The sexual conduct of 'cheap girls', who fell foul of these boundaries, provided the 'other', against which the status of women who adhered carefully to the prescribed sexual code was secured. For the middle generation, however, the presence of such public norms to guide conduct was not so pronounced, and sexual codes of conduct had become more a matter of personal responsibility. Without the availability of clear boundaries, this generation claimed that they often found navigating sexuality a confusing experience. Older discourses were still in operation, but they intermingled with emerging norms of individual freedom of choice and responsibility. In contrast, Nielsen argues that the youngest generation have *become* individuals and subjects of desire in ways that disconnect this position from its prior attachment to masculine subjectivity (Nielsen, 2004: 14). Sexual conduct is no longer determined by codes explicitly associated with gender – those external codes that designate what a 'good girl' versus a 'cheap girl' would do. Sexual mores, for this generation, were expressed in highly individualized terms, indicating that decisions about how to conduct sexuality lay with the authority of individual choice; however, sexuality was still regulated through the othering of 'exposed' girls. Instead of claiming their sexuality as individuals, these were girls who 'allowed' themselves to be positioned as sexual objects for the *desire of others*, thus failing to meet the standards of modern subjecthood through the loss of autonomy that this orientation towards external approval brings.

Many of the complications that these young women encountered derived from the continued persistence of gender hierarchies in which women are positioned as objects despite their refusal of this status. Their experience may be characterized as the assertion of their 'own choice', but this is an experience located within a context in which that agency is constrained by conditions that are not of their own choosing; therefore the newly individualized identities of young women are by implication marked by highly ambivalent moments. For example, Nielsen (2004: 20) argues that, in her study, this ambivalence surrounded young women's experiences of embodiment. Adhering to certain aspects of femininity was experienced as pleasurable, for instance in the ways in which femininity was reproduced on the body, through fashion; but caring *too much* about these pursuits jeopardized self-containment. An overt preoccupation with one's appearance, clothes, make-up, and diet was deemed to be indicative of seeking approval from others and was associated with what these young women interpreted as 'the shame of the dependent girl'. Nevertheless, the interest and effort invested in appearance and bodily appearance could be made consistent with the construction of an independent identity, because contemporary discourses of individualization made it possible for these young women to construct their relationship to dieting, exercise, and a concern with appearance as a positive one, one that delivered feelings of creativity and control and 'a feeling of being in a position to create one's real self' (ibid.). Engagement in bodily practices presented an avenue for self-expression; but, to maintain a consistent narrative of self-empowerment, the tremendous amount of self-control needed to achieve cultural body ideals was interpreted as enabling, while the constraints that such a project introduced into young women's daily lives were downplayed. This analysis reveals the highly intricate balance this younger generation sought to achieve between how they felt they *ought* to identify themselves and how they *actually* identified themselves (Nielsen, 2004: 21).

The paradoxes that accompany the formation of female identity are also evident in Baker's (2008) study of fifty-five women in Australia, aged 18–25, from diverse racial and socio-economic backgrounds, with differing levels of educational attainment and varied experiences of motherhood. The aim of the study was to understand how the young women constructed key events in their lives and how they experienced external influences that impacted on their hopes, aspirations, and fears for the future. In general, Baker found that these women shared an optimistic and positive outlook, which they felt was justified by the significant expansion of freedoms and opportunities women have won in the past 40 years. Gender inequality was largely seen to be a thing of the past and male advantage in the present social context was discounted. One of the effects of this understanding was apparent in the participants' tendency to adopt a position of gender neutrality or equivalency when it came to incorporating gender into their own identities. This was evident in assertions that being a man or a woman was no longer as relevant as just being an individual. Baker notes that these positions were established by many of these young women in the face of evidence that clearly suggested that their own lives contained considerable levels of gender-related violence and inequality, particularly in the context of performing childcare and domestic labour.

A belief that gender inequality no longer conditioned women's lives and that women's lives were now largely self-governed meant that these young women invested heavily in a form of self-identity that was distanced from associations with weakness or compliance. As in Nielsen's (2004) study, femininity was often conflated with victimhood, hence the denial of gender was a significant point of reference in the construction of the women's own identities. By emphasizing the centrality of individual choice, these young women articulated the belief that, now that opportunities were available to women, individual effort and ability would bring success within a set of conditions that they saw as being governed by meritocratic principles. Consistent with this belief, the ideology of choice was used to account for others' lack of success, and evidence of social inequality was interpreted as the product of making 'bad' choices. Gender disadvantage, which was experienced in their own relationships with men, was also placed within the frame of individual choice and agency. This strategy was used to bolster individualized identities; to deny structural inequality; and to assert autonomy. So, rather than appear weak, many young women accounted for the visible inequality in their relationships as the result of a choice, for example in situations where doing more than their share of the housework was 'chosen' to avoid conflict with their male partners. As Baker argues, it is more accurate to describe this behaviour as acquiescence to prevailing norms than as a matter of choice or consent (2008: 58).

In Rich's (2005) study of how a group of highly achieving white women in their early 20s produced their identities in relation to a variety of competing and contradictory discourses that promote particular understandings of gender relations, self-identity, and social inequality, many similar themes emerge. Rich (2005: 496) argues that there are at least four major discourses that young women are positioned within, and that these often overlap in ways that problematize femininity. Second wave feminism stress universal equality of access for women. Post-feminist discourses stress that this equality has been achieved and that, if inequality exists, it is largely up to the individual to find a solution. This attitude towards gender inequality sits comfortably alongside the discourse of individualism, which stresses individuality, freedom of choice, and rationality. Finally, traditional gendered discourses also operate in this context and emphasize gendered binaries, biological assumptions about gender difference, and naturalized heterosexuality. These four discourses make a wide range of meanings available to women as they attempt to articulate their own identities, but these meanings are not easily reconcilable, which means having to manage different subject positions simultaneously.

The women in Rich's study constructed narratives that heavily emphasized the value of individual choice. Their strong sense of agency denied the presence of any external controls, and this was tied to a belief that gender in particular no longer operated as a relevant factor in their lives. For working-class women, the narrative of individual choice translated into a discourse of social mobility in which individuals were rewarded for their hard work and perseverance. Gender entered into these narratives through comparisons of their lives with those of previous generations of women in their families, who were seen to be less successful in educational and occupational attainments. Through the deployment of this comparative framework, gender inequality and structural constraint were relegated to the past, while the present was characterized by a range of equally available opportunities. The subject under construction in the narratives of the middle-class participants was also one that was unencumbered by gender inequality. However, in these narratives comparisons with previous generations of women were not made, and there was an even stronger belief that gender had not made, nor should it make, any difference to who the women are or to the life choices available to them (Rich, 2005: 499). While gender was denied as a structuring force in their lives, various discourses of gender nonetheless entered into their own narratives and shaped them in complex ways. For example, to maintain consistency in their narratives and to support their belief in individual agency, an active distancing from the status of 'victim' was evident. This materialized as disdain for women who might be perceived as weak, this weakness being seen as the reason why *other* young women failed to take advantage of the choices now available to them. The 'weak' women, referred to by one participant as 'girly girls', were denigrated for being *too feminine,* and therefore traditional stereotypes of feminine passivity were invoked. While gender was denied as a factor that influenced them as individuals, they used implicitly gendered binaries and familiar gendered storylines to position themselves in relation to other women, particularly those they perceived as lacking agency (Rich, 2005: 502).

While these women attempted to locate themselves outside of the structures of gender, they often found themselves securely positioned by others within them. Many of the participants reported experiences which indicated that normative expectations associated with femininity were used to police and regulate them. For instance, the women in the study participated in non-traditional sport and physical education, and often found that their identities were not granted legitimacy by others because their successful performance in these sporting activities did not conform to traditional gendered expectations. Thus they had to negotiate a double bind, by asserting their individuality while retaining certain aspects or signifiers of traditional femininity to receive social recognition for their identities. Femininity had to be managed through such things as bodily comportment, dress, and facial expressions. As Rich (2008: 505) explains, 'the women were much aware of having to tread an extremely thin line between not being victims, exercising their agency and choice, and remaining "feminine"'.

These studies illustrate the often complex requirements demanded by emergent forms of femininity. The difficulty, and indeed impossibility, of reconciling what are often contradictory interpellations has a series of significant implications for the ways in which women construct their identities. Furthermore, the effects of these negotiations raise important questions about the relationship between feminism and gender in late modernity. Third wave feminism argues for starting from women's experiences and proposes a number of strategies for re-articulating feminism through the varied contradictory discourses discussed here. What is less evident in third wave feminist personal theorizing is how to think critically about the effects of structurally ambivalent gender identities.

Dynamics of disavowal

As Gonick (2004: 206) argues, idealized 'successful' femininity is constituted by conflicting demands for relationality and autonomy. The experience caused by this tension is often one of confusion and distress for young women, who find relief by denying that an incongruity exists. The performance of this denial results in a disavowal or splitting off of parts of the self, which exacts both a psychic and social cost. In the process affective ties are compromised, as coherence in one's self-narrative is preserved by one's separating off from the traditions of families and communities. In the research of Walkerdine et al. (2001), Walkerdine (2003), and Rich (2005), these dynamics often produced ambivalence for young women from working-class backgrounds. Living out the effects of neoliberalism requires the construction of a consistent narrative of achievement that obliges young women to position themselves against or 'beyond' their parents and families, who are associated with traditional gender arrangements. In Rich's (2005: 501) study, young women from working-class backgrounds claimed independence and embraced the social mobility associated with discourses of individualization, while they portrayed their own mothers as lacking agency and independence – representing, as was the case for one participant, 'the pathetic female'.

Misrecognition of inequality

The individualizing tendencies of a post-feminist social constellation have contributed to the tendency for differential levels of both success and failure to be lived as matters of personal responsibility and ability to make choices correctly (Baker, 2008; Walkerdine, 2003). This places tremendous demands upon individuals to work out a strategy for ensuring success while avoiding personal failure. In practice the young women in Baker's study often expressed ambivalence about how they might achieve this, but, rather than recognize the impossibility of the social demands being placed upon them, these young women blamed themselves for being poor decision-makers and for lacking the critical ability to be decisive. Baker suggests: 'there is a poor fit between young women's decision-making experiences and the abstract voluntarism, autonomous, goal seeking and purposive behavior of the masculinist rational choice theory underpinning neo-liberalism' (Baker, 2008: 61).

The emphasis upon choice sets us an illusory relationship to social contexts by implying that, by constructing oneself as autonomous, one can choose to stand outside the conditions of one's own regulation (Gonick, 2004). The inability to engage with discourses such as feminism, which allow for a social rather than individual explanation for inequality, works to secure women's participation in their own oppression. In Baker's study, when the participants encountered injustice, 'an articulation of the often profoundly gendered or racialized nature of their situation' was 'rejected in preference for a focus on the role of personal determination and extracting a positive outcome from an unjust experience' (Baker, 2008: 60). Rather than challenge the conditions that produced social disadvantage, the young women narrated their experiences of disadvantage as opportunities to display personal strength and resilience. Baker concludes: 'notions of neo-liberal choice and assumptions about de-traditionalization and liberation converge to create new modes of subordination which work at a psychological level' (Baker, 2008: 62).

Impossible identifications

Rich (2005) also found that, while the young women in her study asserted equality in their lives and resisted the various forms of inequality they encountered, they were very reluctant to align themselves with feminism. They associated feminism with disadvantage and male domination and, by implication, making a positive association with feminism would 'rupture a powerful sense of self-determination so intimately bound with the discourse of individualization' (Rich, 2005: 504). Feminism, coded as 'unfeminine', also represented a threat to the traditional aspects of femininity that, if adopted, granted these young women access to social recognition. Having the desire to be assertive, but not too demanding, meant that these young women had to tread

> an extremely thin line between not being victims, exercising their agency and choice, and remaining "feminine". The ambiguity they have to manage therefore is trying to distance their identities from feminist labels, whilst at the same time attempting to maintain a "system of equality" and the ability to exercise individual rights. (Rich, 2008: 505)

While the endorsement of gender equality has become the norm in contemporary Western society, research carried out by Volman and Ten Dam (1998) illustrates the ongoing significance of gender differences and how the role these play in structuring social interaction confounds the norm of equality. The secondary school students in their study rarely constructed gender in terms of inequality, and yet they often adhered to quite conventional notions of gender difference when providing explanations for boys' and girls' performance in specific subjects such as information technology and computing literacy. The girls in particular were aware of gender specific behaviour in the use of computers, and many were able to offer social and historical explanations for why boys were more attracted to computers than girls – one girl remarked, for example, that computer games tended to be about male characters and therefore were of less relevance to girls. Despite expressing this level of understanding of how gender difference is produced through social processes, when the subject of difference was *explicitly* introduced into the interviews, the majority of students strongly denied that ability or skill differed in girls and in boys.

On the one hand, it was evident that the experience these students had of specific subjects such as computing was organized through traditional notions of gender difference. On the other hand, they adhered to a belief in gender equality and had to work quite hard to maintain this belief in the face of the gender differences that they witnessed. The students were unable to distinguish between the differences expressed in the *descriptive* statements they made about gender and the differences expressed in *normative* statements; they refused to identify gender differences openly because they thought that gender differences, understood as inequality, should not exist (Volman and Ten Dam, 1998: 542).

> The key contradiction faced by these students is that multiple forms of masculinity and femininity exist, but the legitimacy of difference between gender groups that implies inequality is under pressure, whereas equality in the sense of sameness is unthinkable. (Volman and Ten Dam, 1998: 539)

Gendered character ideals

These studies demonstrate that the destabilization of traditional gender norms within contemporary cultures of individualized selfhood has differential effects on young women and young men. McLeod (2002) argues that the subjectivities made possible by individualization are not gender neutral, because 'in cultures saturated with knowledge of gender difference, and particularly the feminization of affect and "relationships", such therapeutic techniques of the self are going to resonate differently for girls and boys' (McLeod, 2002: 214). The new character ideals dictated by neoliberal discourses may be somewhat easier for young women to achieve, because these new identities for women coincide with both feminist ideals of emancipation and neoliberal discourses, which simplistically link success and individual effort. Young women can serve as metaphors for social mobility and transformation in a discourse of gender equality and progress (Ringrose, 2007, Harris, 2004a, McRobbie, 2004, quoted in Harris, 2004a). For young women, freedom of choice signals social progress and the possibility of being able to do something different from what was possible in the past. It is questionable whether young men are similarly incited to 'choose' to reconcile individuality with the requirements of relationality and care for others. The limits of the demands placed upon young men by the gender emancipation discourse may not go beyond acknowledging that they should not discriminate against women (Volman and Ten Dam, 1998: 542).

There is some evidence that the expansion of the affective dimension of the public sphere is considered to have differential effects on young women and on young men. Whereas female success is celebrated, this very success is seen to be materializing at the expense of young men, who are disadvantaged by the 'feminization' of educational and workplace settings, and this results in a moral panic over 'failing boys' (Burman, 2005; Phoenix, 2003; Ringrose, 2007). This discourse relies upon narrow and simplistic measures of success by setting up a uniform category of 'girls' in opposition to a uniform category of 'boys'. This gendered binary of success/failure obscures the complicated intersection of categories of social class, 'race', and ethnicity: when examined more closely, the latter reveals that that it is only *some* girls who are currently outperforming *some* boys, and that the ways in which the category of gender is articulated with other axes of identity renders a more accurate analysis of educational achievement.

Positive subjectivities: Realigning gender relations

Gender discourses are being re-articulated in ways that are continuous with previous gender inequalities; but alongside these effects discontinuities are also evident. This has led some commentators to suggest that gendered subjectivities also present opportunities for young women to think about their lives in ways not possible for previous generations of women, particularly with regard to the exercise of female agency (Budgeon, 2001; Duits and van Zoonen, 2007: 161).

> Pride in what women have achieved, conviction about one's rights and confidence in the legitimacy of one's choices may not always seem appropriate to us, but are nevertheless potentially-empowering elements in the gender identities of girls in our research group. (Volman and Ten Dam, 1998: 541)

A certain degree of caution is needed in delivering a wholly negative evaluation of the ambivalent nature of contradictory femininities and of the reconciliation of these competing demands through the ideal of 'choice'. While the ideology of choice operates within neoliberal systems of governance in pernicious and limiting ways, 'choice' is also a concept that underpins feminist critiques of the limitations traditionally associated with femininity. From the perspective of third wave feminism, the experience of negotiating choice complicates identities, offering opportunities for a feminist self-transformation. This conviction begs the question of how to work productively with the category of experience. Scott (1992: 37) advises against doing away with the word 'experience' despite the tendency for it to be used in ways that essentialize identities and reify subjects. It is simply too central to the ways in which individuals produce knowledge and render everyday life meaningful. Therefore, we should seek to understand the politics of its construction by asking how particular experiences are produced, but also what experiences women have and why (Ramazanoglu and Holland, 2002).

Conclusion

Siegel (1997a: 57) suggests that autobiographical writings are best analysed as part of the rhetorical project of third wave feminism and that, to understand their significance, we must read them as emerging out of 'concrete material situations' and out of 'a series of historically specific contradictions'. The analysis of new femininities in this chapter reveals that the identities many young women are constructing within the contemporary gender order share several of the characteristics also associated with third wave autobiographical writings – characteristics that include a sense of individuality, agency, and empowerment. In addition, these studies reveal that a significant level of ambivalence is produced in the pursuit of idealized femininity in late modernity. These texts provide a point of entry into the contradictions that constitute the contemporary post-feminist constellation. Empirical evidence indicates that these contradictions are producing a subject position for young women that is difficult to negotiate; furthermore, these dynamics thwart positive identifications being made with feminism. What can third wave feminism bring to this analysis, emphasizing as it does the centrality of personal experience, individuality, and ambivalence?

Personal theorizing can invite an examination of the rhetorical deployment of subjectivity in a way that draws critical attention to its discursive and social construction. The aim is to inquire after the construction of the first person within the rhetoric of one's argument, so that subjectivity is politicized rather than simply authenticated. As Bernstein explains, 'rather than a plaintive quest for an authentic female voice mirroring some interior or exterior "truth", confessing feminist theory – used with reflexive analytic caution – can explore the politics of subject construction' (1992: 142). To work productively with individual experience, third wave feminism should aim to move beyond affirming experiences by making them visible. The aim is to go further and interrogate why young women are having particular experiences. In particular, a framework for understanding how experiences might be transformed into more politicized subjectivities is lacking. This requires that personal narratives are used in 'primarily a questioning mode, one that imposes self-vigilance on the process of subject positioning both in language and discourse and at a specific historical moment or a particular cultural space [...] reflexive confession registers its own complicity with the institutions that structure its representation' (Bernstein, 1992: 140). Adopting this strategy acknowledges the importance of taking a critical approach to third wave feminism's own representational practices rather than presenting the experiences of young women as 'more real' than their representation in established second wave discourses. Greater reflexivity and self-critique also guard against reducing feminism to a personalized expression and demand engagement with a series of critical questions. How does third wave feminism propose to move from individual 'truth telling' to a sustained analysis of what social conditions needs to change? How is this to be achieved? How might practices of self-reflection become transformative of social relations? In Chapter 5, the production of experience and identities discussed in this chapter will be examined in relation to the 'politics of subjectivity' promoted by third wave feminism.

5
A Politics of the Self

On the one hand, third wave feminism includes in its list of political concerns many issues that clearly are discernible as established feminist issues. These are 'racism, child abuse, rape, domestic violence, homophobia and heterosexism, ablism, fatism, environmental degradation, classism, and the protection of healthcare rights, reproductive rights, and equity' (Garrison, 2000: 143). On the other hand, the relationship of third wave political practice to many established forms of feminist political organization and activism is one of dissonance, because third wave feminism sits uneasily with a politics based upon making a common identification with the category 'woman'. The emphasis within third wave feminism is on the myriad positionings occupied by women, which produce different experiences of these issues. While third wave feminism identifies substantive areas of concern for a feminist politics, the relationship that any individual woman has to these concerns will be defined in terms that escape homogenization. This recognition requires a politics based upon the dynamics of social and cultural difference rather than a politics organized through the expression of commonalities. It is also a politics that is located in the spaces of everyday life rather than in formal political institutions.

> One way that the third wave distinguishes itself from the second wave is through its emphasis on paradox, conflict, multiplicity and messiness. This generation's feminism is often informed by postmodern, poststructuralist theories of identity; as a result, we are able to see the constructed nature of identity as well as

the ways in which gender may be a performance that can be manipulated and politically altered as it is performed. Because this theoretical framework calls into question the very idea of a unified self, it allows for a playful incorporation of performed identities, even when they contradict one another. (Dicker and Piepmeier, 2003: 16)

This quotation expresses three core assumptions underpinning third wave political practices. The present chapter is concerned with examining these assumptions more closely, together with their implications for third wave politics. The first assumption is that identity categories are complex and contradictory, as they are constituted within conditions of indeterminacy and, as such, are characterized by ambivalence and hybridity. Secondly, these conditions allow for the possibility that dominant meanings attaching to identity categories like gender can be re-appropriated and reworked so as to resist and subvert hegemonic definitions of femininity. These practices attempt to problematize the stability of oppressive gender norms by re-coding or reconfiguring their meaning. Thirdly, a privileged site for this politics of resignification is individual identity projects.

Some of the features of third wave feminist politics will be explored to offer a critical account of four related issues. Firstly, in a politics that relies upon the appropriation of dominant representational practices, it may be the case that not all terms are equally open to appropriation and reversal. A second and related issue is that the context of any particular re-appropriation will influence the efficacy of that re-appropriation as a form of counter-hegemonic practice. Thirdly, a critical approach to using resignification as a form of political practice should consider the relationship between the individual agent's intention and the extent to which this intention guarantees the effects of any particular act of re-appropriation. Finally, it should be considered whether states of ambivalence necessarily create a progressive space, one that opens out the possibility for innovative and resistant elaborations of identity. Third wave feminism emphasizes conditions of indeterminacy; however, the degree to which the sites where power operates are 'open' is debated alongside questions about the direction in which this openness may be resolved. Some of these solutions may be progressive from the point of view of advancing women's interests, but the logic of appropriation may also operate to resolve ambivalence in ways that consolidate anti-feminist positions and bolster neoliberal forms of selfhood.

Third wave feminism begins from the position that the relationship between feminism and women's lives can only be understood by acknowledging women's wide-ranging differences (Heywood and Drake, 1997: 9). Third wave feminists explain that, because they have come of age in a society that is transgender, bisexual, and interracial, they 'have trouble formulating and perpetuating theories that compartmentalize and divide according to race and gender and all other signifiers' (Walker, 1995: xxxiii). This is a world constituted through hybridity, in which 'lines between Us and Them are often blurred', making identities 'that accommodate ambiguity and our multiple positionalities' a necessity' (ibid.). Because these social conditions complicate identity formation, Reed (1997: 124) argues, 'one of the strengths of third wave feminism is its refusal of the singular liberal–humanist subjectivity'. Heywood and Drake (1997: 3) echo this refusal when they explain that the impossibility of escaping contradictions 'marks the desires and strategies of third wave feminism'.

Given the emphasis on the multiple and unpredictable positions that constitute women's identity, third wave feminism tends to place particular emphasis on the principle of inclusivity in defining how a feminist practice or identity might be defined. Third wave feminism seeks to work with a proliferation of feminine subjectivities and multiplying forms of feminist affiliation, including 'power feminism'; 'victim feminism'; black feminism; women-of-colour feminism; working-class feminism; and pro-sex feminism (Heywood and Drake, 1997: 3).

> Since no monolithic version of 'woman' exists, we can no longer speak with confidence of 'women's issues'; instead we need to consider that such issues are as diverse as the many women who inhabit our planet [...]. (Dicker and Piepmeier, 2003: 10)

Multiplicity is endorsed often at the expense of definitional consistency or reliability, which had led many critics to accuse third wave feminism of lacking a concrete political agenda that can be backed up by serious strategies for political engagement. In defense against this criticism, it is argued that the positive effect of opening out definitional boundaries is an increased awareness of, and recognition of, the spaces within which feminist identities are now being practiced in everyday life. It is argued that, because there are numerous ways in which one may be a feminist, there can be no one 'right' way of being one. As Walker states (1995: xxvi), 'there are an infinite number of moments and experiences that make up female empowerment'. This pronouncement invites questions regarding what the term 'empowerment' might mean within a late modern post-feminist social constellation and how the potential for any such claim is circumscribed by the dynamics of power that constitute this constellation. Third wave practices are informed by a 'prevailing awareness that the world is increasingly complicated by the intricate workings of power, and we are all too implicated by its web to fit into the model of a perfect feminism, which is, of course a fictitious construct' (Purvis, 2004: 105). Because power is seen to be dispersed, feminism both accesses and deploys power, even as it encounters oppositional power relations and forces. Many of the strategies for resistance advocated rely upon moving away 'from thinking and acting in terms of systems, structures, fixed power relations, and thereby also "suppression" – toward highlighting the complexities, contingencies and, challenges of power and the diverse means and goals of agency' (Krolokke and Sorensen, 2005: 21).

The theme of 'empowerment' runs through third wave discourse, drawing both upon second wave critiques of gender inequality *and* upon a postfeminist discourse that downplays gender inequality and emphasizes the establishment of individualized female success instead.[1] The simultaneous influence of second wave feminism and post-feminism is key to interpreting third wave politics. Proponents of third wave have come of age in a context where 'feminist *language* is part of the public dialogue, but authentic feminist *struggles* are not accounted for in that dialogue except in terms articulated by the mainstream, which still perpetuates a conservative and sexist status quo' (Kinser, 2004: 135) As explained by Dicker and Piepmeier (2003: 11), third wave feminism is likely to differ from second wave feminism in its aims and style of politics, because 'those of us who have reached adulthood in the late twentieth century have grown up in a world not only shaped by feminism but also saturated with backlash rhetoric and politics'. As such, third wave feminism is founded upon an experience of 'hard fought feminist gains as fundamental rights, without recognizing the efforts that went into securing those rights' (ibid.). This analysis of gender inequality is complicated by the experience of growing up with a 'sense of entitlement' largely due to the successes of second wave feminism (Findlen, 1995: xii). Alongside their awareness of gender inequality, third wavers encounter complex depoliticizing discourses, which dismiss the need for feminism in favour of encouraging women to embrace their 'empowerment'. Not surprisingly, third wave analyses of gendered power relations are often uneven as the attempt is made to argue that gendered dynamics of power and resistance have been reconstituted – but not necessarily in ways that are consistent with the excesses of a post-feminist position that discounts the relevance of gender politics.

As will be discussed further in Chapter 7, third wave narratives regularly construct the relationship to second wave feminism in terms of generational difference, the result being a relationship fraught with associations of obligation, debt, and failed legacies. While the use of a generational metaphor has been comprehensively criticized for inadequately capturing the relationship between the so-called 'waves', the reference to familial symbolism can be useful for understanding the emphasis that is placed on the struggle for self-definition in third wave discourses. Within a familial staging of feminist generations, feminism always has a presence that makes itself known as a pre-existing set of identifications, practices, and political positions (Orr, 1997: 42). For a younger generation of women, therefore, feminism initially exists not as something of their making but as something they must come to terms with as they negotiate their own identities. Figuring out the contours of a feminism that isn't simply adopted but allows for the expression of one's own experience has become a rite of passage that signals the coming of age for younger women. This negotiation is now taking place in a social context where discourses of selfhood have become pervasive and both feminism and post-feminism have become established elements of that discursive context. Third wave feminism offers insights into how the presence of feminism and of resistance to it finds its way into the production of young women's identities.

Third wave politics proceeds from the claim that women's oppression is not systematic enough to produce a uniform structural position, a similar experience of oppression, and a shared identity. As such, a 'foundational project of naming shared themes' has become too complicated for third wavers to pursue with any confidence, and the kinds of issues that third wave feminism casts as politically relevant do not necessarily translate as 'women's issues' in a straightforward way (Siegel, 1997b: 57). Rather than rely upon a shared identity that is the effect of structural relations, third wave discourses conceive identity as a complex project, which individuals engage with knowingly, by drawing upon a range of cultural resources. Because these are selves defined through difference, the politics of third wave feminism is constituted through practices that not only allow for the expression of difference, but invite further complication through an acceptance of ambivalence and paradox.

Populism and cultural activism

At the same time as feminism increasingly became institutionalized in the 1990s, early third wave writers tended to place an emphasis on the practice of feminism outside of the academy, within a populist politics that was made accessible to young women through a range of everyday sites (Orr, 1997: 41). The cultural politics of third wave feminism focuses on both the production of activist cultures and the consumption and re-appropriation of popular texts and representations to challenge dominant constructions of femininity. This is a distinctly different feminist project, but it builds upon and selectively uses aspects of second wave feminism in pursuing a broadly defined political project. For instance, Heywood and Drake (1997) argue that third wave feminism embraces second wave critiques of beauty regimes, popular culture, and sexual politics, but does so at the same time as equally embracing the pleasures and desires associated with participating in practices that form the object of feminist critique. This inconsistency is illustrative of a core assumption – namely that new forms of femininity are fractured by an ambivalence that may be used as a resource in forging resistant identities. Since there is no 'pure' definition either of the category 'woman' or of feminist,[2] there can be no 'real' feminist identity that transcends the culture within which it is produced. Identity projects have only the cultural resources within which they are embedded as tools for resistance. This is a practice in which the objects of feminist critique – such as sexist representations of women's bodies – are knowingly re-appropriated and reworked in counter-hegemonic ways. This creates a brand of activism that may not be recognizable as feminist to those who would require that third wave feminism have greater consistency with previously established definitions of 'feminism'. However, these apparently contradictory practices are a central site where third wave feminist politics are enacted. It is envisioned that, through various forms of self-expression, feminist agency is continually created within and across cultural sites, and that these expressions are enactments of resistance.

Feminism and popular culture

Feminism has a long-standing interest in how women use popular culture in ways that undermine traditional gender norms. Feminist cultural critique has challenged the tendency to denigrate 'mass culture' for its association with the feminine and has drawn attention to the need to take seriously ordinary 'feminine' cultural forms. These analyses have not only highlighted the largely invisible character of many of these practices, but have also yielded insight into their complexity. Far from being sites of unilateral patriarchal domination, many of the activities associated with feminine popular culture reveal that the meanings produced in the act of consumption are contradictory and as such offer moments of protest and resistance by generating of a critical awareness of gender relations. Examples include McRobbie's (1991) critical response to analyses of youth sub-cultures in the 1970s, which omitted young women and instead tended to construct sub-cultural rebellion as a masculine pursuit. The exclusion of young women from these practices was, she argued, the result of women's differential access to sub-cultural spaces. The distinction between public, masculine spheres and the private, feminine sphere structured both the opportunities for participation and the types of relations that young women sought to resist. McRobbie's research on the private, and hence invisible, 'bedroom cultures' of young women illustrated that, far from being absent from sub-cultural activities, young women produced their own distinctive responses to their gendered, classed, and generational experience. McRobbie's research into cultures of femininity revealed that, when young women participated in these sites, they were often able to 'win space' for themselves as they negotiated the norms and ideologies associated with femininity. The product of this negotiation was often the reproduction of a gender ideology that prepared young women for the traditional role of wives and mothers, yet McRobbie's work also showed that young women's practices did not simply conform to external expectations but often challenged gender orthodoxies and allowed for moments of resistance (Hollows, 2000: 166). Similarly, Modleski's (1984) and Radway's (1987) research on activities associated with women's consumption of romance fiction drew attention to the resources that feminine popular cultural forms make available to women in the private sphere. Their research challenged dominant conceptualizations of women's practices as a form of passive consumption to examine the intricate workings of women's agency. These studies revealed that women's reading practices were often performed in ways that subverted passive acceptance of the gender *status quo* and, far from acting as spaces where gender ideology was consumed uncritically, romance fiction generated opportunities for women to reflect upon their discontent and to think about their lives differently.

Whereas this tradition of feminist cultural analysis rendered perceptible invisible but resistant practices, the visibility of young women within popular culture has intensified significantly since the early 1990s. Accordingly, a shift has taken place in feminist analyses, away from uncovering covert strategies of female resistance and towards documenting more active and overt expressions of feminist sensibilities, made present for example in the form of female-positive hip hop and Riot Grrrl music space, both of which signalled 'that young women were creating their own publicly visible subcultures or that more fluid gender systems were being developed within youth cultures' (Harris, 2008: 6). This has taken place alongside the rise of a more general socio-cultural interest in young womanhood, which McRobbie argues has arisen as feminist values are being incorporated into 'a range of institutions including law, education, to an extent medicine, likewise employment, and the media', and whereby the 'high profile or newsworthy achievement of women and girls in these sectors shows the institutions to be modern and abreast with social change' (McRobbie, 2004b: 257). This highly visible discourse of female success aligns with the construction of young women as a powerful consumer group; and, as Harris (2003: 40–41) points out, 'while young, attractive women have always been used to sell products, a particular young, assertive and sassy woman has become an advertising icon' and 'girl power' has 'seen girlhood transformed from the evocation of passive innocence to a potential for knowing and acting'.

The increased visibility of young women within popular culture has not taken place in a wholly consistent fashion, either in terms of challenging or perpetuating gender hierarchies. Indeed the terrain of popular culture is increasingly complicated by the multifaceted representational practices through which idealized femininity circulates and, unlike in the 1970s and 1980s, when feminism occupied a much more oppositional space in relation to the mainstream, it has now become a part of the cultural realm of everyday life. Feminist values are present across a wide range of sites, including advertising, talk shows, television programmes, popular cinema, websites, and magazine articles. What makes this terrain particularly complicated is that, with this movement of feminism into the mainstream, the demarcation between feminism and femininity has been problematized and, along with it, questions have arisen about what constitutes a feminist representation of femininity and whether an 'authentic' feminist space is possible and/or indeed desirable. Gill (2007a, 2007b) argues that we are witnessing a particularly distinctive articulation of gender within the media, which is characteristic of a 'postfeminist sensibility'. Because feminism has not been incorporated into the cultural field in a consistent manner, both feminist and anti-feminist messages are 'entangled', such that feminist 'ideas are at the same time articulated and repudiated, expressed and disavowed' – a situation resulting in the profoundly contradictory construction of contemporary gender relations (Gill, 2007a: 163).

> On the one hand, young women are hailed through a discourse of 'can-do-girl power', yet on the other hand, their bodies are powerfully reinscribed as sexual objects; women are presented as active, desiring social subjects, but they are subject to a level of scrutiny and hostile surveillance which has no historical precedent. (Ibid.)

Third wave feminism is drawn to these contradictions – a preoccupation that is evident in the practices, representations, and resources that constitute 'girl' culture. Rather than have these contradictions confound feminism, from a third wave feminist perspective they simply are a part of the cultural landscape within which feminism is located.

> In spite of its homogenized media representations – and second wave reception – 'girl' culture is an extremely eclectic phenomenon which includes the Riot Grrrls of the punk movement, the Hello Kitty-accessorized, and lipglossed Girlies exemplified by the writers of zines such as *Bitch* and *BUST*, as well as the more anodyne mainstream proponents of 'girl power' identified with the Spice Girls. Although these various groups are not always politically aligned, they do have in common a vigorous reclamation and recuperation of the word 'girl' as no longer a simply derogatory and disrespectful term but one that captures the contradictions shaping female identity for young women whose world has been informed by the struggles and gains of second wave feminism. (Gillis and Munford, 2004: 169)

A politics of feminist resignication

Dominant consumer culture offers up 'a historically situated repertoire of cultural objects and images, codes, and signs' ready to be appropriated and deployed in self-consciously political ways (Garrison, 2000: 143). Readily available tools include 'print and visual media; music genres, technologies, and cultures; girl-positive and woman-positive expressions; revolutionary and social justice discourses; shock tactics; nonviolent actions; and the Internet' (ibid.). Particular attention is given to those sites in which lived contradictions associated with new femininities reveal the instability of gender categories and create the possibility for reclaiming femininity through the resignification of its dominant codings.

> Our politics reflects a postmodern focus on contradiction and duality, on the reclamation of terms. S-M, pornography, the words cunt and queer and pussy and girl – are all things to be re-examined or reclaimed. In terms of gender, our rebellion is to make it camp. The underground music community has served as a particularly fertile breeding ground for redefining a feminism to fit our lives. (Klein, 1997: 208)

By advocating a politics based upon appropriating terms used to devalue the feminine, third wave feminism advocates for reworking the power relations that those terms carry. This is a position consistent with Butler's politics of resignification (1997), which Lloyd

(2007: 129) defines as 'politics apprehended (in part) as the capacity to recite language oppositionally, so that hegemonic terms take on alternative, counter-hegemonic meanings'. The abstract potentiality for terms to be seized and used in counter-hegemonic ways resides in the citationality of language – signs are effective because they are repeatable. However, while the success of signification relies upon the convention of past usage that history only conditions the meaning of particular terms to a certain extent, the meaning of words can never be fully secured, and, when decontextualized, they can be deployed to unconventional ends, hence altering their meaning in unanticipated and novel ways. It is this *abstract* feature of language that provides for the possibility of a politics of resignification.

An example of the strategic decontextualization of hegemonic signs of femininity is at work within 'Girlie' culture, which centres upon adopting previously tabooed symbols of women's enculturation – including high heels, make-up, fashion magazines, and Barbie dolls (Baumgardner and Richards, 2000). Unlike the affirmation of the feminine associated with cultural feminism of the 1970s, Girlies do not advocate for the creation of a separate space to validate femininity. For a 'culture-driven generation', the message that equality can only be won by rejecting these traditional signs of femininity is overturned by 'holding tight to that which once symbolized' women's oppression (Baumgardner and Richards, 2000: 137).

> Girlies are girls in their twenties or thirties who are reacting to an antifeminine, antijoy emphasis that they perceive as the legacy of Second Wave seriousness. Girlies have reclaimed girl culture, which is made up of such formerly disparaged girl things as knitting, the color pink, nail polish, and fun. (Baumgardner and Richards, 2000: 80)

Girlies celebrate and work with the accoutrements of highly stylized femininity because in so doing they assert that practices once regarded as instruments of patriarchal power can now be wielded by woman to express strength and agency.

The articulation of a third wave feminist politics through practices of cultural production is exemplified for many third wave writers by Riot Grrrl, a 'young feminist (sub)cultural movement that combines feminist consciousness and punk aesthetics, politics and style' (Garrison, 2000: 142). The name itself represents a 'feminist reclamation of the *girl* with a less polite and more assertive political stance'; this is a move that undermines the perceived passivity of girls by reconfiguring the word 'girls' with an angry 'growl' (Rosenberg and Garofalo, 1998: 809). This form of feminist activism originated in Washington, DC, in 1991, as a response to the experience of marginalization felt by young women within what was a predominantly white, male punk scene. Since then, Riot Grrrl has evolved and expanded into a transnational grassroots network established through the circulation of self-published zines, newsletters, magazines, and websites for and about young women (Harris, 2003: 45). The practices of Riot Grrrl express a DIY (do-it-yourself) ethic of self-empowerment, independence from authority and the embodiment of an ethos that is consistent with third wave feminism's interest in the instability of identity categories. Third wave feminism is interested in how spaces can be created so that young women are able to engage in projects of self-definition. Throughout the writings on third wave activism, this theme of self-expression and definition comes to the fore.

There are three main dimensions to Riot Grrrl culture that have provided a template for third wave politics. In the first instance, a third wave politics of cultural production encourages women to become *active producers* within a dominant culture, where women are primarily positioned as passive and compliant consumers. Activities such as music production, performance, making and distributing zines, designing websites, and blogging provide spaces where highly personal experiences may be explored and expressed. The range of issues that appear is considerable; these include but are not reduced to racism, sexism, classism, and various forms of privilege, rape, child abuse, domestic violence, sexuality, eating disorders, sex industries, media spectaclization, AIDS, apathy, girl power, consumer pacificism, self mutilation, self defense, and zine production (Garrison, 2000: 155; Rosenberg and Garofalo, 1998: 810).

A second principle of third wave activism is an emphasis upon democratic participation and a resistance to formalized or centralized organizing structures. Third wave activism expresses an ethics of inclusivity, which dictates that women have the right to name and construct their own feminist identity without 'becoming the sole owner of what counts as feminism or feminist consciousness' (Garrison, 2000: 160). This ethic is extended as an invitation to other women to identify and express those issues that are central to their daily lives, leaving open the space for other women to enter and share their experiences. Third wave feminism is thereby constituted by a refusal to 'claim ownership of feminism' while allowing for the acknowledgement of one's own and other 'feminist-identified individual's tactical subjectivity' (ibid.).

> When we understand that feminism is not about fitting into a mould but about expanding our ability to be revolutionary from within the worlds and communities and scenes we move around and through, then collective action becomes possible across differences that affect people differently. (Garrison, 2000: 160)

The refusal to claim ownership results in a 'polymorphous' feminism – one that is inherently mobile and tactical, yet one that connects women through an ethics of democratic participation based upon the inclusivity that comes from recognizing that women occupy multiple locations and identities (Garrison, 2003). This democratic impulse is reflected in the forms of cultural production promoted by third wave activism. These are 'low tech' methods that use widely accessible materials and can be independently taken up by anyone. Zines, for instance, 'provide an opportunity to explore women's cultural production in a format unconstrained by commercial or organizational restrictions' (Bell, 2002: 188). The aim is to use these methods to challenge the dominant representational practices of Western culture and to subvert the regulative force of those images and the limits they place upon women's right to represent their own experiences in more authentic, if often contradictory, ways.

A third principle of third wave politics is that a politicized identity is produced through the act of self-expression. Following on from the assertion that gender identity is not reducible to a unifying experience, the content of third wave cultural production is highly personal. Significance is accorded to the empowering and transformative effects of self-expression, made possible through the creation of spaces where young women's concerns are legitimized by the recognition of their right to decide for themselves who they are.

In so doing they challenge the existing confines of a dominant culture that seeks to define and validate their experiences in narrow and oppressive ways.

> While other feminist movements have been geared more toward political action, Riot Grrrl, although remaining staunchly political, also pays attention to the personal and the everyday. It focuses more on the individual and the emotional than on marches, legislation, and public policy. This creates a community in which girls are able to speak about what is bothering them or write about what happened that day. (Rosenberg and Garofalo, 1998: 810)

The aim is not to develop a feminism that makes representational claims on behalf of women, but to advance a politics based upon a way of being feminist that is generated from within one's identity project according to one's unique experiences, so that 'what may appear to be a splintering in this generation often comes from an honest assessment of our differences as each of us defines her place and role in feminism' (Findlen, 1995: xiii). As one third wave feminist says, 'rather than thinking of feminism in terms of a movement or a theory or a text, which can be intimidating, women should be encouraged to express their own feminist perspectives' (Harde and Harde, 2003: 117).

By embracing the ambiguity that results from refusing to be positioned in binary terms, third wave feminism recalls earlier feminist strategies such as Anzaldúa's 'mestiza consciousness' (1987). This concept was used to represent the experiences of living on the margins, where consciousness emerges in-between and through multiple meaning systems, and as such is able to operate effectively within and beyond the force of dominant ideologies (Sandoval, 1991). Licona (2005) borrows the notion of this 'third space' from US third world feminism to explain the ways in which forms of third wave cultural production may be understood as a set of practices that make transcendence of dualities possible. These practices create 'fertile and reproductive spaces where subjects put perspectives, lived experiences, and rhetorical performances into play [...] unlike dualistic language structures (b)orderlands' rhetorics move beyond binary borders to a named third space of ambiguity and even contradiction' (Licona, 2005: 105).

These are spaces governed by a logic of both/and, which challenges notions of purity and authenticity and, as such, facilitates the view of third wave feminism that there is no 'authentic' feminism, but only the possibility of working from within dominant culture in contradictory and often ambivalent ways. Subjects formed in these spaces constantly 'slip and slide across both sides of a border to a third space, between the authentic and the inauthentic, the legitimate and the illegitimate, the pure and the impure, and the proper and the improper' (Licona, 2005: 106). These spaces are *subversive* because, by deploying disruptive discursive strategies, third wave subjects create self-representations that evade the effects of phallogocentric representational practices. These spaces are also *generative* because they allow for the exploration of new subjectivities and for the legitimation of new forms of knowing (Licona, 2005: 106).

The strategies proposed for working productively with ambivalence, diversity, and contradictions through individualized acts of subversive re-appropriation need to be evaluated by being situated more clearly in the socio-historical context in which they operate. As already stated, this is a context where a range of competing discourses seek to define gender relations in conflicting and often irreconcilable ways. Post-feminist writers downplay gender inequality by perpetuating a discourse of female empowerment in which women are positioned as autonomous agents of their own destinies. The influence of this discourse is apparent in the individualizing tendencies of third wave feminist politics. Early post-feminist proponents such as Roiphe (1993: 6) argued that 'the image that emerges from feminist preoccupations with rape and sexual harassment is that of women as victims', and Wolf (1994: 147) similarly claimed that the culturally dominant form of feminism has become 'victim feminism', which incites women to seek power through an 'identity of powerlessness'. However, the 'postmodern individualism' characteristic of third wave discourse is also, partly, the legacy of second wave feminism, which has made female ambition a more realizable project (Heywood and Drake, 1997: 5). Located in tension with second wave feminism and post-feminist discourses, third wave feminism represents one strategy for negotiating the contradictions that constitute a late modern female empowerment discourse; but, far from being neatly compatible with feminist goals, the strategies promoted by third wave feminism require interrogation. As argued in Chapter 4, this is a context in which new femininities offer far from straightforward subject positions. These positions produce both possibilities and troubles for young women as these attempt to manage the difficulties of enacting ideals associated both with traditional femininity and with masculinity (Ringrose, 2007). This tension places demands on young women that are difficult to resolve within current social arrangements, and the contradictions that result are not lived unproblematically, but are experienced as ambivalences that seek resolution often through highly individualized strategies, which do not necessarily work to women's advantage or result in the expansion of their capacity to exercise autonomy.

Despite the assertion that individuality is now more important than one's gender, many aspects of gender difference continue to be valued and, as such, are required of women who wish to be recognized as 'successful'. Traditional dictates of femininity, including physical attractiveness, bodily ideals, and heterosexuality, are not easily rejected as matters of individual 'choice'. Furthermore, many norms associated with traditional femininity operate to cordon off particular choices, which threaten the coherence of its boundaries – including the choice to be a lesbian, childless, single, or a feminist (Baker, 2008; Rich, 2005). Contrary to the claim that traditional norms associated with femininity may be reworked, studies on emerging femininities indicate that female empowerment must remain consistent with those norms and as a consequence, women's relationship to empowerment is often *contained* within the parameters set by regulative norms.

Findings from various studies also indicate that young women's lives are often characterized by a series of ambivalences and that many lack resources that might allow them to manage the gendered dilemmas they face in daily life. Complex contradictions that constitute the discourse of female success are socially systemic in nature and as such cannot be resolved through biographical solutions (Gonick, 2004). Negotiating this discourse and its incitement to construct oneself through the ideal of unencumbered 'choice' places significant demands on third wave political strategies. As discussed here, third wave feminism places ambiguity and hybrid subjectivities at the centre of its politics. According to this analysis, by straddling the intersections of what are often impossible sets of demands, new femininities potentially destabilize prevailing gender norms. However, as the studies discussed in Chapter 4 show, rather than produce such a destabilization, contradictions are not left open as sites of production. Instead their resolution is sought in often highly unsatisfactory ways, which limit positive identifications with feminism. The potential attributed to third wave spaces to produce new articulations of a *feminist femininity* therefore demands closer examination.

Reclamation and reversal

Here we return to the questions posed at the beginning of the chapter. Are all words equally available for appropriation and resignification? What are the factors that influence the processes by which the power invested in those terms may be reversed for subversive ends? It is useful to think about these questions in light of the debates that have built up around Butler's 'politics of the performative' (Butler, 1997). In this analysis Butler argues that there is no necessary relationship between an utterance and its effect. The meanings that terms carry, therefore, are not guaranteed by those who speak them but rely upon conventions and prior utterances, which are recalled when words are spoken in the present. But conventions only partially condition the way specific terms are used; and the instability of signification means that, when circulating in a different context, words can connotatively have meanings that diverge from those of prior utterances. Because speech has the potential for decontextualization, a politics of resignification is based on the citational structure of language, which allows terms to be used across different contexts in ways that deviate from their prior usage (Lloyd, 2007: 131). Terms are open to failure, which makes them available for appropriation by those who refuse to identify with the derogatory meanings attaching to particular terms.

However, the extent to which all terms are equally open to resignification has been debated, as some terms may be more 'fixed' by the conventions that govern their prior usage. It is these conventions that, when sedimented over time, lend force to particular terms. The force of language is 'to a large extent, given by the conventional nature of the terms and by the way in which relations of power are embedded within and reproduced through the speaking of terms' (Mills, 2000: 268). These power relations are part of the 'historicity' that is intrinsic to a given term and is invoked when a term is deployed (Lloyd, 2007: 131). When a derogatory term is used, it is the force of this history that is brought to bear, in the form of repetition of hurtful past utterances.

It may be the case that certain terms cannot be tactically resignified and reversed to work against this historicity. While any particular deployment of a term exceeds the moment of its deployment and is, therefore, open to strategic reversal, the force relations that 'lie behind linguistic conventions survive the momentary refusal of a subject to be named in its terms' and may contain or limit the efficacy of that reversal (Mills, 2000: 268). Lloyd similarly argues that reversals

> tend to be implicated in the same mode of thought that they are laboring against since one of the ways they operate is by accepting the legitimacy of certain key elements of a discourse. Being able to turn a discourse around in order to argue for a position or behavior that is initially condemned or pathologized, or deploying certain 'naturalized' assumptions against the grain, does not necessarily displace the discourse in question. (Lloyd, 2005: 104)

Because attempts to reverse discourse are culturally embedded, 'there is no place outside of their historical location from which to work, which means that the discursive formations that structure those locations also inform the kinds of resistance that are possible' (p. 105). Indeed Disch (1999: 556) notes that linguistic agency may be at its most effective when backed by hegemonic institutions. A successful reversal, therefore, is tied to the historical specificity of the context of its deployment; otherwise the reversal exists only as a *potential*.

An examination of the contextual specificity of any particular act of resignification is likely to reveal that the effectiveness of these acts is highly contingent. While it is the abstract features of language – 'the capacity of all speech for decontextualization' – that provides the ontological conditions for agential change, in practice the potential for language to signify in any number of a multitude of ways is shaped and bounded by the specific social and political conditions that operate to facilitate particular acts of iteration and resignification (Lloyd, 2007: 132). To interrogate fully the potential that acts of resignification may have to produce effective resistance, an analysis must move beyond an abstract account of the features that allow language to be deployed in subversive ways, towards an account that attends to the historically specific conditions within which *actual* deployments of language are made. Close analysis of this context will illuminate why certain deployments may produce a subversive, counter-hegemonic resistance to dominant norms, while other instances will result in a conventional and hegemonic repetition. Lloyd's argument suggests that a genealogical method can produce an analysis of the contingent factors that converge to produce the conditions of possibility for an effective reversal of the power inscribed in terms. This may include pre-existing or emerging discourses, previous practices or prior norms, which are reiterated in specific utterances. Effective recitation is instituted and shored up by these conventions and pre-existing, recognizable modes of intervention (Lloyd, 2007: 137), and this is what distinguishes the *potential* of resignification from its *actualization*. The point here is that effective counter-hegemonic deployments of language are only partially attributable to the abstract features of signification. Their potency relies upon a series of contingent factors:

> Even 'transgressive' reinscriptions may [...] be turned to other, nontransgressive ends. Indeed it may only be in retrospect and with the aid of genealogical analysis [...] that it is possible to gauge how effective an intervention or an expropriative reinscription has been. Given the iterability of language, one crucial factor of course is [...] the extent to which a reinscription is able to break with its 'prior context'. (Lloyd, 2005: 144)

This caveat also applies to the strategic use of parodic performances to oppose power. A parodic performance of gender seeks to destabilize the norms that serve to naturalize gender; but, because it is not possible for those performances to take place outside of gender, 'politically parody may actually reproduce what it seeks to displace' (Lloyd, 2005: 141). For any potential audience, a performance of gender is only made intelligible through the existing discourses that parodic performances seek to subvert, therefore any performance of gender, parodic or not, may have the effect of re-idealizing norms and existing conventions. The intention behind the parodic performance has limited efficacy where the outcome of its reading is concerned. This is why the progressive promise of parody is limited, finding its most successful realization within sub-cultural sites, where those performances are intelligible as transgressive because of their specific context. Parody is neither always transgressive nor always politically progressive. Furthermore, resistance in itself does not necessarily furnish the grounds for political transformations and social change.

As outlined in Chapter 2, a genealogical feminism draws attention to the historically contingent shifts in power relations within which feminism has operated. While power is reconceptualized in more dispersed and dynamic terms within third wave feminism, McNay draws attention to the need to interrogate contingent power relations; for, just as this contingency creates the condition for a destabilization of terms, it is also the case that the primacy given by Butler to processes of 'symbolic identification results [...] in a disregard of the specificity of socio-historical power relations and the connections between the two spheres' (McNay, 1999: 181). As she points out, 'there remains a tendency to valorize the linguistic act of resignification per se as inherently subversive at the expense of a more sustained consideration of the extent to which attendant social relations are dislodged or reinforced by such an act' (McNay, 1999: 181).

Squires (1999: 4) states that the normative task for a feminist politics of the subject is to reveal the extent to which gendered identities are themselves products of particular political discourses and to explore the 'convolution of gender and power' (Coole, 2000: 42). There is a tendency in the third wave literature to undertheorize this complexity and hence to analyse adequately the contested context within which its strategic interventions are made. Third wave feminism is constituted through its negotiation of both the conventions of second wave feminism and the values of neoliberal post-feminism, which emphasize individualism. Where a strategy based upon the reversal of power is concerned, this convergence complicates the efforts to enact counter-hegemonic re-appropriations of negative terms attached to femininity and may limit the effects of parodic performances.

Two main challenges demand consideration. Firstly, the spaces that third wave feminism claim to be sites for the production of empowered female identities must provide opportunities to evade the co-optation and commodification of pro-girl discourses (Kinser, 2004;

Riordan, 2001). Because the effects of resignification are contingent upon specific economic, political, and social relations, these effects must be analysed in relation to the 'structures of consumerism', which not only play a key part in the creation of identities but render these identities open to commodification and recuperation (McNay, 1999: 182). Female empowerment has been transformed into an extremely attractive commodity, which 'contributes to rearticulating dominant patriarchal and capitalist values, while not substantially disrupting power relations' (Riordan, 2001: 282). The consumption of female empowerment in its various forms merely offers 'a celebration of what girls already do rather than encourage girls to seek power through direct economic and political means' (Riordan, 2001: 291). 'Buying' into feminine empowerment may enhance a sense of agency associated with individualized identity, but it leaves little room to develop an awareness of the full complexity of self-empowerment or to develop a sustained critical understanding of the social context where female empowerment and feminist values are appropriated in the name of reproducing the *status quo*. This appropriation occurs at the expense of understanding the classed and 'raced' divisions that render empowerment discourses so problematic. As McRobbie (2004a: 260) effectively states, to count as a 'modern sophisticated girl' who is free to choose, young women must withhold critique and maintain 'an uncritical relation to dominant commercially produced sexual representations which actively invoke hostility to assumed feminist positions from the past in order to endorse a new regime of sexual meanings based on female consent, equality, participation and pleasure, free of politics'.

These critiques suggest that third wave feminism must go beyond advocating women's right to choice and self-expression and interrogate the substance of those choices in a critical way; but third wave feminism is often uncertain about the role of prescription in feminist politics. This is manifest in the rhetorical strategies that the third wave deploys to differentiate itself from second wave feminism, which is now almost customarily characterized as overly dogmatic – and hence incompatible with new feminist subjectivities. As one of the early proponents of third wave feminism explains:

> Young women coming of age today wrestle with the term [feminist] because we have a very different vantage point on the world

than that of our foremothers [...] For many it seems that to be a feminist in the way that we have seen or understood feminism is to conform to an identity and way of living that doesn't allow for individuality, complexity, or less than perfect personal histories. (Walker, 1995: xxxii–xxxiii)

This position explains why the specificity of individual experience is repeatedly placed at the centre of third wave politics. Ideally, spaces of self-exploration and creation offer women the opportunity to lay claim to personalized feminist identities without facing judgement or condemnation; but is laying claim to the legitimacy of one's experience always a feminist act? Third wave spaces are located within a context where the undertaking of a project of self-definition is valued in and of itself, and such a context is consistent with the contemporary normative expectations that regulate 'modern', liberated femininity.

Herein lays the second challenge. Contemporary femininities are celebrated, by definition, for the skills that constitute them: self-definition, self-responsibility, and *independence* from a collective identification with gender or feminism. Third wave feminist political strategies must deliver a more sustained and judicious account of how the late modern incitement to engage uncritically in a project of self-definition that simply celebrates individualized female success differs from the individualized, self-determining, strong femininity emphasized in many of its own statements. Regressive tendencies within post-feminist popular discourses continue to suggest that feminism places limits on women's ability to construct their own identities in ways they feel suit their circumstances best; but being able to engage in self-expression does not necessarily stand up to scrutiny as a form of feminist politics. Post-feminism has ascended to become one of the dominant logics of late modernity therefore third wave feminism requires a more strategic position to be developed so that the projects of self-definition that it valourizes do not simply become conflated with taking up a position that is limited to the celebration of individualized experiences of empowerment.

To produce feminist articulations of femininity, third wave feminist political strategies must offer opportunities to transcend the ideological incitement to engage *uncritically* in a project of self-definition based upon individualized female success and values such as choice, freedom, and self-sufficiency that have been co-opted by this discourse. It is a difficult task to give recognition, simultaneously, to the multiple positionings, experiences, and priorities that constitute women's lives *and* to place limits on the ethics of inclusivity to demarcate where a feminist articulation of identity lies. The risk for third wave feminism in not exploring how this might be negotiated is that a call to the practice of inclusivity easily mutates into an indiscriminate invitation to construct any claim to feminist membership as equally valid or radical.

> Resistance per se does not equal feminism; consumerism for women does not equal feminism. Some choices *are* more compromising to women's lives than others, and third-wave feminists have no business shutting down the discussion about which choices accomplish what all in the name of pluralistic thinking. Pluralism, multiplicity, polyphony, all of these suggests a willingness to hear;' they do not imply *ipso facto* acceptance of what is heard. (Kinser, 2004: 145)

Current social conditions require a sustained analysis of how definitional boundaries might be drawn around a *feminist* project of resistant self-transformation. The problem third wave feminism must consider further is that 'anything that looks like one is casting off any cultural restriction whatsoever, and in particular if the one doing so is female, counts as feminism' (Kinser, 2004: 144). Acts of resignification, therefore, may be experienced as subversive and resistant; but the efficacy of this experience may be overestimated by a misplaced investment in individual intentionality. The meaning of terms such as 'girlie' or 'slut' is not exhausted by their reclamation, and to suggest that they are would presuppose an agent who is able to control the meaning of acts of resignification. Having an intention to perform a particular act cannot be conflated with an ability to fix the effects of those actions (Mills, 2000: 276). Indeed, if a politics of resignification relies upon the indeterminacy of language for its strategies of re-appropriation and reversal, then these deployments are as likely to fail – or perhaps even more so, since they are working against the force of established conventions and hegemonic institutions. Furthermore, it is difficult to know whether a speech act that was intended to be subversive is successful or results instead in the re-inscription of existing power structures, particularly since the effects of any acts are mediated and therefore may not reach the audience in the form intended.

The success of any such act is dependent on the reception of these acts by others within specific and determinate contexts.

> The question is not just about what parodic intervention signifies but also where, when and to whom it signifies in the ways that it does. Parody may be transgressive from the perspective of the specific linear history of practices that constitute a particular individuated subject... This does not guarantee, however, that it is parodic when seen in the context of others. (Lloyd, 1999: 208)

The resources made available by 'girl culture' are in many ways significantly overdetermined by their historicity and by a present post-feminist sensibility that would seek to create the impression that historicity has been transcended. McNay (2000: 68) points out that we should be wary of analyses that invest ambivalent subjectivities with inherent progressive potential, because to do so is to elide a 'dynamics of symbolic destabilization with processes of social and political transformation'.

> A consideration of gender shows that whilst there may have been a loosening of dominant images of femininity, the transformatory impact of these images upon women's social status is from certain... rather than being self-evidently emancipatory, the destabilization of images of femininity may be indicative of more insidious forms of subordination. (McNay, 2000: 68–69)

A critical understanding of the relationship between resistance and agency would question whether the two are synonymous and it would seek to examine the relationship of both to power. As Mills (2000: 274) states, 'while agency is ostensibly a precondition for resistance, resistance does not necessarily follow from agency nor refer to the same relation or action *vis-à-vis* relations of power'. Post-feminism reduces politics to the right to self-expression regardless of its form or substance, but just the fact that a particular act is experienced as resistant does not make it a feminist act *per se*. There is a propensity, within a politics of resistance, to put an accent on *individualized* agency (Riordan, 2001: 283) – which is why resistance has also become the preferred idiom of post-feminism, whose discourse of empowerment relies upon casting off prescriptive codes, particularly those associated with so-called 'victim feminism' (Denfeld, 1995; Roiphe, 1993; Wolf, 1994). Third wave feminism should avoid the supposition that '"[w]e feminists" has come to mean, unilaterally and unequivocally, "we victims"' (Siegel, 1997b: 63).

A final matter for further interrogation is the role that ambivalence plays in third wave strategies of reversal. The endorsement of hybrid identities suggests that contradictions are consistently, and perhaps even inherently, laden with a progressive potential. Critics have, however, suggested that the political force of ambivalence that results from not belonging to dominant social categories is often overstated. Those who argue that being in-between categories of fixed identity is politically productive do so on the basis that these identities are ultimately undecidable, and therefore unsettling for the dominant order; but Ang (1996: 46) points out that 'ambivalence is not only a source of power but also a trap, a predicament' – because ambivalence can be recoded positively and managed as an expression of 'tolerance' towards those who are different. For example, in Ang's (1996: 45) discussion of multicultural Australia, structural ambivalence does not overturn the binary opposition between self and other, but re-inscribes this relation in a different fashion, so that being a minority subject in Australia means being positioned in the grey space where inclusion and exclusion are 'almost the same but not quite'. It is a position that is imposed to contain difference – a position of embracing it symbolically but keeping it in an in-between space. The inside/outside dynamic that advocates of hybridity seek to harness is not merely of their own making, but is also imposed on subjects, as an act of regulation within a space in which minority subjects are both discursively confined and at the same time symbolically embraced (Ang, 1996).

Conclusion

The aim of third wave politics to move away 'from thinking and acting in terms of systems, structures, fixed power relations, and thereby also "suppression"' (Krolokke and Sorensen, 2005: 21) towards the strategic engagement with contingent operations of power is an attempt to avoid deterministic analyses that lend explanatory primacy to one type of power. Instead, consideration is granted to the non-systemic and multiple operations of force relations. Diffuse power effects may interconnect, but this is not necessarily reduced to singular explanations, and responses to the operation of power are similarly dispersed points of resistance. By problematizing some of the excesses that are the result of a third wave reliance upon a logic of contingency, the intention in this chapter is not to suggest that a more viable alternative would be found in theorizing gendered social relations as a social totality organized by a logic of necessity linked to the operation of patriarchy or capitalism. On the other hand, claiming that in the contemporary gender order power flows through disparate and multiple force relations can lead to an underdeveloped account of how it is that power can and does materialize in systematic ways to produce particular effects. The challenge is to theorize power as diffuse and non-systemic, and yet to be able to account for how particular continuities emerge and form patterned effects. Disparate mechanisms of power can converge in particular places to produce a hegemonic effect (Lloyd, 2005), and these convergences can be traced and analysed by using a genealogical method to

> elucidate ways in which specific elements converge in contingent historical fashion to produce women's oppression in its variety and persistence. An analytic of power, that is, can be deployed that enables us to explore how specific force relations intersect and, crucially, where there are gaps or contradictions (and there will be many) in this intersection. (Lloyd, 2005: 84)

This approach involves ascertaining the actual interconnections that have formed between what are otherwise disparate elements with no necessary connection. As argued in Chapter 3, this is exemplified by the interconnections that constitute the post-feminist constellation where, for instance, feminist deployments of principles such as 'choice' converge with neoliberal deployments, seemingly to endorse a shared social good. However, the meaning of a word like 'choice' carries a considerably different import when used within a feminist context, compared to a context organized by neoliberal ideologies, and will orient users in one context to a completely different set of priorities and aims. The convergence of feminism and neoliberalism is not governed by a logic of necessity; nevertheless, their convergence effects gendered processes of subjectivation and the production of hegemonic femininity as expressed through discourses of 'choice' and 'empowerment'. As Lloyd (2005: 86) argues, 'a system of relations between elements is created not out of necessity but through the accidental confluence of discrete often conflicting, modalities of power'. Third wave feminism has identified that femininity in late modernity is far from unproblematic and presents both opportunities and challenges. While focusing on the opportunities that contradictions might bring to the analysis of new feminities, the third wave project must also engage with the limits set by these contradictions and offer a more critical analysis of how and why they are sustained. Individual empowerment is an important element in transforming current social arrangements, but, while necessary, it is not sufficient. A sense of entitlement is not enough to transform a culture where that entitlement is not yet fully recognized (Orr, 1997: 33).

6
The Limits of Choice

The language of choice now circulates widely as a central element of political discourses, social policies, and consumer practices. In a social context where a proliferation of choices is presented to individuals across a range of spheres in their daily lives, the opportunity to make 'good choices' – those that will lead to an outcome that best reflect one's desires – is deeply valued. The capacity to exercise self-determination and self-governance is achieved through a process of choosing, acting, and living according to what is deemed in some fundamental way to be important to one's sense of self (Friedman, 1997: 41). Autonomous choices are reached through a process of careful self-reflection and, therefore, are seen to be grounded in an authentic expression of what is right or true for that particular person. The significance granted to individual choice is reflected in familiar sayings such as 'be true to yourself', 'be your own person', and 'do what is right for you'. The widespread use of these popular expressions is indicative of how fundamental personal autonomy has become to our common understandings of individual identity and how valued the right to make choices for oneself is.

In Chapter 5 the analysis of third wave political practices raised important questions about the extent to which a post-feminist social constellation makes spaces available for women to achieve greater levels of autonomy through expanded agency and increased opportunities to make choices that are consistent with their goals and desires; but, because the concept of autonomy has traditionally been associated with the constitution of a masculine mode of subjectivity, its utility for alternative feminist theories of gendered subjectivity is often questioned. Indeed a critical analysis of autonomy has been at the core of feminist critiques of Western metaphysics, leading many to reject the possibility that autonomy might inform a strategy for conceptualizing a more positive mode of subjectivity for women. However, the capacity for self-determination that autonomy implies also suggests that its value for feminism is far from exhausted. As a result, many feminist theories that seek to conceptualize gendered subjectivity have had to negotiate a range of issues that the concept of autonomy introduces. Foremost in these accounts is the need to recognize that subjects are embodied and embedded in concrete social relations – thus an account of autonomy that is consistent with that feminist revision of subjectivity has been a central aim. Feminist reconceptualizations of the subject are informed by the political necessity to think how it might be possible for gendered social relations to be reconfigured so that female subjectivity may become a position from which to claim entitlement to self-definition and self-determination – key components of the concept of autonomy.

This chapter will explore current debates regarding the role that choice is playing in the constitution of emerging gendered subjectivities, and whether the discourse of 'choice' currently associated with 'empowered femininities' enhances women's autonomy. It will be argued that choice has emerged both as a *descriptive* and as a *prescriptive* component of idealized forms of late modern femininities, and that this necessitates a critical consideration of autonomy and of its relation to third wave feminism. In so far as gender norms have been reconfigured and allow women to assert their desires in the face of expanded opportunities for self-definition, increased autonomy and choice describe contemporary ideals of femininity. But choice is also prescriptive, insofar as it has become a normative feature of discourses that valorize the entrepreneurial, self-determining subject. Women are incited to make choices by discourses that obscure the conditions that make choice possible – or impossible, for that matter. When these conditions are concealed, the choices that are on offer appear to be 'natural' or inevitable, and therefore beyond the bounds of critique. As argued in Chapter 4 contemporary femininity has become firmly associated with the language of choice and autonomy, but the significance of the term 'choice' alters with the register within which it is located, be that feminist, neoliberal, or libertarian post-feminist appropriations.[1] Appropriations often put forward competing meanings and are harnessed to different ends; therefore there is a need to examine what happens when women engage in the act of choice-making. Choice is a necessary element in the achievement of women's autonomy, but it is not enough. Feminist theory requires an evaluative language to interrogate not only why particular choices are on offer within any given site, but also to analyse critically the choices that women actually make. To act autonomously implies that one is making 'good' choices, or choices that are right for the individual in question; therefore autonomy is constituted by a significant normative dimension, as it requires some basis for assessing the choices that are possible (or are not possible, for that matter) within any given socio-historical context. Third wave feminism requires an evaluative standard to critique those conditions, to stake normative claims about how those conditions should change, and to develop strategies for bringing about those changes.

Debating 'choice'

It has been argued that contemporary social conditions place increased demands on individuals to engage actively in choice-making. Theories of reflexive modernization maintain that processes of social change have weakened the structures that constrain individual agency and mark out the parameters of one's life course. A combination of established authorities and ascribed statuses once limited the need for individuals to navigate alternative life trajectories; however, processes of individualization and detraditionalization have dismantled these external forces. As a result, clear guidelines that make it quite apparent how to live one's life and to define the areas in which individuals have to make decisions are now more difficult to find. With the 'freeing of agency from structure', individuals increasingly participate in the construction of 'elective' or 'do-it-yourself' biographies by drawing upon a wide range of options, but without the certainty of what constitutes the 'right choice'. As argued by Beck and Beck-Gernsheim (2002: 5), 'life, death, gender, corporeality, identity, religion, marriage, parenthood, social ties – all are becoming decidable down to the small print; once fragmented into options, everything must be decided'. Individualization, as a structural characteristic of late modern society, translates into a demand for women to make choices that not only constitute their 'life projects' but express who they are or who they want to be (Budgeon, 2003; Harris, 2004b; McRobbie, 2004a). Critics have maintained that these accounts of late modernity, which rely upon the assumptions of increased individualization and detraditionalization, seriously *over*estimate the extent to which choice is available to individuals, and that focusing upon freedom of choice has led to unjustified prominence being granted to agency and personal autonomy. This 'focus has eclipsed our understanding of how individual lives unfold, and of the contexts and conditions under which individuals make choices which, in classical social science, has [*sic*] been conceptualized as "structure"'(Brannen and Nilsen, 2005: 412).

Baker (2008: 62) argues that this error is particularly acute when young women's lives are viewed through the lens of individualization – a conceptual framework that, in tandem with neoliberal ideology, promotes 'an exaggerated emphasis on *change* rather than *continuity* which conceals the stability (or worsening) of the position of women'. As the ideology of choice has ascended in late modernity, women are encouraged to believe that their lives are determined through acts of volition. This comes at the expense of recognizing how ascribed statuses and external social relations continue to circumscribe agency in ways that actually limit both the freedom women have to exercise choice and the kinds of choices they have access to. Baker (ibid.), like many other critics, is sceptical of how particular choices come to acquire their value and cautions against accepting women's claims that their choices do reflect their own desires, since at times 'certain choices are imposed on young women as more desirable than others and particularly as more necessary to be a "real" woman whose behavior meets the needs of men'. From this perspective, by participating in a culture of selfhood that incites women to construct themselves as self-determining subjects whose choices represent their 'true' selves, and not outcomes of insidious forms of governance, women are made subject to new forms of subordination and regulation.

Gill (2007c) picks up similar themes in her critical evaluation of Duits' and van Zoonen's (2006) analysis of young women's sartorial choices, in which they undertake a comparison between 'headscarves and Porno-chic'. In this analysis they argue that the terms of both public and feminist debates regarding the choices young women make problematically imagine young women as passive victims of patriarchal ideology, thus denying them agency, autonomy, and respect. This error, they argue, results in a failure to acknowledge young women's voices and in a refusal to genuinely attempt to understand what their choices mean. What they find objectionable is that the assertion that these young women are capable of making their own choices is met with such disbelief, particularly by many feminist critics.

> Our project arose out of surprise and irritation about the dichotomy of these debates which are either exclusively concerned with the meaning of the headscarf as a supposedly problematic marker of girls' submission to Islam and male family members, or entirely with the belly button shirt as a sign of rampant sexuality incited by the forces of popular culture. (Duits and van Zoonen, 2007: 161)

For Duits and van Zoonen, to assume that young women's choices are the product of hegemonic forces is tantamount to reproducing the very thing that feminism has long sought to dismantle – the denial of autonomy to women. Gill maintains, however, that her criticism of their position centres upon the tendency for terms such as 'agency', 'autonomy', and 'choice' to be deployed in ways that, she argues, evacuate cultural and social contexts from the analysis and instead fetishize young women as freely choosing individuals. Gill questions the efficacy of these terms for a feminist analysis of the present socio-cultural field, when they are used in a non-critical or self-evident way.

> To what extent do these terms offer *analytical* purchase on the complex lived experience of girls and young women's lives in postfeminist neoliberal societies? Moreover, what kind of feminist *politics* follows from a position in which all behavior (even following fashion) is understood within a discourse of free choice and autonomy? I suggest that, seductive as the call to 'respect' girls' 'choices' is, it remains trapped in precisely the individualizing, neoliberal paradigm that requires our trenchant critique. (Gill, 2007c: 72)

Gill develops her argument not as a refusal to recognize young women's agency, but as a call to complicate the terms of this debate and, in particular, to situate more carefully individuals' accounts of their choices within wider sets of social relations and processes, so that those accounts may be examined and analysed more deeply for what they tell us about the production of contemporary femininity. Demanding that such an interrogation be undertaken is not a sign that young women are being silenced; rather, she argues, it is a sign of *critical respect*, which 'involves attentive, respectful listening, to be sure, but it does not abdicate the right to question or interrogate' (p. 78). Her concern is to attend to the ways power works in and through subjects in the act of making choices. The choices one makes are the effect of the power relations that work to structure one's subjectivity. Therefore, that which is often claimed to be 'authentically' known by individuals does not necessarily express what is in the best interests of securing self-determination. Gill's response to Duits and van Zoonen challenges the sense of self, so often defended as the foundation for what is known to be 'right for me'. In models that fail to interrogate the language of choice, 'the autonomous, freely choosing subject appears peculiarly affectless, apparently not governed by any forces other than those she could fully articulate if asked to do so' (p. 76). 'Authenticity', a value that may seem above reproach, is often deployed to secure the legitimacy of one's choices; but, because claims based upon that value are placed beyond question, they must be examined further. Analyses of the processes through which such claims are made require that a third wave feminist politics of autonomy avoid re-instating the rational, unencumbered, and self-regulated subject of liberal discourse, which feminism has so thoroughly problematized.

Where Gill raises questions about whether the choices made by young women can be adequately understood as their own, Duits and van Zoonen argue that they are less interested in questions of autonomy and more concerned with understanding 'agency', defined as 'the purposeful actions of individuals, leaving aside the question whether these actions are autonomously arrived at, or are the results of structural factors' (2007: 165). It is a mark of respect, they maintain, to seek to understand the meanings young women give to their own choices over and above granting analytical primacy to the effects of top-down discourses. They conclude their argument with the observation that a younger generation of feminists feel 'irritated' by the denial of their agency by older feminists, especially as the self-image they identify with is one of having a strong sense of self and agency (Duits and van Zoonen, 2007: 168). Gill's frustration is partly caused by a wish to interrogate the content of those choices and, by implication, the social context in which they emerge. Her critique suggests the need for a critical language or vocabulary that will facilitate an *evaluation* of those choices and of all the associated ramifications.

This exchange represents the ongoing debates taking place within feminism about the extent to which the language of 'choice', in circulation within popular discourses, actually reflects transformed social arrangements and women's levels of autonomy. The two positions fall on either side of the long-running philosophical debate regarding the extent to which subjects enjoy free will on the one hand, or, on the other, are determined by factors beyond their control. In the remainder of this chapter the concept of autonomy will be interrogated by picking up on key themes raised by Duits and van Zoonen's analysis of young women's choices. Firstly, feminist debates regarding the utility of the concept of autonomy will be examined, particularly as the concept has been rethought in the context of theorizing power, gendered subjectivity, and feminist politics. Secondly, an issue that is central to these debates is that autonomy is linked to critical capacities, namely to the ability to reflect upon choices and to evaluate the circumstances in which choices are made. This critical capacity not only guides feminist agency but also provides the basis for a feminist politics. For many feminists, despite the association of autonomy with masculine modes of subjectivity, autonomy retains a value, but requires reworking for us to take stock of its social and relational nature. Finally, even when adopted in a revised way, the concept of autonomy proves problematic unless conditions are placed upon its exercise. The capacity for acting autonomously is linked to moral autonomy therefore one's choices are not meaningful in isolation, but gain moral import when situated within specific social contexts and sets of social relations.

Autonomy, Agency, and gendered subjects

In the mid-1990s the often uneasy relationship between postmodernism and feminism provided the backdrop for important feminist debates about gendered subjectivity, sharing as they did an extensive critique of the transcendent Cartesian subject of Western metaphysics (Benhabib et al., 1995; Braidotti, 1991; Nicholson, 1990). However, where post-structuralist thought laid bare the problematic nature of purporting to be a subject who was fully self-present, unified and, above all, defined through the capacity for rational thought, feminism pushed this critique further by pointing out that the Cartesian subject was not only premised on a number of questionable grounds but was also implicitly gendered. Feminist critique established that modernity was inherently constituted through the force of a gendered exclusion – an exclusion of all those who fall outside the bounds of what is recognized as belonging to the position of a rational, knowing, autonomous, and implicitly *masculine* subject. While the feminine operated as man's devalued other, 'the place of the free-willed subject who can transcend nature's mandates is reserved exclusively for men' (Alcoff, 1995: 434–35).

Given that the critique of the subject of modernity represents a crisis of modernity only insofar as these critiques disrupt the masculinist foundations of classical subjectivity, it is not surprising that the so called 'death of the subject', initiated by male thinkers such as Foucault, Lyotard, and Derrida, was not experienced as a loss by feminist theorists. Yet simply to deny the utility of maintaining the possibility of an autonomous subject presented a series of problems for feminism. Braidotti offers an apt summary of this challenge: 'One cannot deconstruct a subjectivity one has never been fully granted […] in order to announce the death of the subject one must first have gained the right to speak as one […] one must first gain access to a place of enunciation' (1991: 122). To the extent that classical subjectivity has been problematized for its association with masculinity, feminism had either to reject or to reassess the core assumptions which constitute this model. Feminist critiques have, therefore, focused on how structures might be remade to support women's entitlement to self-definition and self-determination – key components of the concept of autonomy. However, theories of autonomy and their relationship to women's agency and choices continue to cause discord within feminism, as the exchange between Duits and van Zoonen (2007) and Gill (2007c) so clearly illustrates.

Mackenzie and Stoljar (2000: 3) summarize the long list of problems that feminism encounters with the concept of autonomy: it is 'inherently masculinist [...] inextricably bound up with masculine character ideals, with assumptions about selfhood and agency that are metaphysically, epistemologically, and ethically problematic from a feminist perspective, and with political traditions that historically have been hostile to women's interests and freedom'. As Meyers argues, 'the view of the self that has dominated contemporary Anglo-American moral and political philosophy is that of homo erectus – the free and rational chooser and actor whose desires are ranked in a coherent order and whose aim is to maximize desire satisfaction' (1997: 2). Lorraine Code (2000) has maintained that a 'hyperbolized' version of autonomy, associated with self-mastery and self-reliance, dominates the social imaginary of white western societies and thus promotes a form of unbridled individualism, which is at odds with feminist ideals. This hegemonic form of autonomy, which materializes in incitements such as 'just be yourself', promotes self-sufficient individualism, whether or not such an ideal is possible or desirable. This account problematically privileges an instrumental mode of being – a mode of being that fails to recognize connections to others; denies the social nature of the self; presupposes that the self is coherent, unified, and transparently self-aware; and values reason over emotion (Friedman, 1997: 42). This liberal conception of selfhood provides the basis for self-constitution and self-mastery.

> It is difficult, if not impossible, to engage with the concept of autonomy without some articulated version of the kind of person, or subject, attached with this notion [...] Who, then, is the autonomous person? What does he or she look like? A number of themes recur in the literature: self-definition, self-mastery, self-determination, self-directedness, self-rule, self-respect, living in harmony with one's (true) self, authenticity and procedural independence in defining and identifying with the substance of these terms. (Di Stephano, 1994: 387)

These themes problematically suggest the existence of a 'self' whose autonomy depends upon self-containment and the ability to disengage from social relations and contexts. Feminist insistence on the embeddedness of the subject in concrete historical, social, and cultural contexts constitutes one of the key overlaps of feminist theorizing of the subject with post-modern critiques of the transcendental subject of Western metaphysics. Benhabib (1995a: 19), for instance, argues that the various practices that contribute to the constitution of gender form 'one of the most crucial contexts in which to situate the purportedly neutral and universal subject of reason [...] in its deepest categories western philosophy obliterates differences of gender as these shape and structure the experience and subjectivity of the self'.

By interrogating the processes through which gendered subjects come into being within concrete social conditions, feminist accounts of subject formation endorse the assumption of relationality and a rejection of transcendence, but have developed different strategies for thinking about the interrelationships of sex, gender, and subjectivation. In these accounts, many of the key issues that emerge in the more recent exchange between Duits and van Zoonen (2007) and Gill (2007c) crystallize in disagreements about how to theorize the production of gendered subjects and the capacity for autonomous critique and political agency. Benhabib (1995a), for example, initiates her theory of the subject with the argument that the subject is one who is always socially situated, and as such is not untouched by 'contingencies of difference'. While her position shares with postmodernism the rejection of a universal, transcendent subject, she argues that feminism cannot dispose of the concept of the subject altogether; for to do so would necessitate a simultaneous loss of many ideals that feminism cannot afford to abandon. Feminism would cease to retain its political efficacy without certain characteristics traditionally associated with the subject in Western philosophical thought – including 'self-reflexivity, the capacity for acting on principles, rational accountability for one's actions and the ability to project a life-plan into the future, in short some form of autonomy and rationality' (Benhabib, 1995a: 20).

The relationship between agency and the conditions within which that potential originates is a key issue for feminist theory; and it is evident that, while autonomy, as a political ideal, is important to endorse, there is a

> very great distance between the ideal of autonomy and the heteronymous reality of many women's (and men's) lives. This suggests two mutually elusive possibilities: that 'autonomy' carries a critical force and emancipatory appeal that should be of use to

feminists; or that 'autonomy' fails to make reasonable contact with the difficult and complex dimensions of a gender system which functions not merely as a system of socialization but, more deeply and pervasively, as a system of enculturation within which selves are constituted, emerge and take gender – (as well as other) differentiated shapes. (Di Stephano, 1994: 388)

Feminist positions within these debates have fallen along a continuum defined by the axes of voluntarism and determinism – both of which, taken to their furthest conclusion, prove unworkable. Benhabib, for instance, argues that systems of signification structure gendered subjectivities through narrative forms, which shape identities according to the social and cultural context in which those identities are articulated. This does not mean, however, that situated subjects are *determined* by this context or by their position within systems of signification. In this regard Benhabib retains a subject who is the 'author' of a self-narrative and, although 'heteronymously determined', is one who 'strives toward autonomy' (Benhabib, 1995a: 21). Against Butler, she states that to argue that subjects are not authors but rather 'merely another position in language' is to suggest that the subject 'can no longer master and create that distance between itself and the chain of significations in which it is immersed such that it can reflect upon them and creatively alter them' (p. 20). Benhabib is explicit about her commitment to a subject who is capable of self-determination; a conviction that leads her to question the efficacy of Butler's theory of performativity, which she argues has no 'doer' behind the deed and therefore undermines feminist politics.

Where Benhabib insists on the subject being *situated* in the social, Butler argues that the subject is *constituted* by the social (Fraser, 1995: 42). For Benhabib, constitution equates with determination, thereby disallowing agency and failing to account for human agents' capacity for self-reflection and self-determination. Butler, however, is critical of Benhabib for 'investing subjects with the capacity to deliberate or act outside of their cultural context' (Webster, 2000: 11). She problematizes autonomy by defining it as an illusionary relation to the self, produced as an effect of the process through which subjects are constituted.

> The subject is constituted through an exclusion and differentiation, perhaps a repression, that is subsequently concealed, covered

over, by the effect of autonomy. In this sense, autonomy is the logical consequence of a disavowed dependency, which is to say that the autonomous subject can maintain the illusion of autonomy insofar as it covers over the break out of which it is constituted. This dependency and this break are already social relations, ones which precede and condition the formation of the subject. (Butler, 1995b: 46)

From Butler's perspective, we always act from within culture, and we are constituted by and through those acts. As for agency, Butler is clear in her formulation: 'No subject is its own point of departure' (Butler, 1995b: 42). The subject, therefore, cannot be taken as the origin of its own action and, despite the criticism of determinism often levelled at her theory of agency, Butler maintains that this theorization does not foreclose on agency *per se*. In the theory of gendered performativity, the moment of action and signification are coincident; therefore the 'constituted character of the subject is the very precondition of its agency' (p. 46). Agentic potential flows from the subject's constitution in power and discourse, and not from a capacity that exists prior to the subject's constitution. The subject is 'the permanent possibility of a certain resignifying process, one which gets detoured and stalled through other mechanisms of power, but is power's own possibility of being reworked' (p. 47). As gender is never fixed but brought into being as the product of an ongoing reiteration, the conditions for resistance are always possible (Webster, 2000). Butler does not intend to dispense with the notion of the subject, but challenges us to 'ask after the process of its construction and the political meaning and consequentiality of taking a subject as a requirement or supposition of theory' (Butler, 1995b: 36). To claim a subject with an 'ontologically intact reflexivity' is to attempt to secure a foundation that places beyond question the very positing of that subject and of the political programmes that flow from it.

That the possibility of a subject position comes into being only through the displacement and disavowal of abject others requires feminism to attend to its own claims, made on behalf of the subject 'woman'. Butler's solution is to call the subject into question so as to open it up as a site of contestation, thereby making it available for 're-usage or redeployment that previously has not been authorized' (1995b: 49). Leaving the category 'woman' open as an 'undesignatable field of differences' relieves the category of its foundational weight, making it a 'site of permanent political contest' (p. 41). Starting from uncertainty releases the term from normative constraints, so that new significations and configurations become possible. Many feminists have been reluctant to leave such a fundamental issue exposed for misappropriation, but Butler argues that the radical democratic impulse of feminist politics requires this uncertainty and that the contestations that women engage in over the content of the term can thereby offer an 'ungrounded ground' or a contingent foundation for feminism.

This debate highlights one of the key points of contention that has troubled feminist theorizing of subjectivity within the context of debates concerning the utility of postmodernism for feminism. While a Foucaultian analysis of the constitution of subjects through relations of power has been widely and productively taken up by feminism in order to critique gendered relations, theorizing subjects as *constituted* seems to undermine the *constituting* capacities of subjects; and it is these capacities that form the basis for feminist social critique and transformation.

While Benhabib wants to claim that Butler's performative theory of gender constitution is ultimately deterministic, Butler criticizes Benhabib for offering an account of agency which implies that subjects are at some point capable of action which transcends the limitations of the situation or context from which they act and, most significantly, through which they are constituted. (Webster, 2000: 8)

Both theorists are committed to placing agency within specific social and historical contexts; but the accounts of agency given vary – firstly, in terms of the relative strength or capacity for freedom associated with agency; and, secondly, in terms of where that agency is located. In Benhabib's account, agency is a capacity that *subjects have* for choice and self-determination. For Butler, agency is the possibility for resistance, *located within the process* by which subjects come into being. These differences have profound consequences for feminist political practice, particularly with regards to the extent to which the subjects envisioned in these accounts are seen to have control over their actions and choices (Webstser, 2000: 11–12). Benhabib clearly retains a subject who has the capacity for self-reflection and choice, but Butler's concerns lay more with how agency comes into being through the activity of repetition and, in terms of a political practice, how that repetition might be subverted and destabilized. As Webster (2000) argues, these accounts matter to feminism because they raise questions about the possibility that subjects might be transformed along with cultural and political relations. A sufficiently compelling account of agency is required in order to theorize

> what role subjects may actively play in their construction as gendered, on what grounds they might strengthen that role in the political arena through collective action and how they might set up appropriate aims and objective that contest their determination by the highly gendered relations of power in which they are situated. (Webster, 2000: 18)

Ultimately, Webster contends that Butler's performative account of agency, which requires that signifiers be left strategically empty, is not robust enough to provide 'a programmatic vision for a feminist politics' (Webster, 2000: 15). Webster draws on the work of Wendy Brown (1995) to mount a convincing critique of Butler's theorization of agency, focusing particularly on whether her account of agency as resistance is 'inadequate for accounting for the sort of resistance which might be required in order for subjects to avoid wholesale social determinism' (Webster, 2000: 16). Brown argues that, although resistance exists, its presence is not in itself sufficient to contest power successfully, because by itself resistance 'does not contain a critique, a vision, or grounds for organized collective efforts to enact [...] Resistance-as-politics does not raise the dilemmas of responsibility and justification entailed in "affirming" political projects and norms' (1995: 49, cited in Webster, 2000: 17). This latter point echoes Benhabib's claim that Butler's theories lack a standard for evaluating the adequacy that any particular resignification might have for achieving feminist goals (Benhabib, 1995b: 110). For Butler, the terms of critique that feminists may use are always already implicated in the field of power; therefore to 'establish a set of norms that are beyond power is itself a powerful and forceful conceptual practice that sublimates, disguises, and extends its own power play through recourse to tropes of normative universality' (Butler, 1995b: 39). For Benhabib, however, feminist social criticism requires 'normative foundations' – 'the conceptual possibility of justifying the norms of universal moral respect and egalitarian reciprocity on rational grounds; no more and no less' (Benhabib, 1995b:118). There is nothing concrete in Butler's framework that can meaningfully respond to the normative questions it raises (Fraser, 1995). For example, are all resignifications progressive? Are subjects only brought into being through exclusion? Are all exclusions equally problematic?

> '[R]esignification' is not an adequate substitute for 'critique,' since it surrenders the normative moment. Likewise, the view that subjectivation necessarily entails subjection precludes normative distinctions between better and worse subjectivating practices. Finally, the view that foundationalist theories of subjectivity are inherently oppressive is historically disconfirmed [...] feminists need to develop an alternative conceptualization of the subject, one that integrates Butler's poststructuralist emphasis on construction with Benhabib's critical–theoretical stress on critique. (Fraser, 1995: 69)

Fraser's comments underscore two core issues that are relevant to the present discussion of gendered choice in late modernity. Firstly, that feminist theories of the subject necessarily include a theory of how particular subjectivities come into being through social processes; and, secondly, that a normative standard, which allows critique of the type of subjects that actualize under particular conditions, is required. This critique must be able to extend to an analysis of the exercise of agency and, by implication, to the connection between agency and choice. As made evident in the recent exchange between Duits and van Zoonen (2007) and Gill (2007c), women's relationship to agency and the extent to which their choices are governed by their own interests remain a site of contestation within feminism; 'how do we speak about people as constructions of the social order on the one hand, and as constructing agents or actors on the other, without erring on either side?' (Jones, 1997: 262, cited in Hughes, 2002: 98). Where Duits and van Zoonen wish to hear about the choices young women want to make, Gill would rather analyse those choices as the basis for developing a critique of the social and discursive relations from which specific choices emerge and are granted social recognition as 'good' or 'proper' choices for young women. Listening carefully to what women's choices mean to them is a necessary point of departure for understanding women's agency within late modernity; however, as Gill (2007c) maintains, the meaning and significance of these choices only become apparent when it is recognized that the origin of those choices is not the rational, choosing subject, but a subject whose autonomy emerges as *the product of social processes*. In short, Gill's response to Duits and van Zoonen seems to be saying: how can we respect choices, if we have no way of evaluating their significance? Her critique demands a normative language that will facilitate critical evaluation of the conditions and processes that make particular kinds of selves and choices possible.

These debates indicate that the concept of autonomy, if it is to be a viable third wave feminist ideal, must be reconceptualized in a form that neither blindly privileges the independence of individual will nor generates an overly deterministic account of individual capacities for self-reflection and agency. Di Stephano (1994: 398) succinctly summarizes the dilemma involved in rejecting the notion altogether.

> Posing the question of the obsolescence of autonomy risks a peculiar kind of paradox, for the very thought that we have a choice or responsibility to accept, modify or reject the discourse and ethos of autonomy is itself a feature of the modern autonomous mindset. Political vocabularies 'speak us' even as we imagine that we are 'speaking them'. We cannot, then get over ourselves even, and precisely as, subjects who have been constituted, however fictitiously as 'autonomous'. To the extent that women have been less than unambiguously embraced within the discursive reach of autonomy, we should not be surprised to find that autonomy has emerged as a question for feminism.

Relational autonomy

Feminist efforts to retrieve the concept of autonomy have done so primarily by reworking it as a *relational* concept. One of the aims of these approaches has been to develop a more comprehensive and nuanced account of agency, located in concrete socio-historical and cultural conditions. Many mainstream theories of autonomy make sense only if one accepts an abstract agent; but, because self-identity develops through a condition of intersubjectivity affected by social conditions, so too must autonomy be rethought as a capacity that does not belong to subjects *a priori*, but comes into being through dynamic social processes. The first consideration taken into account by relational theories is that the 'characteristics and capacities of the self cannot be adequately undertaken without attention to the rich and complex social and historical contexts in which agents are embedded' (Mackenzie and Stoljar, 2000: 21). Relational accounts, therefore, enable an analysis of the effect social relations and contexts have on the individuals' sense of themselves; their beliefs and motivations; the capacity for self-reflection; and their ability to act on their desires. Autonomy theorized in this way delivers a much richer account of agents and their capacities (Friedman, 1997, 2000, 2003; Mackenzie and Stoljar, 2000). The values and wants that individuals comprehend as their 'own' are actually social in nature, arising as they do from established social norms, practices, and relations.

Secondly, relational accounts depend upon the claim that selves can be said to exist as meaningful entities. Indeed autonomy as *self*-determination would cease to exist if selves were not consequential; therefore in the course of everyday life selves are assumed to exist: 'selves are agents, each one distinct from others of the same kind, who can be the authors of doings and whose doings are to be explained and understood in terms of intentional states that characterize them' (Friedman, 2003: 31). However, fictional selves are deemed, or not deemed, to be in theoretical debates Friedman (p. 35) points out that '"we" are far from being able to get along in everyday life without the discourses that do presume the existence of selves' and that, as long as discursive practices that posit or construct selves continue to operate, there is analytical purchase in assuming that talk about selves makes sense and that selves exist. Thirdly, because relational theories of autonomy assume the social nature of the self, they challenge the mainstream position that autonomy *necessarily* requires independence and separation from others. Autonomy is a capacity that is socially conditioned, thereby challenging the assumption that autonomy is necessarily tied to individualism and emotional detachment. Human interrelations are necessary to its realization. Nedelsky (1989: 7–11, cited in Friedman, 1997: 45) summarizes the aim of relational approaches – to 'combine the claim of the constitutiveness of social relations with the value of self-determination'. From this perspective, our capacity for self-determination is only possible because of the social relationships that foster it.

Relational autonomy and choice

In her basic account of relational autonomy, Friedman (2003: 4) explains that, for choices and actions to be considered autonomous, the 'choosing and acting self as the particular self she is must play a role in determining them. The self as a whole, as the particular self she is, must somehow (partly) determine what she chooses and does.' This definition contains three elements deemed central to the exercise of autonomy. Firstly, autonomy has been achieved when an individual's actions are consistent with a sense of self that is deeply held by the individual. Secondly, this consistency is achieved through a process of self reflection: a 'process in which, roughly, a whole self takes a stance toward particular wants and values she finds herself to have [...] a person's self reflections give a crucial imprimatur to the wants and concerns on which they focus approvingly. Those wants and concerns become more truly a (whole) person's "own"' (p. 5). Finally, self-reflection of sufficient quality ensures that actions are governed by a particular self, which represents 'who one really is'. The act of self-reflection underpins self-determination, because it functions as a reaffirmation of what one really cares about and, by implication, of what can be deemed authentic.

Because relational approaches are underpinned by the assertion that autonomy is a socially conditioned capacity, the effects of this conditioning are of particular concern. It is possible that social relationships may enhance this capacity, but it is also the case that autonomy can be hindered by social conditions that compromise the independence of reflection; therefore autonomy depends upon a *procedural requirement* that this process of self-reflection is of sufficient quality and orientation – that it has not been coerced or distorted by external forces. In procedural accounts, then, what is important is that the 'agent has subjected her motivations and actions to the appropriate kind of critical reflection' (Mackenzie and Stoljar, 2000: 14) and is able to engage in sufficient self-reflection, unimpeded by coercive conditions.

Theories concerned with procedural independence focus on the *quality* of self-reflection, but not on its *content*. These substantively neutral approaches have been useful from a feminist perspective because, contra mainstream approaches, substantive neutrality makes it possible to rethink autonomy as interconnectedness instead of separation. The nature of the relations that one must have to others is not specified, and the action that results from the process of self-reflection is neither necessarily condoned nor condemned. Nor do substantively neutral approaches dictate the nature of choices that someone must make to achieve autonomy. From this perspective, choices that are based upon one's dependence on, and commitments to, others may be perceived as autonomous.

However, substantively neutral approaches raise some interesting challenges for feminism. Many critics have argued that focusing solely on procedural issues while ignoring substantive ones results in an approach that is not robust enough to account for the effects of oppressive social conditions. Relational approaches to autonomy are explicitly concerned with the effects of oppressive social relationships and processes of socialization, and this concern manifests on three levels (Mackenzie and Stoljar, 2000: 22). The first level refers to the role 'social norms and institutions, cultural practices, and social relationships play in shaping the beliefs, desires, and attitudes of agents in oppressive social contexts' (ibid.). The second level consists in analysing the effects of oppressive conditions on the development of agents' capacities for self-reflection, self-direction, and self-knowledge. Thirdly, relational accounts are concerned with the agent's ability to act on those autonomous desires. This includes not only examining the restrictions that social contexts may place on an individual's freedom, but also evaluating the impact that social norms, institutions, practices, and relationships may have in effectively limiting the range of *significant* options available to them (ibid.).

If actions are taken on the basis of desires that are the product of oppressive socialization, then can those actions really be conceived of as autonomous? Meyers (1997: xi) expresses the dilemma that feminists face when she asks: 'If women's professed desires are products of their inferior position, should we give credence to those desires? If so, we seem to be capitulating to institutionalized injustice by gratifying warped desires. It not, we seem to be perpetuating injustice by showing disrespect for those individuals.' In Meyer's account not all desires should be granted equal recognition, particularly those that have been accepted uncritically as in the case when an individual habitually consents to established expectations and gendered social norms. Mackenzie and Stoljar (2000: 18–21) question whether in this case a procedural account is really sufficient for feminism. Desires could only be objected to on the basis that they have not been reached through sufficiently independent reflections, but not on the basis of their *content*. Therefore, critique of any particular desire is restricted to procedural considerations. For example, in a procedural account a woman's decision to enter into a repressive relationship could be conceived of as autonomous as long as this choice was freely made, in other words it was made following a process of self-reflection and it was consistent with the woman's established self-identity. This has led some feminists to argue for a theory of autonomy that considers the content of particular desires and choices and holds them to a standard of evaluation not required by procedural theories. For many feminists procedural accounts are limited in their ability to account for the effects of oppressive socialization; and, because they are substantively independent, these theories seemingly grant legitimacy to desires and choices that may in practice run counter to feminist principles and values. Substantive theories, on the other hand, require a more normative view of what is needed for women to flourish in society. Procedural independence must be augmented by further non-neutral conditions, which are either placed on the specific content of an agent's preferences or applied to the constraining context within which choices are made, so that those choices are 'substantively guided by a commitment to autonomy as a value or, at least, devoid of commitments that are inconsistent with a commitment to autonomy' (Friedman, 2003: 20).

The significance of substantive theories is most apparent in situations where social relationships can impact adversely upon an agent's ability to reflect critically upon norms they have internalized and accepted even when these norms are false or incorrect. From this perspective, 'preferences influenced by oppressive norms of femininity cannot be autonomous' (Stoljar, 2000: 95). The key here is the development of a *critical* capacity for reflection and the question of how contemporary social relations support or impede the development of this capacity. A second concern is that substantively neutral autonomy takes for granted and accepts the selves that are *already in existence* rather than promoting a more radical critique of these selves, as evaluated against those that might come into existence under different social conditions. As Friedman states (1997: 54), 'at this historical juncture, rather than promoting autonomy, we might be better off urging that some of us *change* what we "really" are'. After all, feminist theories of gendered selves have been undertaken to critique the content of the selves that social relations, institutions, and norms produce. A third consideration is whether we may want to rank the choices on offer or to apply some evaluative standard to the selves that may come into being as result of making particular choices. A substantively neutral model of autonomy can offer no grounds for critiquing the content of choices or behaviours that result from exercising autonomy (p. 53).

This discussion of autonomy speaks to many of the concerns raised by Gill in her critique of Duits' and van Zoonen's championing of young women's choices. Is it sufficient that young women are making choices they claim to be their 'own'? Alternatively, is it necessary to question the consistency of those particular choices with the value of self-determination, understood here as promoting a condition of flourishing? Gill's comments suggest a degree of scepticism towards the suggestion that choices can be 'authentic' or reflect an authentic self just because the individual making those choices claims those choices to be 'true'. This claim for authenticity implies that personal autonomy also carries a claim to moral autonomy.

Prior to the eighteenth century, differences between persons were not accorded moral significance; rather the importance accorded to individuals derived from the value given to the social role or status they occupied. In modern conceptions of the subject, however, the ideal of authenticity has become intrinsic to the formation and expression of identity. Authenticity as an ideal implies that each individual has an original way of being human, which requires that each of us discover what this inner sense of ourselves consists of. The moral weight of the ideal of authenticity resides in the right of every person to discover and express this inner feeling of what is right for them. When we lose the capacity to listen to our inner self, for instance when we conform to external pressure, we lose access to what makes us unique, and in so doing we cease to live the life we ought to live. As Taylor (1991: 29) explains, 'being true to myself means being true to my own originality, and that is something only I can articulate and discover. In articulating it, I am also defining myself. I am realizing a potentiality that is properly my own.' The moral force of authenticity relies upon two conditions that a quest for mere self-fulfilment lacks.

Firstly, for the differences that we claim for ourselves to matter – those differences that constitute our unique identities – they must be given substance against a 'horizon of significance' that exists anterior to choice. This is to say that choices are only really important because some issues are more significant than others. For instance, if the choices we make merely express an individual preference, like choosing which shoes to wear at work, this choice doesn't really matter in the sense of us having to justify why it is more valid to have chosen a black pair over a brown pair. In instances such as these, differences are not held to be significant beyond what the individual desires, and as such the significance of those choices is minimal. For choices to matter beyond individual preference and to be esteemed as worthy or valuable, they have to take on significance against some standard or shared understanding. If this condition does not hold up, then self-choice becomes inconsequential. Furthermore, the standard by which we evaluate significance cannot be self-generated. Instead, the moral force of authenticity can only be achieved within conditions where the self is engaged with demands that emanate from beyond the self (Taylor, 1991: 39–40).

> I can define my identity only against the background of things that matter. But to bracket out history, nature, society, the demands of solidarity, everything but what I find in myself, would be to eliminate all candidates for what matters. Only if I exist in a world in which history, or the demands of nature, or the needs of my fellow human beings, or the duties of citizenship, or the call to God, or something else of this order *matters*, can I define an identity for myself that is not trivial. (Taylor, 1991: 40–41)

Sometimes, in discourses that elevate choice as a social good in itself, the principle of recognizing the equal value of different ways in which individuals may choose 'what is right for them' is often invoked. This can, however, lead to a distorted version of autonomy, because the affirmation of choice is deployed as the overriding criterion for assigning value. Taylor (1991: 37) explains this as a situation in which 'all options are equally worthy, because they are freely chosen and it is choice that confers worth'. This logic risks a slide into relativism, where the significance of difference and diversity is lost. To recognize difference, it is not enough to value the right to make different choices, because mere difference, in itself, can't provide the ground of equal value. Recognizing difference as significant requires a horizon against which that significance is made intelligible. Therefore, if differences are to matter, beyond the acknowledgement that all individuals should have the equal right to make choices, a substantive condition must also be met.

> To come together on a mutual recognition of difference – that is, of the equal value of different identities – requires that we share more than a belief in this principle; we have to share also some standards of value on which the identities concerned check out as equal. There must be some substantive agreement on value, or else the formal principle of equality will be empty and a sham. (Taylor, 1991: 52)

Secondly, the moral force of authenticity is linked to the dialogical nature of identity. Authenticity requires the generation of an inward sense of uniqueness, but this can only be done through dialogue and negotiation with others. Seeking self-fulfilment without regard for the ties we have to others undermines the condition required for authenticity because our identities rely, in crucial ways, on recognition from others. Unlike forms of recognition conferred on individuals through formal social roles or positions, 'inwardly derived, personal, original identity doesn't enjoy this recognition a priori' (Taylor, 1991: 48). Recognition is generated through dialogical relations; therefore individuals are intrinsically dependent on others. Discourses of choice that preserve the formal recognition of difference – that is, the right to make individualized choices based on individual experience – but deny the validity of holding up the substance of these choices for scrutiny can be problematic.

Conclusion

These discussions illustrate how the language of agency, autonomy, and choice is a minefield for third wave feminism. These concepts are all vulnerable to misappropriation and misuse, certainly; but even when deployed with the force of genuine intent behind them they involve extremely difficult debates for feminism, and consequently the 'complex ambivalence' (Di Stephano, 1994) that the concept of autonomy creates for feminism continues. For third wave feminism, these debates centre upon the tension that defines the relationship between autonomy and interdependence. New femininities, the product of processes of detraditionalization within late modernity, constitute femininity through the lens of increased individualism, in combination with the influence of feminism and of a culture infused with neoliberal values that increasingly incite women to remake themselves in the image of free and successful individuals (McLeod, 2002). The convergence of competing discourses around the notion of 'choice' greatly complicates a feminist analysis of women's agency in late modernity. Rather than clarify the nature of that complexity, third wave discourses often invoke contrasting and incompatible versions of the ideal of autonomy. Within the contemporary post-feminist constellation, there are at least three versions or forms that are in circulation. Firstly, there is the autonomy accorded to neoliberal entrepreneurial selves. Secondly, there is a presumption of autonomy, of the sort associated with the individualized reflexive do-it-yourself biographies of late modernity. Thirdly, there is the distinctive value of autonomy advocated by feminism, which recognizes and critiques the relations of power that result in individuals having differential access to conditions that support the realization of autonomy. The conflation of these positions dehistoricizes the significance of claims made on behalf of women, and in so doing it depoliticizes the concept as well. We must ask what the effects of making particular choices are. Whose values define what the good choices are? Who has the authority to determine how choices should be negotiated?

Third wave feminism faces the challenge of generating a critical response to the emergence and celebration of women's choice – one that draws a distinction between choice for the sake of choice and choices that increase women's autonomy. This is a challenge undertaken from within a post-feminist social constellation in which the mainstreaming of feminist choice complicates the constitutive role that autonomy plays in the formation of gender identities and relations.

As discussed in Chapter 5, within third wave discourse there is an often apparent unease associated with making statements that may be deemed to be overly prescriptive, as this is believed to lead to the exclusion of different expressions of feminism. Drawing on a post-structuralist sensibility, third wave constructs the feminist subject through multi-vocality, ambiguity, and the possibilities inherent in non-dichotomous thinking. However, beyond the generality of terms such as 'multiple feminisms', 'diversity', and 'contradiction', the substantive content of the definition of third wave feminist identity lies largely with the individual. Therefore, it is the individual who is privileged as the site of access to what third wave feminism means. The analysis undertaken in this chapter, however, highlights the complicated nature of feminist critique and the need for evaluative standards to be in place if choices and difference are to have any substantial import. These standards are social and cannot be generated from the individual taken in isolation. There are two primary risks associated with the failure to develop strategies for engaging critically with the language of choice and autonomy, which has become a prevalent feature of late modernity. Firstly, third wave feminism may become defined by an 'anything goes' ethos, in which the only way respect may be granted to women's choices is by valuing the act of choice itself. This is a form of 'soft relativism' whose guiding principle is the right of each individual to discover and assert what is right for them and to pursue their self-fulfilment accordingly. Definitional matters and evaluative standards rest with each individual and therefore cannot be subject to criticism or appraisal by others, for 'what this consists of, each must, in the last instance, determine for him – or herself. No one else can or should try to dictate its content' (Taylor, 1991: 14). The second risk that must be negotiated is that of 'moral subjectivism' – a position taken when it is asserted that what may be deemed as right or good for each individual cannot be grounded in reason or in the nature of things. Instead, that which is regarded to be right is the product of what each individual prefers and adopts accordingly, merely by being drawn to that preference (p. 18). From this position it would not be reasonable to make judgements about or to debate the content of what each deems to be right for him or herself. In contrast, theories of relational autonomy proceed on the basis that what we value and what we 'know' to be good for us is socially produced and therefore has to be open to evaluation and critique, as particular social configurations will produce conditions that are better than others for realizing collective aims, whether expressed in terms of social justice, of a good life, or of human flourishing. Third wave discourses, in emphasizing the individualizing dimension of autonomy, operate with an underdeveloped conceptualization of the social. For example, a focus on how contemporary social conditions produce a feminine subject position that is internally contradictory is present in many third wave texts, but this discussion stops short of a critical analysis of those contradictions, tending instead towards the affirmation of contradiction as inherently subversive while simultaneously paralysing the critical capacities of subjects and of feminism itself.

7
Generational Dynamics and Feminist Futures

Third wave feminism positions itself against a post-feminist backlash, which has denigrated feminism for its purported perpetuation of women as 'victims'.[1] In opposition to this backlash, third wave feminists advocate the continued need and indeed viability of a feminist identity; however, it is claimed that this is a distinct identity, which is discontinuous with the identities associated with second wave feminism. The construction of a distinction between a second wave and an emergent third wave is a vital constitutive element in third wave's narration of feminism history and in its own positioning within different feminisms.[2] The relegation of second wave feminism to the status of a necessary but outdated stage in feminism's trajectory serves to legitimate many of the claims made by third wave particularly as it presents itself as a corrective to feminism's shortcomings. Yet by invoking the wave metaphor a relationship with the established enterprise of feminism is also suggested. So on the one hand, third wave feminism seeks to establish a radical figuration of feminist subjectivity that is *not reducible* to second wave principles and problematics. Yet on the other hand, invokes a *reproductive temporality* by constructing its place as a successor to second wave within feminism's time. By charting feminism as a linear movement through consecutive waves, third wave feminism relies upon a 'then and now' binary logic, which sets up a third wave as an antidote to the failure it attributes to the second wave, to deal adequately with conditions that demand feminism to encompass contradiction, multiplicity, and non-unitary identities. This chapter offers a critique of the relationship that third wave feminism constructs with other forms of feminism by analysing how the proclaimed discontinuous identity of this wave is established through a logic of negative difference and disavowal, which is at odds with the desire to establish an irreducible third wave feminist identity.

[margin note: N.B. B's analysis]

To develop this argument, it is necessary first to provide a critical account of the generational metaphor that has been used to narrate feminism's history, and to examine how its associated logic of reproduction increases antagonisms between feminisms. A logic of reproduction relies upon feminism being 'passed on' intact (Adkins, 2004) and, when it is successful, it acts as a guarantor for bringing a feminist future into being. Therefore, the disjuncture that exists at present between different 'waves' of feminism is often posited as a site of loss and crisis. A lack of unity across feminisms is interpreted as one of the factors that contribute to the sense that feminism has not been successfully passed on. The third wave, with its claim to discontinuity with second wave feminism, is often positioned as part of the problem of feminism's present failure. Advocating for new feminist subjectivities that are irreducible could move third wave feminism out of a linear temporality that holds feminism in a state of 'crisis'; but such potential is ultimately negated by the ways in which third wave literature positions itself *against* second wave feminism. This relationship is constructed through a set of binary terms joined through an oppositional logic in which one term is negated to establish the other. Such logic is incompatible with a non-linear temporality, which would support the claim for feminist identities that do not negate other identities. To take third wave feminism's claim to offer a radical figuration of a feminist subject seriously requires a concept of difference that does not collapse back into a binary opposition. The possibility of thinking about feminism in terms of alternative and non-reductive temporalities should be taken on as part of the third wave feminist project.

The limits of reproductive time

Third wave feminism is concerned with gender relations but establishes itself as a critique of feminism, and therefore much of the third wave literature is focused on defining its relation to feminism and on setting out the terms of its own perspective on the significance of gender in contemporary social conditions. This requires third wave to negotiate a precarious space, which exists in tension with both second wave feminism and a post-feminist backlash (Kinser, 2004: 124). In third wave literature the generational metaphor is often used as a temporal register to organize our understanding of relations between women and to construct the relationship between feminism and time in a particular way (Gillis and Mumford, 2004; Purvis, 2004). A common point of reference for the construction of a third wave position is the suggestion that a new sensibility is required by women who are located on one side of the divide defined by generational difference.

> Young women coming of age today wrestle with the term [feminist] because we have a very different vantage point on the world than that of our foremothers. We shy from or modify the label [feminist] in an attempt to articulate our differences while simultaneously avoiding meaningful confrontation [...] for many of us it seems that to be a feminist in the way that we have seen or understood feminism is to conform to an identity and way of living that doesn't allow for individuality, complexity, or less than perfect histories. (Walker, 1995: xxxiii)

By signalling that second wave feminism is an embodiment of the past, this narrative is organized by one of the dominant frameworks used for understanding feminism's complexity – a generational metaphor underpinned by the logic of reproduction (Bulbeck, 2001; Henry, 2003; Looser and Kaplan, 1997; Roof, 1995, 1997; Wiegman, 2000). The generational metaphor, however, with its logic of succession and teleological ordering, has exacerbated the sense that the present moment for feminism represents a serious disjuncture between its past and its future. Feminism is defined in significant ways by the aim of bringing a future into being that is different from the present, and as such is a future that may be embraced wholeheartedly (Grosz, 2005). In debates about whether or not third wave feminism contributes to this feminist project, the present is often assessed in terms of the absence of signs of this promised future (Purvis, 2004). The problematic of present time in feminism is apparent in the emergence of a 'crisis narrative' that depicts feminism as having lost its coherence and sense of purpose. There is a spectre of failure that haunts contemporary feminism and has dominated the political imaginary of academic feminism since the 1990s

(Wiegman, 1999/2000). This perceived failure of feminism's present is attributed to various factors, but foremost amongst these has been the assertion that the object of feminism, along with its goals and self-definition, is less coherent and less transparent than was once thought. Kavka expresses this sentiment thus:

> Feminism ain't what it used to be. Perhaps with some nostalgia, many of us who call ourselves feminists look back to the peak of the second wave in the 1970s, to a feminism that in retrospect seems to have had a clear object (women), a clear goal (to change the fact of women's subordination), and even a clear definition (political struggle against patriarchal oppression). Such clarity is a trick of memory, no doubt [...]. (Kavka, 2001: ix)

It is implied in the crisis narrative that feminism was once a uniform and unified project and that the possibility that feminism might continue to be a clearly recognizable entity has been counteracted by the loss of certainty that critiques of modernist principles such as progress, universality, and truth have brought to bear on feminist knowledge claims. Perhaps the clearest blow to this certainty was delivered as the object of feminism came under increased scrutiny from within feminism itself. The more that feminism has become self-conscious, the more anxious it become about itself (Elam and Wiegman, 1995). For Adkins (2004), this shift represents an engagement with a contemporary social formation in which feminism's objects of critique are increasingly taking on the characteristics of feminist critique itself. As discussed in Chapter 2, feminism has been incorporated into the object of its inquiry through an increased self-consciousness marked by internal reflexivity. This development, Adkins argues, has created unease amongst some feminists, because it is interpreted as a turning away from feminisms' *proper* object and associated political project – 'a movement away from the subject–object problematic (reflection on and critiques of the world) towards a subject–subject dynamic (internal reflection and critique)' (Adkins, 2004: 433).

The crisis narrative is structured by a set of binaries that are implicitly organized in temporal terms, to indicate that a profound shift has taken place as feminism has moved its focus away from collectivity to fragmentation; from 'real' world activism to academic institutionalization; from socialism to post-structuralism; from identity to difference; from a politics of doing to a theory of knowing; from social inequality to subjectivity; and from the material to the cultural (Adkins, 2004). For feminists such as Segal (2000), these shifts do not represent progress but indicate the loss of a utopian political vision collectively shared and sought after. From Segal's point of view, 'difference based feminisms' or the 'new' feminism of the 1990s, which draws heavily upon 'poststructuralist theorizing, phallogocentrism or on women's nomadic, multifarious but ineluctable "otherness" ', is determined to distance itself from the 'old equal-rights feminism' of the 1970s (2000: 22).

> Time, one might think, for a renaissance of feminist politics. But few women have the time, even if they had the inclination (in these days when only instrumentalized self-serving is applauded) to sift through the potentialities and perils of differing versions of feminism. This leaves only a contentious minority of women attempting to map out and assess which different pieces in the jigsaw of feminism get picked up, leaving us to ask just who is selecting the fragments and whose particular interest their delivery serves. (Segal, 2000: 36)

This perceived failure to bring the future to its utopic completion renders the present as a site of mourning inhabited by a 'melancholic orientation', which refuses to come to terms with the present but instead remains lodged in the past, forever attached to its lost object (Adkins, 2004; Brown, 1999). When what was hoped for in the past is absent from the present, an unhealthy attachment to that past may form. In addition, Wiegman (2000) argues that the failure of the present invokes a *loss of the future*. In this narrative of 'apocalyptic time', the current generation of feminists is often seen to have betrayed 'the ethos, intentions, and critical dimensions of a purportedly more activist feminist past, a time prior to both the academic institutionalization of feminism and its public-sphere decline' (Wiegman, 2000: 805). Within the register of apocalyptic time, the proliferation of feminisms and of debates about its proper object is often linked to the ways in which feminism has dealt with difference.

> It is safe to say that, at the beginning of the new century, academic feminism finds itself so deeply troubled about the internal

dynamics of 'difference' that women's very incommensurabilities with one another serves as one of the most powerful forces in narrating feminisms' apocalyptic end. (Wiegman, 2000: 808)

In debates about the relationship between separate waves of feminism, the primary source of incommensurability, which holds feminism within apocalyptic time, is the differences between women that are accounted for by the logic of generational difference. These are differences that are constructed according to a teleological narrative that requires origins and successions. Since the present moment defies an orderly handover of the past into the present, then into the future, failed reproduction is the issue that lies at the heart of the apocalyptic narrative. The generational metaphor holds feminism within a deeply problematic temporality and places demands upon feminism that, due to its complexity, it cannot meet. Social progress within this model depends upon the replacement of the past with the present, which is then similarly overcome and replaced. This movement over time disallows variations, and when new experiences or concerns emerge women can be found in opposition to each other, thereby preventing the formation of relations between equals (Roof, 1997: 72).

Generational binaries frame such oppositions. On the one hand, if progress is understood as emerging through replacement, then the logic of succession introduced by the mother/daughter trope means that an older generation of women become the object of disavowal and dis-identification (Henry, 2003). On the other hand, the mother/daughter trope and its accompanying familial connotations present feminist relations as being caught up in a heteronormative Oedipal drama in which the language of inheritance and debt strains relationships. Indeed the notion of ownership is often implicit in competing versions of feminism. Within a generational chronology, those who come later are bound by the reproductive logic of cause and effect to remain 'dutiful' (Eisenhauer, 2004; Roof, 1997). Feminism becomes something that is inherited or bequeathed intact rather than created.

Importing the full force of Oedipal rivalry, recrimination and debt, generation is neither an innocent empirical model nor an accurate assessment of a historical reality. Rather, generation reflects and exacerbates Oedipal relations and rivalries among women, relies on a patriarchal understanding of history and a linear cause–effect narrative, and imports ideologies of property. (Roof, 1997: 71)

Detloff (1997) points out that the generational metaphor encourages fractures in women's relationships within academia and shores up those conditions that generate a 'politics of contempt' between women who find themselves on opposite sides of a gap defined as generational. Within the academy, 'sufficient individuation and an ability to dispense with the work of one's precursors are still the hallmarks of academic success' (Detloff, 1997: 81). Operating from this mode, rooted as it is in a logic of self versus other, limits one's capacity to engage with difference and erects a barrier to the furthering of feminist scholarship. This dialectical model of individuation, which resolves difference through its elimination, hinders dialogue, and inhibits generous exchange between women whose differences are complex and multiple, but get reduced to being generational.

The overly simplistic and reductive image of feminism perpetuated by the generational metaphor inadvertently colludes with anti-feminist forces that seek to depict feminism as fractured, impotent, and obsolete. The suggestion that differences within feminism result in profound incompatibility fuels a stalemate that confines feminism's main problem within its own borders and deflects attention from other, more productive sites of analysis. This model of relations between feminisms

> ... with its chimera of order and all-too-real Oedipal drama focuses blame, energies, and even the dilemma of women's relationships in the wrong place: among women themselves. Instead of looking to larger institutional and cultural forces that perpetuate sexism, foster rivalry, and undervalue women's contributions, we look to ourselves and to what we see as a family drama as the cause of our dysphoria while thinking that a correct and orderly disposition of generational history and appropriate recognition would solve the problem. Of course, this isn't a fitting model at all but, rather, contributes to the production of a tension that might otherwise not be so prominent, while preventing the emergence of other, less hostile, more charitable models. (Roof, 1997: 85)

Third wave subjectivities

The reproductive logic that lies at the core of the generational metaphor compels feminism to operate in a self-identical mode, as this secures certainty and serves the aim of predicting and controlling the future. To guarantee futurity, this model of time requires origins, history, and a continuity that translates, for feminism, into 'a story of maternal order and generational succession, thereby reproducing a model of feminist subjectivity that requires it to be self identical across time' (Wiegman, 2000: 809). Feminism has often relied upon the privileging of individual experience and consciousness as a foundation for making knowledge claims. The desire for knowing the future, therefore, becomes grounded in a particular origin – the feminist subject or the authorial 'I'. The epistemological position that follows assumes that 'feminist consciousness has a consistent content and that the processes and practices of its enunciation are already known' (Wiegman, 2000: 819). Within this model the means for mechanically reproducing the past into the future is a self-identical feminist subjectivity, which is fashioned in a mimetic relation to those already in existence. Identities and practices that deviate from what feminism 'already knows' are therefore treated as 'nothing less than betrayals, of both the personal and the political kind' (Wiegman, 2000: 813). The 'real' feminist subject bases the criteria for success on what was 'right back then' and is able to judge the present as a failure of reproduction.

When it operates within a reproductive temporal register, feminism is prone to acting as a disciplinary force by granting recognition only to what is already known – which makes feminist subjectivities that may not be self-identical unintelligible. Therefore generational metaphors disallow feminist subjectivities that emerge spontaneously as specific sites of resistance within particular historical conditions. These dis-continuous or non-originary productions exist out of sync with a teleological organization of feminism's political time.

> To think about feminism's political time as nonlinear, multidirectional and simultaneous [...] means engaging with a highly mobile and non-identical feminism, one whose historicity is not captured

by crafting for feminism an identity based on continuities of feminisms' political time. (Wiegman, 2000: 811)

The identities that are constructed in third wave feminist discourses are suggestive of such irreducibility. As argued in Chapter 2, third wave feminism emerged in the early 1990s – a decade in which feminist theory became increasingly concerned with producing adequate accounts of the intricate constitution of gendered subjects in light of critiques of the foundational status of the category 'woman'. Third wave discourses have tended to embrace the uncertainty that surrendering a belief in universals brings about and have articulated the grounds for a renewed feminism from this position of undecidability. Drawing on a post-sructuralist sensibility, third wave feminism embraces multi-vocality, ambiguity, and the possibilities inherent in non-dichotomous thinking. Key advocates of third wave have argued that 'we are the products of all the contradictory definitions of and differences within feminism, beasts of such a hybrid kind that perhaps we need a different name altogether' (Heywood and Drake, 1997: 3).

Embracing contradiction and multi-vocality as the basis for a new form of feminism had been a key strategy for counteracting claims that diversity has brought fragmentation and the demise of feminism. Furthermore, in the face of the backlash politics of the 1990s and of the portrayal of feminists as a group of extremists who, in the name of feminism, have 'embarked on a moral and spiritual crusade that would take us back to [...] the nineteenth century values of sexual morality, spiritual purity, and political helplessness' (Denfeld, 1995: 10), third wave feminists have claimed a feminist identity, but they are doing so by refusing to be bound by a feminist ideal not of their own making. The heavy reliance on post-structuralist theories of non-unitary identities informs an advocacy for 'a playful incorporation of performed identities, even when they contradict one another' (Dicker and Piepmeier, 2003: 16). It is claimed that these strategies will 'change the face of feminism as each new generation will, bringing a different set of experiences to draw from, an entirely different set of reference points, and a whole new set of questions' (Walker, 1995: xxxiv). Third wave feminism is constituted by claims that 'this generation of feminists wants its own institutions and a right to its own attitudes and interpretations' (Baumgardner and Richards, 2000: 138).

As explored in Chapter 4, autobiographical accounts feature strongly in third wave discourse and are a privileged medium for making claims about how this brand of feminism shapes everyday life. In these writings the experiences associated with the conscious embodiment of contradictions that come from living in late modernity are presented as a form of 'lived theory' and are intended as a response to the shortcomings of both second wave feminism and post-feminism. A focus on individualized contradictions in particular and on the role these play in the production of gendered subjectivities forms the basis for a third wave politics that often coalesces around the production of new femininities, characterized by amalgamations of contradictions and by the bringing together of seemingly incongruous elements. Resistance is expressed in a politics of performative transgression, undertaken through the re-appropriation of derogatory terms like 'bitch' or 'slut', so that they can be recast as descriptors of confident identities for women. By embodying and enacting contradictions, third wave femininities aim to disturb the repetition of dominant signifying practices and to open up new realities (Krolokke and Sorensen, 2005: 18).

This performative politics is illustrated in one strategy that seeks to reconfigure feminine subjectivity by placing emphasis on the pleasurable and knowing performance of ironic femininity. Baumgardner and Richards (2000), two of the primary advocates for reclaiming and resignifying the word 'girl', argue for the establishment of a new feminist identity, which calls into question the binary of girl/woman.

> Girlies are adult women, usually in their mid-twenties to late thirties, whose feminist principles are based on reclaiming girl culture (or feminine accoutrements that were *tossed out with sexism during the Second wave*), be it Barbie, housekeeping, or girl talk. (Baumgardner and Richards, 2000: 400; emphasis added)

This strategy of valourizing feminine culture is reminiscent of the 'gynefocal aesthetic' of the cultural feminism of the 1970s, which challenged androcentric privilege by celebrating traits traditionally denigrated by their association with femininity. Similarly, the intent is to release femininity from its encoding as frivolous, trivial, or inconsequential within dominant culture; but Baumgardner and Richards (2000) make clear that this celebration of femininity is not like that of the second wave. They argue that the celebration of the feminine associated with second wave feminism advocated a *separate* culture; a utopia or, as they say, a feminine 'ghetto'. For third wave feminism, 'having or loving our own culture isn't the same as cultural feminism [...] it's just feminism for a culture-driven generation' (Baumgardner and Richards, 2000: 134). The generational logic used here sets third wave against the second wave; indeed these identities depend quite literally upon casting second wave out of the present moment. Performed identities are produced through the re-appropriation of what *previous generations* of feminists critically dispossessed.

> Girlie says we're not broken, and our desires aren't simply booby traps set by the patriarchy. Girlie encompasses the tabooed symbols of women's feminine enculturation – Barbie dolls, makeup, fashion magazines, high heels [...] Young women are emphasizing our real personal lives in contrast to what some feminist foremothers anticipated their lives would – or should – be: that the way to equality was to reject Barbie and all forms of pink-packaged femininity. (Baumgardner and Richards, 2000: 136–137)

The embrace of attitudes, values, and behaviours once considered decidedly non-feminist raises questions about the boundaries of feminist identity. Can a girl be a feminist, or is a girl someone who becomes a feminist after gaining the requisite experience and knowledge? How does one become a feminist? What is the nature of such a process? These questions reveal one of the central, and most interesting, tenets of the third wave – a commitment to engage critically with the foundational concepts of feminism by asking who the representational subject of feminism is (Siegel, 1997a). Eisenhauer (2004: 87), for example, argues that the 'girl' operates as a crucial site for critiquing many of the normative assumptions of feminism. Rather than ask what feminism mean to girls, she suggests that a more productive line of inquiry would proceed from asking what girls mean to feminism. She argues that, within feminism, an exclusionary logic produces a binary in which Woman is constituted in opposition to Girl, and that girlhood is portrayed as a state that must be overcome through a progressive 'enlightenment' if one is to arrive at and become included within the subject of feminism. This logic reduces girls to a one-dimensional category, defined by lack of genuine experience, critical abilities, and agentic force (Taft, 2004: 70), and produces a set of hierarchal binaries that correspond to the dichotomy woman/girl, including 'effective/ineffective, real/imaginary, agent/victim/ and whole/divided' (Eisenhauer, 2004: 87). Against this logic of negation, third wave feminists defend a feminist identity that is irreducible and, as such, places this feminist subjectivity outside of a temporality in which binary terms are set against each other, with one term repudiating the other. This form of exclusionary logic is one that third wave feminism claims to be particularly attuned to, and it suggests that third wave feminism aims to short-circuit the kinds of generational logics which underpin the anxious expression of feminist 'crisis narratives'. A sensitivity to the limits of binary thinking is at the core of its advocacy for a feminism that is inclusive of women's difference from each other. Relations internal to feminism and to the differences that constitute women's experiences are the object of concern in how third wave narrates its own position and commitments.

Upon close examination, however, it can be seen that the claim to inclusivity that is constitutive of third wave feminism relies upon a logic that actually reproduces the dynamics of inclusion and exclusion. This problem arises, specifically, in the way in which third wave feminism distinguishes itself from second wave feminism. The claim is made that a defining distinction between the second and the third wave is the latter's ability to encompass difference, while the former is – implicitly and at times explicitly – characterized as unable to operate inclusively of women's differences. For third wave feminism, respecting and working with difference requires the 'development of modes of thinking that can come to terms with the multiple, constantly shifting bases of oppression in relation to the multiple, interpenetrating axes of identity, and the creation of a coalition politics based on these understandings' (Heywood and Drake, 1997: 3). In short, third wave feminism defines itself and its difference from second wave through its self-proclaimed ability to work constructively with 'paradox, conflict, multiplicity, and messiness' (Dicker and Piepmeier, 2003: 16).

The defining principle of accommodating difference is at its most explicit in the claim that one of the major corrective tasks faced by third wave feminism is that of moving beyond the essentialist conceptions of 'woman' put forward by the second wave. Heywood and Drake (1997: 8) describe the 'definitional moment' of third wave feminism as proceeding from critiques levelled at the white (second wave) women's movement by women of colour and by US's third-world feminisms. Once this moment is chosen as the origin of third wave feminism, second wave feminism is left behind, constructed as too narrow in its focus and perceived as ethnocentric, heterosexist, exclusionary, and overly prescriptive. Therefore, the association of second wave feminism with simplistic and essentializing tendencies renders it obsolete and relegates it to the past. The next wave is left to negotiate a new gender order and set of social conditions constituted by diversity and increased complexity. This construction of second wave feminism simultaneously justifies third wave arguments and legitimates the 'truth' of the claims put forward because they are constructed as *progressive*.

> With no utopic vision of the perfectly egalitarian society or the fully realized individual, third wave feminists work with the fragmentation of existing identities and institutions. If third wave feminism distinguishes itself from the second wave in any definable way, it is in its emphasis on making room for contradictions. We struggle to accommodate the differences and conflicts *between* people as well as *within* them. (Reed, 1997: 124)

The construction of feminism in these terms is exemplified in a discussion, published in one of the popular third wave anthologies, *Catching a Wave* (2003), between a mother and a daughter who debate the relationship between second and third wave feminism, each generation representing what is being discussed as clearly divergent forms of feminism. In this conversation Erin, the daughter, purposively distances herself from second wave when she says: 'I'm lucky to have the opportunity to explore and assert my feminism. But unlike you and other second wavers, I will never be able to define my feminism clearly because of the erratic nature of the third wave, and I'm comfortable with that' (Harde and Harde, 2003: 123). Here contradictory identities are presented as a specific feature of the times in which these women came of age. Defining identity in this way assumes that a set of historical conditions produce a particular set of experiences, which then lead to a consciousness that third wave articulates in ways that second wave is unable to muster because it belongs to a different time. The disjuncture between a consciousness formed in these conditions and the feminist consciousness expressed in the second wave of feminism is seen to be caused by conditions of increased complexity, which prevent coherent and consistent identities from coming into being. The suggestion is implicit that this move, from a time of non-contradiction to a time of inescapable contradiction, is a chronological move.

Third wave feminism claims to be capable of operating comprehensively within and across a wide variety of social differences and is, therefore, able to accommodate the contradictions and ambivalence that may result. This position ought to be compatible with the simultaneous operation of different waves of feminism. However, in third wave discourse it is evident that these two distinctive waves of feminism are not accommodated or imagined to co-exist as irreducible forms of feminism. The distinction that is made between third wave and second wave feminism is one that suggests linearity, defined by the progressive movement from a feminism that imposes unity (essentialism) to a feminism that welcomes contradiction, non-unitary identities, and diversity (difference). In this formulation, second wave feminism belongs not only to a different temporality, but also to one that is *prior* to (and not simultaneous with) the time of third wave feminism. Third wave feminism ultimately reverts to generational time by assigning feminisms to chronologically different temporalities on the basis of the binary of equality versus difference. In the construction of second wave feminism there is an implicit suggestion of 'that was then' and 'this is now'. Second and third wave feminisms are cast as discrete, internally coherent, and mutually exclusive positions, each being one located in a distinct and separate time. Generational difference is constructed in terms that suggest not only discontinuity, but a complete disjuncture between groups of women occupying distinctly separate feminist positions, expressed in terms of consecutive waves of feminism. Such a construction glosses over the existence of internal contradictions and deliberations, suggesting levels of similarity that do not exist, while obscuring continuities between different positions.

Feminist histories

As Hemmings (2005: 118) points out, 'all history takes place in the present, as we make and remake stories about the past to enable a particular present to gain legitimacy'. Telling stories about feminism's present, past, and, by implication, future is a contested practice, but acknowledging that the 'truth' of feminism's history might be constructed differently is a useful starting point for deconstructing generational metaphors and for defusing the injurious effects associated with their deployment. Hemmings (2005) argues that, despite the complexity and variety that characterizing Western feminism, the dominant story told about it is one that is overwhelmingly singular, successive, and linear in nature. In this narrative, feminism moves forward over time, away from a focus on sameness between women towards a focus on difference. This narrative is implicitly endorsed by the generational metaphor that frames the second/third wave relationship. In this chronological narrative feminism is structured in two distinct ways. Firstly, by a temporal movement, which describes how feminism changes over time; and secondly, by a hierarchical relation, which describes a shift away from second wave's exclusion of difference towards a post-modern position, defined by its inclusion of diversity. This relation is hierarchical because it is implied that the nature of such a movement signals evolutionary progress.

> Western feminist theory tells it own story as a developmental narrative, where we move from a preoccupation with unity and sameness, through identity and diversity, and on to difference and fragmentation. These shifts are broadly conceived of as corresponding to the decades of the 1970s, 1980s and 1990s respectively, and to a move from liberal, socialist and radical feminist thought to postmodern gender theory. A shift from the naïve, essentialist seventies, through the black feminist critiques and 'sex wars' of the eighties, and into the 'difference' nineties and beyond, charts the story as one of *progress* beyond falsely boundaried categories and identities. (Hemmings, 2005: 166)

The structuring logic of 'then and now' sets up a series of binaries in which one term is validated at the expense of what the other term represents. Thus feminism is imagined through the tensions expressed in dualities such as closed/open; essentialism/deconstruction; simple/sophisticated – and so on. For advocates of third wave feminism who privilege the second term of these dualities, a narrative of progress is being achieved by feminism as time passes.

> Narratives of either progress or decline
> (both follow linear pattern + obscure complexities)

However, for others to privilege the second term is to contribute to a sense that feminism is in crisis, because it is felt that embracing the values implicit in those terms results in a loss of efficacy for feminism. As discussed earlier in Chapter 2, the crisis narrative is also structured by a set of binaries, but it is one in which integrity is invested in the first term: material/textual; real/linguistic; activism/nihilism. Thus the narrative creates a story of present failure for feminism.

The tendency to narrate feminism as moving from a concern with sameness in the 1970s, through one with identity in the 1980s, to one with difference in the 1990s creates two equally unhelpful and opposing positions (Hemmings, 2005). On the one hand, this linear trajectory permits the relevance of the past to be dismissed in the present moment. On the other hand, the past is romanticized as the time when 'real' feminism existed. Evaluations of feminism that rely upon the linear narrative and its suggestion of decline or progress, depending on where one's commitments lay, erase the ongoing contestations that have constituted the complex genealogy of feminist thought and practice and allow the potential that these debates have to be simply ignored or written off as inconsequential. While third wave feminism labours to argue for irreducible feminisms, the analytical and practical purchase of this strategy is counteracted by a narrative of progress and succession in which legitimacy is sought by denying the past in the present. In this narrative, different forms of feminism are ordered consecutively and coherently rather than made to co-exist in a less orderly and reductive fashion.

Historical narratives of feminism produce particular positions from which it is possible to speak the 'truth of feminism'; thus authorial privilege is granted to some, while other experiences and knowledge are disallowed. Indeed Siegel (1997b: 61) points out that, 'because feminism speaks itself differently at different times and in different locations, narrative chronologies that say "in this wave" tend to erase the heterogeneity of feminisms at any given moment'. When third wave feminism relies upon a generational metaphor to secure its legitimate place as the successor to a feminism whose time has passed, an ideological, historical narrative is re-inscribed – a narrative that was problematic for feminism to begin with.

A more radical telling of the third wave's position within feminism – and one that is more in keeping with the irreducible feminist subjectivity third wave attempts to invoke – would require a different formulation, which does not rely upon the binaries of 'second' wave and 'third' wave and their definitions of 'equality/difference' or 'uniformity/messiness':

> I suggest that we consciously detach history from narrative, that we look closely and ever-vigilantly at the stories *behind* the stories we tell, that we understand history as containing no truth, no knowledge, no enlightenment, that we narrate feminism not as a family affair or generational history but as a partial story with no beginning and no end and no structuring binaries. (Roof, 1995: 68)

Third wave's professed commitment to plurality, difference, and hybridity should be able to operate in such a space, but the potential to do so is limited by the way in which a generational metaphor is used to construct feminism as a developmental narrative of linear progress reduced to the succession of discrete generations. This analysis suggests the need for an alternative temporal register in which the complexity of feminism may be considered in terms which are non-linear, multi-directional, and open. Feminist theorizing of time begins from the premise that, 'like anything else humans consider, time does not exist independently of our observations, and specific approaches to time are thus social and human constructs' (Milojevic, 2008: 332). As a social construct, how time is understood varies across different societies and cultures and alters throughout history. Feminist analyses of time are unified by the 'acknowledgement of the complexity of temporal experience and the affirmation of this multiplicity and diversity as a vehicle of knowledge' (Leccardi, 1996: 175).

These analyses have challenged the socially dominant conception of time defined as linear, singular, and continuous, functioning so as to order, regulate, and synchronize social life. This privileged model, constructed around industrial work and machine time, has the effect of subordinating non-work and unpaid work time to 'productive' work time. By drawing attention to the co-existence of distinct experiences of time, feminist theory has shown that, although this fact remains largely unrecognized, dimensions of time and space are gendered and, as such, men and women will often be differentially positioned within the social realm. Historically this has meant the subjection of 'women's time' and experiences to the register of patriarchal time, which eventually 'smothered time's very richness, discontinuity, multiplicity and qualitative non-homogeneity' (Leccardi, 1996: 171). These alternative approaches to time, which incorporate gendered knowings, are marginalized in relation to dominant, hegemonic time.³ This 'hegemonic time is the approach that "wins" over all the others, and becomes naturalized as objective phenomena' (Milojevic, 2008: 333). Within such a system the principles of rationality and mechanical causality assume dominance, while alternative subjectivities are ignored and discounted.

Perhaps the best known analysis of the gendering of time is presented by Kristeva (1981) in her influential essay *Women's Time*, in which she argues that feminism's relationship to time varies according to three generations. The political goals of the suffragists and 'existential' feminists centred upon women's right of entry into historical time. Access to the subject position embedded in public space allowed women equal participation in the realm of time, which was taken for granted as natural, but in actuality privileged men. This demand for 'insertion into history' expressed a 'logic of identification' with the 'logical and ontological values' of existing malestream society. Demands for equality were universalized to all women, despite 'the problems of women of different milieux, ages, civilizations, or simply of varying psychic structures (Kristeva, 1981: 19). The generation of women who came to feminism after 1968 rejected the androcentrism of the privileged temporal register of social time and sought instead to construct a distinct feminist identity and 'consequently of temporality as such' (Kristeva, 1981: 19). Rather than seek to be included as equals in the register of masculine, historical time, they aimed to undermine the logic of the symbolic order itself in favour of articulating the specificity of sexual difference and women's particularity, which is sacrificed within the symbolic order. This required recognition of the irreducibility of sexual difference – a difference 'without equal in the opposite sex and, as such, exploded, plural, fluid, in a certain way nonidentical' – therefore outside of linear time (Kristeva, 1981: 19). This perspective expressed a need to 'give a language to the intrasubjective and corporeal experiences left mute by culture' and to validate 'women's time' which is cyclical, mythical, or 'monumental' time (ibid.). Kristeva, however, advocates another relationship between feminists and temporality. For a third generation, she argues, the task will be to combine the former two attitudes into a position that includes the insertion into history, as well as the 'radical refusal of the subjective limitations imposed by this history's time'. This attitude would operate within both linear time *and* reproductive time, within machine time *and* corporeal time as a whole, and it would require an acknowledgement of the specificity of each woman as well as of her multiplicity (p. 20).

Although Kristeva draws on the language of generations to examine variations in women's time and the positions that feminism has taken to challenge hegemonic time, she defines generation as a 'signifying space' and, most importantly, ends her analysis with the recognition of the parallel existence of different temporalities and of the possibilities produced by their interconnections within this space. Purvis (2004: 112), therefore, cites Kristeva's account as an example of how the relationship between feminism, temporality, and difference might be constructed in terms that resist paradigmatic closure. In this reading of Kristeva, the generational metaphor serves to distinguish different feminist *political* agendas that are *perspectival* rather than *sequential* and, as such, model 'a politically efficacious vision of the political time of third-wave feminisms, or a third-wave feminist consciousness', which are irreducible to other times and identities (Purvis, 2004: 114). It is because the concept of feminist generations is so contested that Purvis suggests retaining it; a strategic use of the concept can invite debate and encourage critical inquiry into the narratives that feminism deploys to represent its constitutive relations. Other readings of this essay, however, maintain that Kristeva's analysis remains too firmly entrenched in a reproductive logic to offer a really useful reinvention of feminism's time. Roof for example (1997: 83) maintains that Kristeva lands the force of her 'nongenerational generational history' on a third generation; a generation that will combine the 'linear and the monumental, the local and the global, the symbolic and the imaginary aesthetic. The third generation is imagined as a chip off the old' block.

> First-generation linear time spawns second-generation monumental time. Both defined by their times, both become dangerous in time. These opposites can do nothing other, in the ideology

of the production narrative, than, in a curious hetero-lesbian metaphor, together spawn a third generation of feminists, one that is an admixture of the first two, evidence of the operation of the oppositional, reproductive narrative. It is with this final filial product of the ironic union of two generations of feminists that Kristeva ends her generational history. (Roof, 1997: 84)

If the generational metaphor does not capture the complexity of feminism and its existence within and across time, how might we imagine this complexity otherwise? It has been argued in this chapter that there is a tendency within the third wave literature to rely upon a generational metaphor, underpinned by a negative concept of difference, to establish a relationship to second wave feminism. The 'then and now' binary that constructs this relationship establishes a third wave on the basis of a disavowal of feminism's past. At the same time the feminist subjectivities that third wave feminism claims to represent seek to be non-identical with those of second wave feminism and, as such, their establishment should not have to rely upon a negation. This is a contradiction that can be remedied by returning to feminist critiques of hegemonic social time.

Different times

The concept of 'women's time' has been developed precisely for the purpose of challenging binary structures and introducing an analytical approach that is better able to recognize complexity and difference. These are models that define time in polysemic terms and their development has served to make female time visible, as dominant formulations of patriarchal social and historical time have obscured experiences associated with women's activities. These models have also sought to establish the specificity of female time, 'starting from the non-hierarchic multiplicity of the dimensions of female temporality, closely interlaced with one another and unable to be conceptualized separately' (Leccardi, 1996: 175). The feature held in common by feminist theories of women's time is the complexity and diversity of temporal experience, which serves as an important element in producing feminist knowledge (ibid.). Proceeding from this perspective, it has been possible to reveal that linear time is not neutral but defined by a forward-looking momentum, driven by a desire to control the future and by a propensity to deny or suppress social and culture differences. Odih (1999: 33) points out that linear time presumes to be innocent, but its commitment to a single time means that it 'knows no Other'. Because hegemonic time suppresses difference and marginalizes experiences that fall outside of its linear parameters, the insistence that 'Other times' exist simultaneously has been a powerful strategy for challenging this hegemony. However, by categorizing different temporal registers as 'male' or 'female', these theories may inadvertently reinforce and reproduce the very exclusionary logic that is the object of feminist critique. Even though these theories are progressive insofar as they undermine masculine rationality by insisting upon the recognition of differential feminine knowledges, that difference is contained within a gendered dualism and, therefore, the strategy remains entrenched in 'a space already prepared for it by the intellectual tradition it seeks to reject' (Lloyd, 1984: 104, cited in Odih, 1999: 34).

> Whilst feminist suggestions of distinct 'male' and 'female' times draw our attention to the significance of gender to the discursive construction of linear time, their dualistic suppositions need to be treated with immense caution. By transforming what are merely heuristic categories into reified ontological realities, these feminist discourses attend to representational epistemologies and in so doing, often unintentionally, reinforce the hegemony of linear time. (Odih, 1999: 33)

Braidotti (1997: 28) similarly argues that attempts to claim the positivity of difference that rely upon a Hegelian framework are limited to a strategy of reversal where the best one might hope for is that the balance of power between the opposing poles will shift in a more favourable direction. Against this strategy, Braidotti advocates an approach based upon 'sexual difference' – a critical practice that begins from the assertion that the terms that constitute the opposition in a gendered dualism 'are *not* reversible, either conceptually or politically' (ibid.). These terms belong to a pre-existing system, formulated through asymmetrical power relations, and they 'carry built-in structural inequalities' (ibid.). Given this limitation, feminists working from a sexual difference perspective argue that an alternative structure is required in order that these terms be freed from their determination in a system that holds the terms in a negative relationship. A central concern here is to redefine difference in terms that are not contained within a binary which dictates that one term must necessarily occupy the place of the 'devalued other', and where being 'other than' does not equate with 'being-less-than' (p. 29).

Grosz (2005) draws upon such a conception of difference when she advocates the need to think about the future of feminism from within a new conceptual framework. Throughout Western thought the feminine is that which been negated, 'represented as a lack, the opposite, the same as, or the complement of the one subject' – the masculine (Grosz, 2005: 174). Within this economy, woman can only ever be the Other to the One. The aim is to dislodge difference from this negative relationship, so that it might be rethought in positive terms. Irigaray (1993), for example, argues that sexual difference is not what we have known in the past as such, nor is it the difference we understand today. Rather, because women have never been granted a time or space for themselves *as women*, sexual difference has yet to take place. This is not the same as arguing that women have never had an identity, indeed 'phallocentrism is explicitly *not* the refusal of an identity for women (on the contrary, there seems to be a proliferation of identities – wife, mother, teacher, nun, secretary, whore, etc.), but rather, the containment of that identity by other definitions and other identities' (Grosz, 2005: 174). At issue are the limitations of past and present representational systems and symbolic orders that allow for only one sex and its counterpart. If women are to be more than an 'afterthought', they need access to alternative conceptualizations and autonomous representations of sexual difference that are irreducible to one sex. This conceptualization releases difference as an effect of negation, allowing it to be rethought as an ontological positivity whose fullness is yet to be realized.

> Sexual difference is that which has yet to take place, and thus exists only in virtuality, in and through a future anterior, the only tense that openly addresses the question of the future without pre-empting it in concrete form or in present terms. Sexual difference does not yet exist, and it is possible that it has never existed. The sexes as we know them today have only model, a singular and universal neutrality. At best, equal participation is conceptualized [...] the existence of *at least* two points view [...] has yet to be considered. (Grosz, 2005: 175–176)

Sexual difference carries with it the implication that, at minimum, there are two 'ways of doing *anything*, without being able to specify in what ways they may develop or what form they may take place' (p. 166). This perspective invites a strategy for developing new modes of thought, which draws upon existing concepts, practice, methods, and languages but refuses the conventions associated with their usage, and does so in favour of redeploying them in different ways. Sexual difference operates as a 'provocation' prompting us to examine existing knowledges to understand what has been left out; what might be done differently; what potentials reside within the present but have yet to be actualized.

> It is because sexual difference hides itself in other concepts and terms, other oppositional forms – in the distinction between form and matter, between space and time, between mind and body, self and other, nature and culture, and so on, that it remains the latent condition of all knowledges and all social practices. (Grosz, 2005: 177)

For Grosz, the concept of sexual difference is implicitly linked to rethinking the future from a feminist perspective, as the time of sexual difference is the time of the future and as such orients us to what might become if we were to be no longer held within existing frameworks. Here time is thought of as a force of active variation or continual becoming, 'in terms which liberate it from the present, for time is the force of differing' – the process by which a subject is always in an act of becoming something else (p. 178). What we may come to know or think as the object of feminism may be imperceptible under the terms of our present knowledge and with the means by which sexual difference has been made meaningful up until now.

> This conception of sexual difference as yet to come, as virtual within patriarchy, is not, I believe, a utopian conception [...] rather, Irigaray's claim is ontological. There are (at least) two types of sexual being, irreducibly different, and not adequately representable under a single model or image. (Grosz, 2005: 177)

The future is not one that can be known or predicted on the basis of the present as it departs from and is uncontained by the past and the present. It is future that is yet to be (Grosz, 2000: 1017). In contrast the generational metaphor adopts a model of time and history that ties the future to the past and therefore limits the horizons through which the future may be imagined. A reproductive logic produces the present from the past by assuming that the present is essentially like the past; therefore the more knowledgeable we can become about this past, the better equipped we are to deal with the future. Following this logic, the future is then conceived as something we *already know* and can predict, as it is simply a variation on what has come before. Reproductive metaphors constrain our thinking about the future by limiting the possibilities it holds to the tendencies towards what has already been. This model 'inevitably produces a predictable future, a future in which the present can still recognize itself instead of one open to contingency and the new' (p. 1018).

Conclusion

Narrating feminism through a story of generational succession, while not uncommon in accounts of feminist history, has proven to be highly contentious and unproductive. Underpinned by a divisionary logic, generational metaphors can lead to the present being constructed on the one hand as a failure of orderly reproduction, and on the other hand as a site where a rich feminist past is disavowed. Feminist critiques of dominant time with its linear direction and propensity for the exclusion of difference even while assuming progress have, however, alerted us to alternative temporal registers, which introduce complexity to our analyses of feminism's past, present, and future. Redefining time through multiplicity admits of difference, affirms plural subjects, and recognizes 'the simultaneous presence of numerous, concrete and diversified experiences of time' (Leccardi, 1996: 175). It has been argued in this chapter that feminist theorizations of time have brought new models of thought and practices into being, and that these address three primary issues associated with the problematic deployment of a generational metaphor.

Firstly, in feminist re-creations of time, difference is not merely acknowledged and accommodated, but fundamentally repositioned as an ontological condition whose value is not dependent upon another term. From this perspective, differences within feminism need not lead to disintegration, disorderly turmoil, and ineffectual disarray. Ang (1997), for example, argues that the particularities that constitute women's experiences do produce moments of incommensurabilty, but that this need not undermine the unity that feminist political commitment requires. Cultural differences may create instances in which social encounters are marked by the irreducible experiences of individuals. For, despite the extent to which meaningful frameworks, experiences, and knowledge can be reduced to a common vantage point, it is also the case that there may be a 'residue of the particularity that cannot, ultimately, be shared'; however, this does not 'imply an absolute impossibility of communication', but rather such moments 'are precisely what propel us to go on communicating, forever chasing an ultimate fullness of understanding and complete commonality that are never achieved' (Ang, 1997: 59). From this perspective, the 'apparently impossible simultaneity' of incommensurable realities is the very condition that requires a commitment to work together and to take responsibility for ongoing negotiations.

Secondly, transcending generational metaphors opens up new possibilities for representing feminism's past, present, and future. The decolonization of the future rests upon the proliferation of alternative stories, histories, time frames, and methodologies, and a feminism that can tell only one story about itself will be limited in its capacity to contribute to such a project. Indeed, feminism should start by interrogating why particular 'truths' come to constitute its own history while other stories, composed of alternative experiences and knowledge, become obscured or sidelined. Hemmings (2005: 131) calls for thinking of feminism as 'a series of ongoing contests and relationships rather than a process of imagined linear displacement'. Potentially, this would generate a proliferation of stories and would make continuities in feminist values, concepts, and practices visible, strengthening rather than diminishing the resources feminism has for thinking the future. Feminist history cannot, therefore, depend upon a disavowal of the past, for 'the past is never exhausted in its virtualities, insofar as it is always capable of giving rise to *another* reading, another context, another framework that will animate it in different ways' (Grosz, 2000: 1020). Nor should the past be regarded as 'fixed, inert, given, unalterable'; it is 'inherently open to future rewritings', because the 'past contains the resources to much *more* than the present' (p. 1019).

Finally, rejecting a generational account of feminism facilitates the development of a politics of the self, which third wave feminism seeks to promote. This is a politics that can counteract the intensification of hegemonic time and its damaging effects. As Milojevic (2008: 341) argues, there is a need 'to find "liberation" from the globalised, computer-generated compressed time that threatens life itself'. Hegemonic time in the present moment of neoliberalism and individualization is indicative of such a threat. Third wave feminism seeks to examine what kinds of gendered subjectivities might be possible to inhabit in such a time, and insisting on the diversity of feminist temporality promises a greater understanding of how feminism is constituted by irreducible subjects across different times and spaces. Grosz's (2005: 167) exploration of time demonstrates that, rather than build a politics based upon the recognition of known identities, 'feminism may be well served to position the subject not as aim or goal of struggles, but as a sieve or cipher through which dynamic forces struggle to emerge'. Feminism then shifts away from only being able to recognize established and verifiable identities to a struggle for the 'right to act and to make according to one's own interests and perspectives, the mobilization and opening up of identity to an uncontained and unpredictable future'.

8
Closing Reflections

It is challenging to deliver an account of third wave feminism that adequately establishes its objectives, accurately captures its strengths and weaknesses, and satisfactorily assesses its potential. Dean (2009: 335) explains that, insofar as the phrase 'third wave feminism' lacks a clear, substantive referent, the discussions of 'third wave feminism' have tended to deploy this phrase as a 'discursive resource'. The aims pursued throughout the present book are consistent with this observation: the point of the analysis undertaken here is not to identify the clear boundaries of a discrete, empirical entity that can be said to fully and completely represent 'third wave feminism'. Instead, the aim has been to outline a set of general tendencies or features that, taken together, express an approach to thinking through the complex interaction of feminist principles, anti-feminist sentiments, individualizing forces, and neoliberal persuasions that constitute the gender order in the early twenty-first century. Approaching the study of third wave feminism in this way has relevance for how we might analyse the nature of gendered subjectivity, the practice of feminist politics, the production of feminist knowledge, and the performance of feminist critique at this historical juncture.

Third wave feminism has sought to respond to a wide range of economic, political, and cultural features of contemporary Western society, which have affected the ways in which gendered subjectivities are articulated and enacted. Broadly speaking, key factors include the rise of global capitalism, the expansion of information technologies, crises of environmental degradation, 'multiple modes of sexuality, changing demographics, and declining economic vitality' (Dicker and Piepmeier, 2003: 14). Heywood and Drake (2004) explain how a number of demographic and economic determinants shape third wave feminism. New levels of gender parity in educational attainment and occupational success mean that women are as likely, or perhaps even more likely, to identify with their *generation* than with their *gender*. Under these circumstances, a feminism that relies upon intergenerational identification can be less effective than one that speaks to newly forming feminine subjectivities.

Secondly, third wave feminism has developed within a context in which there has been a proliferation of visual culture and the mass circulation of images of femininity. Rather than serve only as an object of critique, popular culture is also seen to simultaneously, provide, a site of pleasure and creativity. By refusing to deploy straightforward codes to designate contemporary gender ideals in terms of simple binaries such as 'good' or 'bad', third wave feminism insists upon the necessity of straddling binaries and of working with the contradictions that result. Negatively coded terms such as 'bitch', 'slut', or 'girl' are strategically re-appropriated in an ironic stance to express new amalgamations of contradictory feminine subjectivities. These emerge in acts of cultural production and consumption that seek to run counter to, and to subvert, dominant representations of femininity; yet they often draw upon the products of popular culture as resources (Garrison, 2000; Klein, 1997; Reed, 1997).

Thirdly, the tenets of third wave feminism are consistent with the view that late modern lifestyles are characterized by increased levels of insecurity and that this state of uncertainty prevents individuals from investing their identities in any one specific site, particularly in a job or in a profession (Heywood and Drake, 2004: 16). The destandardization of life courses in late modernity underscores the multifaceted nature of late modern identities, which by necessity have become more flexible, mobile, and complex (Beck and Beck-Gernsheim, 2002).

Lastly, third wave feminism attempts to articulate a response to qualitative shifts taking place in the restructuring of contemporary power relations. Globalization and the resulting world economic order it fosters have altered the concentration of wealth and power in many complex ways. For third wave feminists, the site for political struggle has been affected in this shift, as the 'enemy' has been increasingly decentralized and patriarchy itself has been dismantled as a primary object of critique (Heywood and Drake, 2004: 16). As such, this third wave of feminism does not privilege gender or sexual difference as its key site of struggle, nor does it limit itself to any single issue.

In addition to mapping out these general features of late modernity, it has been argued in this book that understanding third wave feminism involves, firstly, analysing the conditions that constitute the contemporary Western gender order and, secondly, giving a critical assessment of the theoretical project that third wave feminism promotes as a strategy for comprehending and intervening in those conditions. A genealogical analysis of feminism contributes to this task by illuminating the contingent factors that converge in particular places and at specific times to create concrete socio-historical challenges, which feminism seeks to engage with. It has been argued throughout this book that third wave feminism has emerged in a set of conditions best described as 'post-feminist'. Coole's (2000) concept of 'constellation' is a useful tool for identifying and evaluating the interventions that third wave feminism seeks to enact at this particular historical moment. Any particular constellation will have characteristics that are the product of a specific convolution of power relations. These relations affect political consciousness and impact upon the kinds of agency, identities, and sites of contestation that are possible. A post-feminist constellation is characterized by the cultural acknowledgement of gender equality as a social good; by an anti-feminist backlash, in which that acknowledgement produces the ground for denying the ongoing relevance of feminism; and by the circulation of neoliberal rationalities, which operate both to privatize gender issues and to co-opt feminist values in the service of promoting 'free' and 'responsibilized' gendered subjectivities (Duggan, 2003; Inoue, 2007; Kingfisher, 2007). The forces associated with these key dimensions of post-feminism complicate the production of femininity and, when taken together, provide a focus for feminist critique.

The pursuit of gender equality has been established over the past 30 years as an important global political and social goal. In comparison to a time when feminist politics and activism occupied a countercultural, oppositional position in relation to established social norms and institutions, feminist concepts and values are now manifest in policy and state structures; 'moreover, gender equality is increasingly framed as central to the realization of both modernization and economic efficiency and its achievement presented as a key to good governance' (Squires, 2007: 1). The recognition of gender equality has resulted in the expansion of educational and employment opportunities for women, while widening access to political participation. However, it has been observed that the success of the feminist movement may be partly accounted for by the alignment of particular feminist aims and values with the interests of wider social and economic transformations. Squires (2007: 3), for example, explains that 'egalitarian social movements have long been argued to play an important role in facilitating the consolidation of the institutions of governance that allow the economy to be productive' and, therefore, the current legitimacy granted to gender equality may be in large part due to its consonance with the present economic order.

The amenability that gender modernization has with current governance practices has not translated into any greater recognition and acceptance of feminism, indeed the opposite has taken place as gender equality ideals have gained acceptance. A post-feminist social constellation is organized by a robust rejection of feminism as a justifiable political stance. This is a defining contradiction of the current gender order: the legitimacy of gender equality is granted, but at the expense of openly identifying feminism as a valuable and necessary presence. Tasker and Negra (2007: 2–3) analyse the myriad ways in which post-feminist culture 'works in part to incorporate, assume, or naturalize aspects of feminism', while it also works 'to commodify feminism via the figure of woman as empowered consumer' and it invokes an 'invented social memory of feminist language as inevitably shrill, bellicose, and parsimonious'. In this process feminism is 'othered' and rendered obsolete by the figure of the successful, open-minded, self-determining woman. The impression is given that to 'hang on' to feminism would be misguided, old-fashioned, and senseless. In its place, women are offered newly empowered feminine subject positions and the opportunity to 'choose a self' in the act of encountering a wide range of choices within the areas of work, family, consumption, and the practice of sexuality (Budgeon, 2003). As McRobbie (2004b) has argued, these are choices that are to be embraced by young women as they take up their position as liberated 'modern' women; however, this freedom is granted on condition that both feminism and the critique of those choices and of the social conditions from which they arise are dismissed as a concern of the past.

Instead, gender politics in post-feminist culture is reduced to a programme of individualized choice or a politics associated with the 'self as project' (Tasker and Negra, 2007: 21), in which the significance of feminist values that are consistent with autonomy is evacuated and those values reoriented to align with practices of commodification and consumption.

The cultural features of a post-feminist constellation are also consistent with neoliberal rationalities and with their expansion from an economic programme of market fundamentalism into areas of everyday life that are not explicitly associated with the economy. Of primary concern is the infiltration of 'our "personal" sense of identity, interests, happiness, hopes, and even value of life' by neoliberal principles (Inoue, 2007: 80). In its cultural manifestations, neoliberalism operates as a form of governmentality by which individual conduct is organized by a range of everyday strategies and techniques. Neoliberal governance, therefore, may be conceptualized as a 'set of concrete practices, programs, and calculations by which the individual makes herself into a "sovereign" or "free" subject by choosing self-projects that constitute her individualness' (p. 82) and through which the individual comes to understand herself as particular type of person; 'self-governing, responsible, autonomous, self-sufficient, independent and entrepreneurial' (Kingfisher, 2007: 96). Comprehending the cultural dimensions of neoliberalism is central to understanding how the recognition of gender equality, the post-feminist dismissal of feminism, and a politics of the self that seems to have replaced oppositional feminist politics and critique have coalesced. Neoliberal self-governance is insidious because it 'threatens to align seamlessly with the individual's ethical practice of self-mastery and self-autonomy within feminist and liberal–democratic thinking, thus evacuating the critical edge of the latter' (Inoue, 2007: 82).

It is within this context that practices of gendered selfhood have been analysed, particularly as the figure of the empowered and unencumbered young woman has entered into the cultural imaginary and has invited identifications that necessarily eschew feminism as a condition for becoming a full participant in the culture of post-feminism. Female individualization is a process rife with contradictions, and foremost amongst them is the contradiction that, as femininity has been recoded through the language of choice and autonomy, norms associated with traditional gender dichotomies continue to circulate and shape idealized femininity. The continued significance of retaining particular physical attributes and character ideals can be accounted for not only by the resilience and retrenchment of established gender norms, but also by the celebration of particular 'feminine' traits and the importance accorded to 'people skills', 'emotional intelligence', and 'interpersonal skills', all of which are associated with the feminization of structures of labour markets and public institutions (Burman, 2009: 137). Gonick (2006: 2) points out that in this context discourses are in circulation that interpellate 'feminine/feminist subjects in non-unitary ways'. Contradictory discourses construct young women as both vulnerable and empowered, and produce irreconcilable demands. Idealized late modern femininity therefore requires the simultaneous performance of 'relationality and an investment in relations with others' – with the demands of 'modern subjectivity', which emphasize separation and autonomy (Gonick, 2004: 191). While the presence of contradictions and tensions within the norms of femininity is not a new phenomenon, it is argued that neoliberalism has introduced a distinctly different, structurally ambivalent subject position for women; therefore, as young women attempt to make themselves into the idealized successful subjects of late modernity, they experience a set of problems that are unique to the post-feminist gender order. It is within this order that third wave feminism attempts to promote a politics of the self that can counteract the depoliticizing dynamics that drive post-feminist culture.

There is a long-standing tradition of self-critique associated with feminist thought, which has contributed to the emergence of a third wave perspective. In accordance with that tradition, some of the key tendencies associated with third wave feminism now require scrutiny, particularly as a post-feminist constellation is constituted by a set of features that require a feminist response. How might we deploy a third wave feminist analysis to set a new feminist agenda? What does a third wave perspective offer, and where might those strategies require rethinking? In response to these questions, various aspects of a third wave perspective have been evaluated throughout these chapters, placing particular emphasis upon key *theoretical* assumptions that drive third wave feminism. A central aim of the third wave is to question the foundational concepts associated with second wave feminism – a focus that is made most evident by the ways in which third wave seeks to reconceptualize the subject of feminism and to open out the parameters for feminist identifications. This is achieved by asserting the value of diversity and difference amongst women – a position that not only problematizes collective identifications, but also is evident in the tendency to grant greater significance to individual experience. This shift has a range of consequences for how gender relations are theorized. Firstly, the claim is made within the third wave literature that new feminist identities are emerging, which are linked to, but are not reducible to, the aims and efforts of the second wave. Secondly, this shift manifests itself in a move away from a politics informed by collective norms towards a more individualized ethos, which can be characterized as a 'politics of the self'. A further consequence deriving from a focus on difference is evident in the way in which contradictions and the ambivalence that arise from occupying non-unitary subject positions are interpreted as sites of opportunity for rethinking feminist subjectivity within a more individualized political project. Female individualization is one of the most significant processes driving the re-negotiations of gender relations in late modernity; but it would be an oversight to view this process as indicative of unilateral progress. Delivering a critical understanding of individualization remains a critical issue for the third wave feminist project.

Personal theorizing is advocated by third wave feminism as a starting point for understanding the role that feminism plays in the identifications women make as they negotiate a social context that has been shaped by successful demands for greater gender equality. A return to the category of the personal provides an important focus for contemporary feminism, as idealized femininity is encountered by different women in different ways, and empirical studies reveal the complexity that is involved in the negotiation of this ideal. A feminist critique of this process is required to understand how reworked gender norms provide opportunities for women while also serving to regulate women's lives. The focus on experience and the value accorded to personal theorizing in third wave feminism suggest that, in studying the subjective dimension of newly emerging femininities, we should aim to problematize the selves under construction and to interrogate the social location within which those selves emerge. The value attached to individual experience has methodological and epistemological significance, although these issues are not given as much consideration as they could be given in the third wave literature, and at times experience tends to be reified. However, as a methodological strategy, starting from women's experience is consistent with understanding how gender identities and relations are being remade within the contradictory dynamics that constitute the post-feminist gender order. If experience is to be the starting point for a feminist project, this necessitates asking questions about how particular experiences are made possible at specific historical moments. An analysis of empirical studies of young women's identity projects illustrates how late modern social conditions create a structurally ambivalent feminine subject position, defined through the gendered dichotomy of relationality and autonomy. These studies illustrate just how complicated late modern femininities are and how efforts to make oneself into the 'idealized feminine self' are often confounded. Whereas third wave feminism promotes the value of ambivalence, these studies show that newly emerging subjectivities are constituted by tensions that do not necessarily find resolution in progressive strategies, but tend to lead to explicitly individualized orientations to both achievement and failure and to a dis-identification with feminism.

Third wave feminism's commitment to illuminating the personal and the subjective is also driven by the conviction that women should be granted the space to identify with feminism on their own terms rather than accept a definition imposed from outside. The right to self-representation is claimed on behalf of all women: a right that is inclusive of all differences and meant to generate a diverse range of expressions, which can adequately represent third wave identities. Moving away from collective representations towards these individualized articulations indicates that a fragmented and disparate platform is imagined for third wave politics. This 'politics of the self', is developed primarily within the cultural realm and centres upon creating spaces for counter-hegemonic representations of 'feminist femininity'. As feminist values have become incorporated into popular culture and into the spaces of everyday life, third wave feminism takes a sceptical stance towards the possibility of transcending the culture within which feminism is located and made. Therefore third wave politics focuses on the resources of everyday culture and aims to find strategies for reworking and subverting dominant cultural practices. Often undertaken through the appropriation of dominant representational practices, these strategies work with a conceptualization of power as multiple, contingent, and dispersed, which renders the dominant codings of femininity unstable. Without denying the potential reversibility of meanings, it is important also to develop ways of analysing how power materializes in systematic ways to produce and reproduce gender identities and relations that shore up the depoliticizing dynamics associated with post-feminism. There is nothing inherently radical or subversive about contradictory subjectivities. While language and representation are defined in the *abstract* by the unstable structures of language and meaning, context does matter; and, for a politics of the self to be effective, further analysis of contextual factors is required. As argued above, one of the dominant logics that drive neoliberalism is the appropriation and emptying of feminist values such as 'choice', autonomy, and self-reliance; therefore these terms are continually in circulation as sites of contestation. If a politics of resignification is really to represent a strategy with viable prospects, then a more detailed theorization of the effects that specific contexts have on acts of cultural re-appropriations of hegemonic practices and language needs to be worked out.

Critical attention to context also problematizes the ideal of 'choice' that is currently so pervasive in equality discourses. The assertion that increased choice provides clear evidence that gender relations have changed has generated heated debates. 'Choice' has become a deeply problematic ideal in late modernity, and perhaps represents the ideal that is most firmly lodged within the contested spaces and contradictory forces of the post-feminist gender order. It is an ideal that is extremely attractive, as well as malleable; therefore it acts as a perfect 'strategically deployable shifter' (Urciuoli, 2003). As the values associated with autonomy have increasingly become associated with contemporary femininity too, the assumption is made that the presence of choice, in and of itself, is liberating. Moreover, this assumption is accompanied by the belief that choice is synonymous with agency. However, feminist theories of autonomy reject the individualism associated with many mainstream theories and advocate rethinking autonomy as a social capacity. This perspective has purchase, particularly as femininity in late modernity is constituted through the tension of autonomy and relationality

(Gonick, 2004). By taking into account the social relations that make autonomy possible (or unattainable, for that matter), relational autonomy promises to deliver a more nuanced and contextualized analysis of the identities women are constructing within the tensions of post-feminism. Furthermore, relational theorizing enables a *critical evaluation* of the choices on offer, the choices being made, and the impact of those choices upon self and other. Crucially, this analysis is able to underpin political demands for a different set of conditions, that make alternative choices possible. Without invoking a standard – or a means of arriving at some standard – against which choices can be evaluated, third wave feminism ceases to operate as a critical enterprise. This is particularly pertinent to the context of a post-feminist gender order in which individual choice is upheld as a virtue and as a right over the evaluation of the substance of the choices in question. A further consideration relates to the ways in which power flows through the choices we make, so that these choices are both a site of agency, as is emphasized in many third wave texts, *and* sites of governance. It is the latter dynamic that third wave feminism tends to overlook.

Throughout this book, it has been acknowledged that third wave feminism exceeds the boundaries of a neat and tidy definition. Given the complex nature of the late modern social order, it is advantageous to pursue a similarly multi-dimensional feminism. Dean (2009: 342) argues, third wave feminism can operate effectively as an 'empty signifier' that brings 'a modicum of unity and coherence to an otherwise diverse set of feminist issues, while at the same time maintaining a degree of openness providing critical exchanges among feminists'. This observation identifies an elusive balance that third wave feminism needs to strike. One the one hand, third wave feminism recognizes that the late modern gender order is highly individualized and differentiated. The privileging of individual experience, a politics based on self-representation, and an assertion of autonomy and choice are deeply significant sites where gender relations are being negotiated. It is critical that a feminist response to the post-feminist gender order continues to be elaborated and that coherent engagement with the consequences of those negotiations is sustained. On the other hand, this project must be pursued in ways that recognize the limitations apparent in much of the third wave theorizing. Part of the openness professed by third wave feminism needs to feed back into the self-critical tradition that characterizes feminist thought and practice. It is in that openness that the potential of third wave feminism for further development lies; and it is in that spirit that the analysis of third wave feminism has been undertaken here.

Notes

Chapter 1

1. It is generally the case that third wave feminism is perceived as a distinctly Anglo-American phenomenon.
2. According to Heywood and Drake (2004: 13), third wave feminists are part of the generation born between 1963 and 1974. Other theorists avoid clear demarcations, preferring to engage with the problems that definitional debates present. Siegel (1997b: 77) leaves the phrase relatively open, using it to connote 'the diversity of feminisms articulated and practiced by contemporary young women'. See also the discussion in Gillis et al. (2004).
3. Freedman (2006: 85) points out that, soon after the re-emergence of the women's movement in the late 1960s, American journalists began reporting stories of its demise. This included the 1976 editions of *Harper's*. Similar stories appeared in 1980 in the *New York Times*, for instance 'The Radical Days of Feminism are Gone', and in 1990, when *News Week* announced 'The Failure of Feminism'. This was followed by an episode in 1998, when *Time* magazine asked online readers whether they thought that 'feminism is dead'. These kinds of stories continue as a regular in feature of the popular press in the UK.

Chapter 3

1. Beck and Beck-Gernsheim (2002) do not assert that this is a uniform trend but that the extent to which this is possible is impacted by both social background and educational level.

Chapter 4

1. The concept of a 'lived theory' is borrowed by Heywood and Drake (1997: 14) from bell hooks (1994: 59–75).
2. See critique in Segal (1999: 226–228).

Chapter 5

1. As outlined in Chapter 2, the term 'post-feminist' encompasses a broad set of meanings, including references to the influence of post-modernism and post-structuralism; the recognition of diversity within the category of 'woman'; and an anti-feminism backlash in which second wave feminism is repudiated. While third wave feminism is influenced by all of these

meanings, it is generally the case that it is the latter that is counteracted in assertions that feminism is not outdated *per se* but does require updating.
2. See Reed (1997: 14) for a discussion on the politics of purity as a key feature of third wave feminism.

Chapter 6

1. 'Choice' operates as a 'strategically deployed shifter', as discussed in Chapter 3. See Urciuoli (2003) for further elaboration of this concept.

Chapter 7

1. Postfeminists associated with a libertarian backlash against second wave feminism include Roiphe (1993), Hoff Sommers (1994), Denfeld (1995), and Wolf (1994).
2. Although there is no firm categorization of who belongs to the third wave, many writers refer to women who grew up in the 1970s and 1980s as belonging to the relevant cohort. Similarly, 'second wave' is a problematic category and it is not intended to be used here as though its referent were self-evident. In third wave discourse, second wave usually refers to the feminism established in the 1970s and 1980s; therefore this is how the phrase is used in the present book.
3. Milojevic (2008: 333) defines hegemonic time as 'western, Christian, linear, abstract, clock dominated, work oriented, coercive, capitalist, masculine and anti-natural'.

Bibliography

Adkins, L. (2002) *Revisions: Gender and Sexuality in Late Modernity* (Buckingham: Open University Press).
—— (2004) 'Passing on Feminism: From Consciousness to Reflexivity?' *European Journal of Women's Studies*, 11 (4): 427–444.
Ahmed, S. (1999) ' "She'll Wake Up One of These Days and Find She's Turned into a Nigger": Passing through Hybridity', *Theory, Culture and Society*, 16 (2): 87–106.
Alcoff, L. (1995) 'Cultural Feminism Versus Post-Structuralism: The Identity Crisis in Feminist Theory': pp. 434–456 in N. Tuana and R. Tong (eds), *Feminism and Philosophy* (Oxford: Westview Press).
Alfonso, R., and Trigilio, J. (1997) 'Surfing the Wave: A Dialogue between Two Third Wave Feminists', *Hypatia*, 12 (3): 1–9.
Ang, I. (1996) 'The Curse of the Smile: Ambivalence and the "Asian" Woman in Australian Multiculturalism', *Feminist Review*, 52 (spring): 36–49.
—— (1997) 'Comment on Felski's "The Doxa of Difference": The Uses of Incommensurability', *Signs: Journal of Women in Culture and Society*, 23 (1): 57–64.
Anzaldúa, G. (1987) *Borderlands/La Frontera: The New Mestiza* (San Francisco: Aunt Lute Books).
Arneil, B. (1999) *Politics and Feminism* (Oxford: Blackwells).
Bailey, C. (1997) 'Making Waves and Drawing Lines: The Politics of Defining the Vicissitudes of Feminism', *Hypatia*, 12 (3): 17–28.
Baker, J. (2008) 'The Ideology of Choice. Overstating Progress and Hiding Injustice in the Lives of Young Women: Findings from a Study in North Queensland, Australia', *Women's Studies International Forum*, 31: 53–64.
Baumgardner, J., and Richards, A. (2000) *Manifesta: Young Women, Feminism and the Future* (New York: Farrar, Straus and Giroux).
Beck, U. (1992) *Risk Society: Towards a New Modernity* (London: Sage).
Beck, U., and Beck-Gernsheim, E. (2002) *Individualization: Institutionalized Individualism and Its Social and Political Consequences* (London: Sage).
Beck, U., Giddens, A., and Lash, S. (1994) *Reflexive Modernization: Politics, Tradition and Aesthetics in the Modern Social Order* (Cambridge: Polity).
Bell, B. L. (2002) 'Riding the Third Wave: Women-Produced Zines and Feminisms', *RFR/DRF*, 29 (3/4): 187–198.
Benhabib, S. (1992) *Situating the Self: Gender, Community and Postmodernism in Contemporary Ethics* (Cambridge: Polity).
—— (1995a) 'Feminism and Postmodernism: An Uneasy Alliance': pp. 17–34 in S. Benhabib, J. Butler, D. Cornell, and N. Fraser (eds), *Feminist Contentions: A Philosophical Exchange* (London: Routledge).

―――― (1995b) 'Subjectivity, Historiography, and Politics: Reflections on the "Feminism/Postmodern Exchange"': pp. 107–125 in S. Benhabib, J. Butler, D. Cornell, and N. Fraser (eds), *Feminist Contentions: A Philosophical Exchange* (London: Routledge).

Benhabib, S., Butler, J., Cornell, D., and Fraser, N. (1995) *Feminist Contentions: A Philosophical Exchange* (New York: Routledge).

Bernstein, S. D. (1992) 'Confessing Feminist Theory: What's "I" Got to Do with It?' *Hypatia*, 7 (2): 120–147.

Bertram, V. (1998) 'Theorizing the Personal: Using Autobiography in Academic Writing': pp. 232–246 in S. Jackson and J. Jones (eds), *Contemporary Feminist Theories* (Edinburgh: Edinburgh University Press).

Bhabha, H. (1990) 'The Third Space: Interview with Homi Bhabha': pp. 207–221 J. Rutherford (ed), *Identity, Community, Culture, Difference* (New York: Routledge).

―――― (1994) *The Location of Culture* (London: Routledge).

Blackman, L. (2004) 'Self-Help, Media Cultures and the Production of Female Psycholopathology', *European Journal of Cultural Studies*, 7 (2): 219–236.

Braidotti, R. (1991) *Patterns of Dissonance* (Cambridge: Polity).

―――― (1994) *Nomadic Subjectivity: Embodiment and Sexual Difference in Contemporary Feminist Theory* (New York: Columbia University Press).

―――― (1997) 'Comment on Felski's "The Doxa of Difference": Working through Sexual Difference', *Signs: Journal of Women in Culture and Society*, 23 (1): 23–40.

―――― (2002) *Metamorphoses: Towards a Materialist Theory of Becoming* (Cambridge: Polity).

―――― (2006) *Transpositions: On Nomadic Ethics* (Cambridge: Polity).

Braithwaite, A. (2002) 'The Personal, the Political, Third Wave and Postfeminisms', *Feminist Theory*, 3 (3): 335–344.

Brannen, J., and Nilsen, A. (2005) 'Individualization, Choice and Structure: A Discussion of Current Trends in Sociological Analysis', *The Sociological Review*, 53 (3): 412–428.

Bronfen, E., and Kavka, M. (eds) (2001) *Feminist Consequences: Theory for the New Century* (New York: Columbia University Press).

Brooks, A. (1997) *Postfeminisms: Feminism, Cultural Theory, and Cultural Forms* (London: Routledge).

Brown, W. (1995) *States of Injury: Power and Freedom in Late Modernity* (Princeton: Princeton University Press).

Brown, W. (1999) 'Resisting Left Melancholy', *Boundary 2*, 26 (3): 19–27.

―――― (2006) 'American Nightmare: Neoliberalism, Neoconservatism, and De-Democratization', *Political Theory*, 23 (6): 690–714.

Budgeon, S. (2001) 'Emergent Feminist (?) Identities: Young Women and the Practice of Micropolitics', *European Journal of Women's Studies*, 8 (1): 7–28.

―――― (2003) *Choosing a Self: Young Women and the Individualization of Identity* (Westport, CT: Praegar).

Bulbeck, C. (2001a) 'Articulating Structure and Agency: How Women's Studies Students Express Their Relationships with Feminism', *Women's Studies International Forum*, 24 (2): 141–156.
—— (2001b) 'Feminism by Any Other Name?: Skirting the Generation Debate', *Outskirts: Feminism Along the Edge*, 8: 1–21.
Burman, E. (2005) 'Childhood, Neo-Liberalism and the Feminization of Education', *Gender and Education*, 17 (4): 351–367.
—— (2009) 'Beyond "Emotional Literacy" in Feminist and Educational Research', *British Educational Research Journal*, 35 (1): 137–155.
Butler, J. (1990) *Gender Trouble: Feminism and the Subversion of Identity* (New York: Routledge).
—— (1992) 'Contingent Foundations: Feminism and the Question of "Postmodernism"': pp. 3–21 in J. Butler and Joan W. Scott (eds), *Feminists Theorize the Political* (London: Routledge).
—— (1993) *Bodies That Matter: On the Discursive Limits of Sex* (London: Routledge).
—— (1995a) 'Subjection, Resistance, Resignification: Between Freud and Foucault': pp. 229–250 in J. Rajchman (ed.), *The Identity in Question* (London: Routledge).
—— (1995b) 'Contingent Foundations': pp. 35–58 in S. Benhabib, Judith Butler, Drucilla Cornell, and Nancy Fraser (eds), *Feminist Contentions: A Philosophical Exchange* (London: Routledge).
—— (1997) *Excitable Speech* (London: Routledge).
—— (2004) *Undoing Gender* (London: Routledge).
Byers, M. (2003) '*Buffy the Vampire Slayer:* The Next Generation of Television': pp. 171–187 in R. Dicker and A. Piepmeier (eds), *Catching a Wave: Reclaiming Feminism for the 21st Century* (Boston: Northeastern University Press).
Carver, T., and Chambers, S. A. (eds) (2008) *Judith Butler's Precarious Politics: Critical Encounters* (Abingdon, Oxon: Routledge).
Code, L. (1991) *What Can She Know? Feminist Theory and the Construction of Knowledge* (Ithaca, New York: Cornell University Press).
—— (2000) 'Epistemology' pp. 173–184 in A. Jaggar and I. M. Young (eds) *A Companion to Feminist Philosophy* (Oxford: Blackwell Publishing).
Collins, P. H. (2000) *Black Feminist Thought: Knowledge, Consciousness, and the Politics of Empowerment* (London: Routledge).
Conaghan, J. (2000) 'Reassessing the Feminist Theoretical Project in Law', *Journal of Law and Society*, 27 (3): 351–385.
Coole, D. (1998) 'Master Narratives and Feminist Subversions': pp. 107–125 in J. Good and I. Velody (eds), *The Politics of Postmodernity* (Cambridge: Cambridge University Press).
—— (2000) 'Threads and Plaits or an Unfinished Project? Feminism(s) through the Twentieth Century', *Journal of Political Ideologies*, 5 (1): 35–54.
Daly, M. (2005) 'Gender Mainstreaming in Theory and Practice', *Social Politics*, 12 (3): 433–450.
de Lauretis, T. (1987) *Technologies of Gender: Essays on Theory, Film and Fiction* (Basingstoke: Macmillan).

Dean, J. (2009) 'Who's Afraid of Third Wave Feminism?' *International Feminist Journal of Politics*, 11 (3): 334–352.
Dean, M. (1999) *Governmentality: Power and Rule in Modern Society* (London: Sage).
Delmar, R. (1994) 'What is Feminism?' pp. 5–25 in A. C. Herrmann and A. J. Stewart (eds), *Theorizing Feminism* (Oxford: Westview Press).
Denfeld, R. (1995) *The New Victorians: A Young Woman's Challenge to the Old Feminist Order* (New York: Warner Books).
Detloff, M. (1997) 'Mean Spirits: The Politics of Contempt between Feminist Generations', *Hypatia*, 12 (3): 76–99.
Di Stephano, C. (1994) 'Trouble with Autonomy: Some Feminist Considerations': pp. 383–402 in S. M. Okin and J. Mansbridge (eds), *Feminism*, vol. 1 (Aldershot: Edward Elgar Publishing Ltd.).
Dicker, R., and Piepmeier, A. (eds) (2003) *Catching a Wave: Reclaiming Feminism for the 21st Century* (Boston: Northeastern University Press).
Disch, L. (1999) 'Judith Butler and the Politics of the Performative', *Political Theory*, 27 (4): 545–559.
Driscoll, C. (1999) 'Girl Culture, Revenge and Global Capitalism: Cybergirls, Riot Grrrls, Spice Girls', *Australian Feminist Studies*, 14 (29): 173–193.
Duggan, L. (2003) *The Twilight of Equality* (Boston: Beacon).
Duits, L., and van Zoonen, L. (2006) 'Headscarves and Porno-Chic', *European Journal of Women's Studies*, 13 (2): 103–117.
────── (2007) 'Who's Afraid of Female Agency?' *European Journal of Women's Studies*, 14 (2): 161–170.
Eisenhauer, J. (2004) 'Mythic Figures and Lived Identities: Locating the "Girl" in Feminist Discourse': pp. 79–90 in A. Harris (ed.), *All about the Girl* (New York: Routledge).
Elam, D. (1997) 'Sisters Are Doing It to Themselves': pp. 55–68 in D. Looser and A. E. Kaplan (eds), *Generations: Academic Feminists in Dialogue* (Minneapolis: University of Minnesota Press).
Elam, D., and Wiegman, R. (1995) *Feminism Beside Itself* (New York: Routledge).
Elliott, A. (2002) 'Identity Politics and Privatization: Modern Fantasies, Postmodern Aftereffects': pp. 11–22 in V. Walkerdine (ed.), *Challenging Subjects: Critical Psychology for a New Millennium* (Gordonsville, VA: Palgrave Macmillan).
Eveline, J., and Bacchi, C. (2005) 'What Are We Mainstreaming When We Mainstream Gender?' *International Feminist Journal of Politics*, 7 (4): 496–512.
Felski, R. (1989) *Beyond Feminist Aesthetics* (Cambridge, MA: Harvard University Press).
────── (1995) *The Gender of Modernity* (Cambridge, MA: Harvard University Press).
────── (2000) *Doing Time: Feminist Theory and Postmodern Culture* (New York: New York University Press).

Findlen, B. (ed.) (1995) *Listen Up: Voices from the Next Feminist Generation* (Seattle: Seal Press).

Fraser, N. (1995) 'False Antitheses': pp. 59–74 in S. Benhabib, Judith Butler, Drucilla Cornell, and Nancy Fraser (eds), *Feminist Contentions: A Philosophical Exchange* (London: Routledge).

Freedman, E. B. (2006) *Feminism, Sexuality, and Politics: Essays* (Greensboro, NC: University of North Carolina Press).

Friedman, M. (1997) 'Autonomy and Social Relationships': pp. 40–61 in D. T. Meyers (ed.), *Feminists Rethink the Self* (Boulder, CO: Westview Press).

—— (2000) 'Feminism in Ethics: Conceptions of Autonomy': pp. 205–224 in M. Fricker and J. Hornsby (eds), *Feminism in Philosophy* (Cambridge: Cambridge University Press).

—— (2003) *Autonomy, Gender, Politics* (New York: Oxford University Press).

Gardiner, J. K. (ed.) (1995) *Provoking Agents: Gender and Agency in Theory and Practice* (Chicago: University of Illinois Press).

Garrison, E. K. (2000) 'U.S. Feminism-Grrrl Style! Youth (Sub)cultures and the Technologies of the Third Wave', *Feminist Studies*, 26 (1): 141–170.

Genz, S. (2006) 'Third Way/ve: The Politics of Postfeminism', *Feminist Theory*, 7 (3): 333–353.

—— (2009) *Postfemininities in Popular Culture* (Basingstoke: Palgrave Macmillan).

Genz, S., and Brabon, B. (2009) *Postfeminism: Cultural Texts and Theories* (Edinburgh: Edinburgh University Press).

Giddens, A. (1991) *Modernity and Self-Identity: Self and Society in the Late Modern Age* (Cambridge Polity).

Gill, R. (2007a) 'Postfeminist Media Culture: Elements of a Sensibility', *European Journal of Cultural Studies*, 10 (2): 147–166.

—— (2007b) *Gender and the Media* (Cambridge: Polity).

—— (2007c) 'Critical Respect: The Difficulties and Dilemmas of Agency and "Choice" for Feminism: A Reply to Duits and van Zoonen', *European Journal of Women's Studies*, 14 (1): 69–80.

Gillis, S., Howie, G., and Munford, R. (eds) (2004) *Third Wave Feminism: A Critical Exploration* (Basingstoke: Palgrave).

Gillis, S., and Munford, R. (2003) 'Harvesting our Strengths: Third Wave Feminism and Women's Studies', *Journal of International Women's Studies*, 4 (2): 1–6.

—— (2004) 'Genealogies and Generations: The Politics of Praxis of Third Wave Feminism', *Women's History Review*, 13 (2): 165–182.

Gonick, M. (2004) 'Old Plots and New Identities: Ambivalent Femininities in Late Modernity', *Discourse*, 25 (2): 189–209.

—— (2006) 'Between "Girl Power" and "Reviving Ophelia": Constituting the Neoliberal Girl Subject', *NWSA Journal*, 18 (2): 1–22.

—— (2007) 'Girl Number 20 Revisited: Feminist Literacies in new hard times', *Gender and Education*, 19 (4): 433–454.

Grosz, E. (1995) *Space, Time, Perversion: Essays on the Politics of Bodies* (Sydney: Allen and Unwin).

—— (2000) 'Histories of a Feminist Future', *Signs: Journal of Women in Culture and Society*, 25 (4): 1017–1021.

—— (2005) *Time Travels: Feminism, Nature, Power* (Crows Nest, NSW: Allen & Unwin).

Haraway, D. (1988) 'Situated Knowledges: The Science Question in Feminism and the Privilege of Partial Perspective', *Feminist Studies*, 14 (3): 575–599.

Harde, R., and Harde, E. (2003) 'Voices and Visions: A Mother and Daughter Discuss Coming to Feminism and Being Feminist': pp. 116–137 in R. Dicker and A. Piepmeier (eds), *Catching a Wave: Reclaiming Feminism for the 21st Century* (Boston: Northeastern University Press).

Harding, S. (1991) *Whose Science? Whose Knowledge? Thinking From Women's Lives* (Milton Keynes: Open University Press).

—— (1993) 'Reinventing Ourselves as Other: More New Agents of History and Knowledge': pp. 140–164 in L. S. Kauffman (ed.), *American Feminist Thought at Century's End* (Cambridge, MA: Blackwell).

—— (2005) 'Rethinking Standpoint Epistemology: What is "Strong Objectivity"': pp. 218–236 in A. E. Cudd and R. O. Andreasen (eds), *Feminist Theory: A Philosophical Anthology* (Oxford: Blackwell Publishing).

Harris, A. (2003) 'gURL Scenes and Grrrl Zines: The Regulation and Resistance of Girls in Late Modernity', *Feminist Review*, 75: 38–56.

—— (ed.) (2004a) *All About the Girl: Culture, Power, and Identity* (London: Routledge).

—— (2004b) *Future Girl: Young Women in the Twenty-First Century* (London: Routledge).

—— (2008) 'Introduction: Youth Cultures and Feminist Politics': pp. 1–16 in A. Harris (ed.), *Next Wave Cultures: Feminism, Subcultures, Activism* (New York: Routledge).

Harvey, D. (2005) *A Brief History of Neoliberalism* (Oxford: Oxford University Press).

Hawkesworth, M. (2004) 'The Semiotics of Premature Burial: Feminism in a Postfeminist Age', *Signs: Journal of Women in Culture and Society*, 29 (4): 961–985.

Hemmings, C. (2005) 'Telling Feminist Stories', *Feminist Theory*, 6 (2): 115–139.

Henry, A. (2003) 'Feminism's Family Problem: Feminist Generations and the Mother–Daughter Trope': pp. 209–231 in R. Dicker and A. Piepmeier (eds), *Catching a Wave: Reclaiming Feminism for the 21st Century* (Boston: Northeastern University Press).

—— (2004) *Not My Mother's Sister: Generational Conflict and Third-Wave Feminism* (Indianapolis: Indiana University Press).

Hernández, D., and Rehman, B. (eds) (2002) *Colonize This? Young Women of Color on Today's Feminism* (Emeryville CA: Seal Press).

Heywood, L., and Drake, J. (eds) (1997) 'Third Wave Agenda: Being Feminist, Doing Feminism' (Minneapolis: University of Minnesota Press).

—— (2004) '"It's All about the Benjamins": Economic Determinants of Third Wave Feminism in the United States': pp. 13–23 in S. Gillis,

G. Howie, and R. Munford (eds), *Third Wave Feminism* (Basingstoke: Palgrave Macmillan).

Hoff Sommers, C. (1994) *Who Stole Feminism?* (New York: Simon and Shuster).

Hollows, J. (2000) *Feminism, Femininity and Popular Culture* (Manchester: Manchester University Press).

hooks, b. (1981) *Ain't I a Woman?* (Boston: South End).

—— (1994) *Teaching to Transgress: Education as the Practice of Freedom* (New York: Routledge).

Hughes, C. (2002) *Key Concepts in Feminist Theory and Research* (London: Sage).

Inoue, M. (2007) 'Language and Gender in the Age of Neoliberalism', *Gender and Language*, 1 (1): 79–91.

Irigaray, L. (1993) *An Ethnics of Sexual Difference* (London: Athlone).

Jacob, K., and Licona, A. C. (2005) 'Writing the Waves: A Dialogue on the Tools, Tactics, and Tensions of Feminisms and Feminist Practices over Time and Place', *NWSA Journal*, 17 (1): 197–205.

Johnson, L. (1993) *The Modern Girl: Girlhood and Growing Up* (Buckingham: Open University Press).

Kauffman, L. (1993) 'The Long Goodbye': pp. 258–277 in L. Kauffman (ed.), *American Feminist Thought at Century's End: A Reader* (Cambridge, MA: Blackwell).

Kavka, M. (2001) 'Introduction': pp. ix–xxvi in E. Bronfen and M. Kavka (eds), *Feminist Consequences: Theory for the New Century* (New York: Columbia University Press).

Keating, C. (2005) 'Building Coalitional Consciousness', *NWSA Journal*, 17 (2): 86–103.

Kelly, E. A. (2005) 'A New Generation of Feminism? Reflections on the Third Wave', *New Political Science*, 27 (2): 233–243.

Kingfisher, C. (2007) 'What D/discourse Analysis Can Tell Us about Neoliberal Constructions of (Gendered) Personhood: Some Notes on Commonsense and Temporality', *Gender and Language*, 1 (1): 93–105.

Kinser, A. E. (2004) 'Negotiating Spaces for/through Third-Wave Feminism', *NWSA Journal*, 16 (3): 124–153.

Klein, M. (1997) 'Duality and Redefinition: Young Feminism and the Alternative Music Community': pp. 207–225 in L. Heywood and J. Drake (eds), *Third Wave Agenda: Being Feminist, Doing Feminism* (Minneapolis: University of Minnesota Press).

Kristeva, J. (1981) 'Women's Time', *Signs: Journal of Women in Culture and Society*, 7 (1): 13–35.

Krolokke, C., and Sorensen, A. S. (2005) *Gender Communication Theories and Analyses: From Silence to Performance* (London: Sage).

Leccardi, C. (1996) 'Rethinking Social Time: Feminist Perspectives', *Time and Society*, 5 (2): 169–186.

Licona, A. C. (2005) '(B)orderlands' Rhetorics and Representations: The Transformative Potential of Feminist Third-Space Scholarship and Zines', *NWSA Journal*, 17 (2): 104–129.

Lloyd, M. (1999) 'Performativity, Parody, Politics', *Theory, Culture and Society*, 16 (2): 195–213.
—— (2005) *Beyond Identity Politics: Feminism, Power and Politics* (London: Sage).
—— (2007) 'Radical Democratic Activism and the Politics of Resignification', *Constellations*, 14 (1): 129–146.
Looser, D. (1997) 'Gen X Feminists? Youthism, Careerism, and the Third Wave': pp. 31–54 in D. Looser and A. E. Kaplan (eds), *Generations: Academic Feminists in Dialogue* (Minneapolis: University of Minnesota Press).
Looser, D., and Kaplan, E. A. (eds) (1997) *Generations: Academic Feminists in Dialogue* (Minneapolis: University of Minnesota Press).
Ludvig, A. (2006) 'Differences between Women? Intersecting Voices in a Female Narrative', *European Journal of Women's Studies*, 13 (3): 245–258.
Mackenzie, C., and Stoljar, N. (eds) (2000) *Relational Autonomy: Feminist Perspectives on Autonomy, Agency and the Social Self* (Oxford: Oxford University Press).
Maglin, N. B., and Perry, D. (eds) (1996) *'Bad Girls' 'Good Girls': Women, Sex, and Power in the Nineties* (New Jersey: Rutgers University Press).
Mann, S. A., and Huffman, D. J. (2005) 'The Decentring of Second Wave Feminism and the Rise of the Third Wave', *Science and Society*, 69 (1): 56–91.
Marshall, B. L. (1994) *Engendering Modernity: Feminism, Social Theory and Social Change* (Cambridge: Polity).
McLaughlin, J. (2003) *Feminist Social and Political Theory* (Houndmills, Basingstoke: Palgrave).
McLeod, J. (2002) 'Working Out Intimacy: Young People and Friendship in an Age of Reflexivity', *Discourse*, 23 (2): 211–226.
McNay, L. (1999) 'Subject, Psyche and Agency', *Theory, Culture and Society*, 16 (2): 175–193.
—— (2000) *Gender and Agency: Reconfiguring the Subject in Feminist and Social Theory* (Cambridge: Polity).
McRobbie, A. (1991) *Feminism and Youth Culture: From Jackie to Just Seventeen* (Basingstoke: Macmillan).
—— (2004a) 'Notes on Postfeminism and Popular Culture: Bridget Jones and the New Gender Regime': pp. 3–14 in A. Harris (ed.), *All About the Girl: Culture, Power and Identity* (London: Routledge).
—— (2004b) 'Post-Feminism and Popular Culture', *Feminist Media Studies*, 4 (3): 255–264.
—— (2009) *The Aftermath of Feminism: Gender, Culture and Social Change* (London: Sage).
Meyers, D. T. (1997) *Feminists Rethink the Self* (Boulder: Westview Press).
Mills, C. (2000) 'Efficacy and Vulnerability: Judith Butler on Reiteration and Resistance', *Australian Feminist Studies*, 15 (32): 265–279.
Milojevic, I. (2008) 'Timing Feminism, Feminizing Time', *Futures*, 40: 329–345.
Modleski, T. (1984) *Loving with a Vengeance: Mass Produced Fantasies for Women* (London: Routledge).

―――― (1991) *Feminism without Women: Culture and Criticism in a 'Postfeminist' Age* (London: Routledge).
Mohanty, C. T. (1995) 'Feminist Encounters: Locating the Politics of Experience': pp. 68–86 in L. Nicholson and S. Seidman (eds), *Social Postmodernism* (Cambridge, MA: Cambridge University Press).
Munford, R. (2004) '"Wake Up and Smell the Lipgloss": Gender, Generation and the (A)politics of Girl Power': pp. 142–153 in S. Gillis, G. Howie, and R. Munford (eds), *Third Wave Feminism: A Critical Exploration* (Basingstoke: Palgrave).
Murray, G. (1997) 'Agonize, Don't Organize: A Critique of Postfeminism', *Current Sociology*, 45 (2): 37–47.
Negra, D. (2009) *Fantasizing the Reclamation of Self in Postfeminism* (London: Routledge).
Nicholson, L. J. (ed.) (1990) *Feminism/Postmodernism* (London: Routledge).
Nielsen, H. B. (2004) 'Noisy Girls: New Subjectivities and Old Gender Discourses', *Young*, 12 (9): 9–30.
Odih, P. (1999) 'Gendered Time in the Age of Deconstruction', *Time and Society*, 8 (1): 9–38.
Orr, C. M. (1997) 'Charting the Currents of the Third Wave', *Hypatia*, 12 (3): 29–45.
Parkins, W. (1999) 'Bad Girls, Bad Reputations: Feminist Ethics and Postfeminism', *Australian Feminist Studies*, 14 (30): 377–385.
Phoenix, A. (2003) 'Neoliberalism and Masculinity: Racialization and the Contradictions of Schooling for 11- to 14-Year-Olds', *Youth and Society* 36 (2): 227–246.
Phoenix, A., and Pattynama, P. (2006) 'Intersectionality', *European Journal of Women's Studies*, 13 (3): 187–192.
Pollitt, K., and Baumgardner, J. (2003) 'Afterword': pp. 309–319 in R. Dicker and A. Piepmeier (eds), *Catching a Wave: Reclaiming Feminism for the 21st Century* (Boston: Northeastern University Press).
Purvis, J. (2004) 'Grrrls and Women together in the Third Wave: Embracing the Challenges of Intergenerational Feminism(s)', *NWSA Journal*, 16 (3): 93–123.
Quinby, L. (1997) 'Genealogical Feminism: A Politic Way of Looking': pp. 146–167 in J. Dean (ed.), *Feminism and the New Democracy: Resiting the Political* (London: Sage).
Radway, J. (1987) *Reading the Romance: Women, Patriarchy and Popular Literature* (London: Verson).
Ramazanoglu, C. (2002) *Feminist Methodology: Challenges and Choices* (London: Sage).
Reed, J. (1997) 'Roseanne: A "Killer Bitch" for Generation X': pp. 122–133 in L. Heywood and J. Drake (eds), *Third Wave Agenda: Being Feminist, Doing Feminism* (Minneapolis: University of Minnesota Press).
Rich, E. (2005) 'Young Women, Feminist Identities and Neoliberalism', *Women's Studies International Forum*, 28: 495–508.

Ringrose, J. (2007) 'Successful Girls? Complicating Post-Feminist, Neoliberal Discourses of Education Achievement and Gender Equality', *Gender and Education*, 19 (4): 471–489.

Riordan, E. (2001) 'Commodified Agents and Empowered Girls: Consuming and Producing Feminism', *Journal of Communication Inquiry*, 25 (3): 279–297.

Rita, A., and Trigilio, J. (1997) 'Surfing the Third Wave: A Dialogue between Two Third Wave Feminists', *Hypatia*, 12 (3): 1–9.

Roiphe, K. (1993) *The Morning After: Sex, Fear and Feminism* (London: Hamish Hamilton).

Roof, J. (1995) 'How to Satisfy a Woman Every Time...': pp. 55–70 in D. Elam and R. Wiegman (eds), *In Feminism Beside Itself* (New York: Routledge).

—— (1997) 'Generational Difficulties, or, the Fear of a Barren History': pp. 69–87 in D. Looser and A. E. Kaplan (eds), *Generations: Academic Feminists in Dialogue* (Minneapolis: University of Minnesota Press).

Rose, N. (1989) *Governing the Soul: The Shaping of the Private Self* (London: Free Association Books).

—— (1996) 'Governing "Advanced" Liberal Democracies': pp. 37–64 in A. Barry, T. Osborne, and N. S. Rose (eds), *Foucault and Political Reason: Liberalism, Neoliberalism, and Rationalities of Government* (Chicago: Chicago University Press).

—— (1998) *Inventing Ourselves: Psychology, Power and Personhood* (Cambridge: Cambridge University Press).

—— (1999) *Powers of Freedom: Reframing Political Thought* (Cambridge: Cambridge University Press).

Rosenberg, J., and Garofalo, G. (1998) 'Riot Grrrl: Revolutions from Within', *Signs: Journal of Women in Culture and Society*, 23 (3): 809–841.

Rowe, A. C., and Licona, A. C. (2005) 'Moving Locations: The Politics of Identities in Motion', *NWSA Journal*, 17 (2): 11–14.

Rowe-Finkbeiner, K. (2004) *The F Word: Women, Politics and the Future* (Emeryville, CA: Seal Press).

Sandoval, C. (1991) 'U.S. Third World Feminism: The Theory and Method of Oppositional Consciousness in the Postmodern World', *Genders* (10): 1–24.

Scott, J. W. (1991) 'The Evidence of Experience', *Critical Inquiry*, 17 (4): 773–797.

—— (1992) 'Experience' pp. 22–40 in J. Butler and J. W. Scott (eds), *Feminists Theorize the Political* (New York: Routledge).

Segal, L. (1999) *Why Feminism? Gender, Psychology, Politics* (Cambridge: Polity).

—— (2000) 'Only Contradictions on Offer', *Women: A Cultural Review*, 11 (1): 19–36.

—— (2003) 'Theoretical Afflictions: Poor Rich White Folk Play the Blues', *New Formations*, 50: 142–156.

Short, K. (1994) 'Coming to the Table: The Differential Politics of *This Bridge Called My Back*', *Genders*, 20: 3–44.

Sidler, M. (1997) 'Living in McJobdom: Third Wave Feminism and Class Inequity': pp. 25–39 in L. Heywood and J. Drake (eds), *Third Wave Agenda:*

Being Feminist, Doing Feminism (Minneapolis: University of Minnesota Press).
Siegel, D. L. (1997a) 'The Legacy of the Personal: Generating Theory in Feminism's Third Wave', *Hypatia*, 12 (3): 46–75.
—— (1997b) 'Reading between the Waves: Feminist Historiography in a "Postfeminist" Moment': pp. 55–82 in L. Heywood and J. Drake (eds), *Third Wave Agenda: Being Feminist, Doing Feminism* (Minneapolis: University of Minnesota Press).
Smith, J. (1997) 'Doin' It for the Ladies – Youth Feminism: Cultural Productions/Cultural Activism': pp. 226–238 in L. Heywood and J. Drake (eds), *Third Wave Agenda: Being Feminist, Doing Feminism* (Minneapolis: University of Minnesota Press).
Squires, J. (1999) *Gender in Political Theory* (Cambridge: Polity).
—— (2007) *The New Politics of Gender Equality* (Basingstoke: Palgrave).
Stoljar, N. (2000) 'Autonomy and the Feminist Intuition': pp. 94–111 in C. Mackenzie and N. Stoljar, (eds) *Relational Autonomy: Feminist Perspectives on Autonomy, Agency and the Social Self* (Oxford: Oxford University Press).
Stone, A. (2005) 'Towards a Genealogical Feminism: A Reading of Judith Butler's Political Thought', *Contemporary Political Theory*, 4: 4–24.
Taft, J. (2004) 'Girl Power Politics: Pop-Culture Barriers and Organizational Resistance': pp. 69–78 in A. Harris (ed.), *All about the Girl* (New York: Routledge).
Tasker, Y., and Negra, D. (2007) *Interrogating Postfeminism: Gender and the Politics of Popular Culture* (London: Duke University Press).
Taylor, C. (1991) *The Ethics of Authenticity* (Cambridge, MA: Harvard University Press).
Urciuoli, B. (2003) 'Excellence, Leadership, Skills, Diversity: Marketing Liberal Arts Education', *Language and Communication*, 23: 385–408.
Valverde, M. (2004) 'Experience and Truth Telling in a Post-Humanist World: A Foucauldian Contribution to Feminist Ethical Reflections': pp. 67–90 in D. Taylor and K. Vintges (eds), *Feminism and the Final Foucault* (Chicago: University of Chicago Press).
Volman, M., and Ten Dam, G. (1998) 'Equal but Different: Contradictions in the Development of Gender Identity in the 1990s', *British Journal of Sociology of Education*, 19 (4): 529–545.
Walby, S. (2000) 'Beyond the Politics of Location: The Power of Argument in a Global Era', *Feminist Theory*, 1 (2): 189–206.
—— (2002) 'Feminism in a Global Era', *Economy and Society*, 31 (4): 533–557.
—— (2005a) 'Introduction: Comparative Gender Mainstreaming in a Global Era', *International Feminist Journal of Politics*, 7 (4): 453–470.
—— (2005b) 'Gender Mainstreaming: Productive Tensions in Theory and Practice', *Social Politics*, 12 (3): 321–343.
Walker, R. (ed.) (1995) *To Be Real: Telling the Truth and Changing the Face of Feminism* (New York: Anchor Books).
Walkerdine, V. (2003) 'Reclassifying Upward Mobility: Femininity and the Neo-Liberal Subject', *Gender and Education*, 15 (3): 237–248.

Walkerdine, V., Lucey, H., and Melody, J. (2001) *Growing Up Girl: Psychosocial Explorations of Gender and Class* (Houndmills, Basingstoke: Palgrave).

Webster, F. (2000) 'The Politics of Sex and Gender: Benhabib and Butler Debate Subjectivity', *Hypatia*, 15 (1): 122.

Whittier, N. (1995) *Feminist Generations: The Persistence of the Radical Women's Movement.* (Philadelphia: Temple University Press).

Wiegman, R. (1999/2000) 'Feminism, Institutionalism, and the Idiom of Failure', *Differences*, 11 (3): 107–136.

———— (2000) 'Feminism's Apocalyptic Futures', *New Literary History*, 31: 805–825.

———— (2002) 'Academic Feminism Against Itself', *NWSA Journal*, 14 (2): 18–37.

Wolf, N. (1994) *Fire with Fire* (London: Vintage).

Wong, K. S. (2003) 'Pranks and Fake Porn: Doing Feminism My Way': pp. 294–308 in R. Dicker and A. Piepmeier (eds), *Catching a Wave: Reclaiming Feminism for the 21st Century* (Boston: Northeastern University Press).

Woodhull, W. (2003) 'Global Feminism, Transnational Political Economies, Third World Cultural Production', *Journal of International Women's Studies*, 4 (2): 76–90.

Yuval-Davis, N. (2006) 'Intersectionality and Feminist Politics', *European Journal of Women's Studies*, 13 (3): 193–209.

Zack, N. (2005) *Inclusive Feminism: A Third Wave Theory of Women's Commonality* (Oxford: Rowman and Littlefield Publishers, Inc.).

Zita, J. (1997) 'Third Wave Feminism, Special issue', *Hypatia*, 12 (3): 1–6.

Index

Adkins, Lisa, 31–5, 159
agency *see under* choice
autonomy, 88, 131, 137–9, 147
  and agency, 140–2
  and authenticity, 150–2
  relational, 145–7
  procedural, 147–8
  substantive, 149

Beck, Ulrich, 57–60, 132, 183
Beck-Gernsheim, Elizabeth, 57–60, 132, 183
Benhabib, Seyla, 139–44
Biography, 58–60, 132
Braidotti, Rosi, 49–50, 176
Butler, Judith, 119, 122, 140–3

choice, 88, 94–5, 118, 130, 132–3, 144, 150, 190
  and agency, 134–6

difference, 152–3
  between women, 2, 4–8, 29, 152, 160–1, 168, 170
  gender *see under* gender
  sexual, 173, 176–9

education, 64, 65, 71, 95, 110
epistemology, 78
experience, 2, 25, 53, 77, 79–86
  critiques of 84–7
  and theory, 78–9, 101
  and the personal, 81–4, 188

Fraser, Nancy, 140, 144
femininity, 89
  contradictory, 73, 87
  new, 53, 61, 73, 153
  successful, 16, 50, 66–8, 88, 95, 118

feminism
  death of, 10–11, 157
  future of, 35, 158–60
  history of, 36, 159, 171
feminization, 63, 99, 187

gender
  equality, 2, 20, 10–13, 70, 97–8, 184–5
  difference, 4, 94, 98–9, 118
  inequality, 4, 14, 42, 69, 92–4, 96, 106–7, 117
  mainstreaming, 10–15, 46
  modernization, 10, 12, 53, 66, 69, 185
  order, 10, 18, 22, 47–8, 75
  genealogy, 18, 31, 36–9, 43, 121–2, 128, 171, 184
  generation, 6–7, 26–7, 107, 156, 158, 161, 167
  conflict, 161–2, 169–170
  reproductive time, 157, 169, 172
  political, 7
governmentality, 55–7, 63, 186
Grosz, Elizabeth, 177–80

Harris, Anita, 17, 65, 74
Hemmings, Clare, 169–71

individualism, 9, 16, 24, 88, 94, 138, 146
individualization, 58–9
  and gender, 53, 59–61, 74, 88, 92, 98, 132–3

Kristeva, Julia, 173–4

Lloyd, Moya, 112–13, 120–1